Tish Sommers

Tish Sommers, Activist, and the Founding of the Older Women's League

Patricia Huckle

Foreword by Maggie Kuhn
Epilogue by Susan E. Cayleff

The University of Tennessee Press
Knoxville

The paper in this book meets the minimum requirements of the
American National Standard for Permanence of Paper for Printed
Library Materials. ∞   The binding materials have been chosen
for strength and durability.

Library of Congress Cataloging in Publication Data

Huckle, Patricia, 1937–
　　Tish Sommers, activist, and the founding of the Older Women's League /
Patricia Huckle; epilogue by Susan E. Cayleff. — 1st ed.
　　　　p.　　　cm.
　　Includes bibliographical references and index.
　　ISBN 0-87049-691-3 (cloth: alk. paper)
　　　1.　　Sommers, Tish.　2. Feminists—United States—Biography.
3. Social reformers—United States—Biography.　4. Older Women's League
(U.S.)—History.　　I. Sommers, Tish.　　II. Title.
HQ1413.S65H83　　　1991
305.4'092 — dc20
　[B]　　　　　　　90-46851　　　CIP

For Tish and Laurie, of course,
and for Alita and Tanis

Contents

Illustrations

Foreword

We are living in the midst of two world revolutions which have collided head on—the demographic revolution, where more people are living longer than at any time in human history, and the technological revolution, which has profoundly changed the economic base of America and how we live and work and communicate. Women are the survivors in the demographic revolution, outliving men eight to thirteen years. With the technological revolution, women are established in jobs once considered "men's work," but without equal salaries or opportunities for career advancement. The number of "working wives" and "working mothers" are steadily increasing and will continue to rise, and so is the feminization of poverty. Medical technologies have greatly increased our chances for survival with immunization and organ transplants, but medical technologies have made it difficult to die with dignity.

In the new decade of change, women have a tremendous challenge to lead and nurture a "third revolution"—a political and economic revolution that affirms justice and human values, reorders our national priorities, and rejects all forms of violence, including war.

Tish Sommers was a lifelong revolutionary. She mobilized her passion and energy to work for change. If she had lived, the third revolution would have been at the top of her agenda. I met Tish in Washington at a conference of the National Organization of Women (NOW). She was a participant in a workshop that I was leading on workplace reform. In the lively discussion, it was clear to both of us that we were kindred spirits.

Tish met Gray Panther activists in Oakland, California, where she lived and agreed to join the Gray Panther National Board. There she was at home with others who had been on the same long political journeys through the ranks of socialism and communism in search for justice and peace in a profit-centered, acquisitive society. Our staff and board members were delighted when Tish agreed to write a regular column for *Network*, our quarterly newspaper. Thousands of readers were informed and inspired by her commentary.

In September 1978, I was asked by the U.S.-China Peoples Friendship Association to lead a study tour to the People's Republic of China. Thirty people registered, including twelve Gray Panthers. Tish was one of the first to sign up. On the long flight to Beijing, we organized ourselves into working groups to facilitate interaction with our Chinese hosts and prepare for productive study of Chinese society-education, housing, collective farming, the justice system, and health care. Tish liked the idea and agreed to chair the health group, assisted by a medical student. On the tour Tish's personal struggles to fight cancer increased her interest in China's comprehensive system of mental and physical health, including the use of acupuncture and ancient herbal medicine. Tish was also "the recorder" of our study tour and delighted us with her observations.

On the homeward flight, Tish spoke of her concern for older women—the displaced homemakers, their financial insecurities in a competitive job market. She wanted to organize midlife and older women and practice what she had been proclaiming: "Don't agonize, organize!"

So OWL, the Older Women's League, was launched and has been flying high ever since. I was delighted to address the organizing conference and present Gray Panthers' good wishes.

Tish Sommers and Laurie Shields and I kept in touch by letter and telephone. They were my loving friends. I had a very sad phone visit with Tish a few days before she died. Her spirit still triumphed.

—Maggie Kuhn

Preface

There was no organized plan when we began the project that became this book. Three friends—Tish Sommers, Alita Letwin, and I—sat down one weekend, none of us knowing we had entered a collective dialogue that would last three years, and for Alita and me an ongoing inquiry over another five years.

My initial purpose was at first very limited. I wanted my students in women's studies to hear the story of a woman who had lived in "interesting times," as a dancer in Nazi Germany and then as a radical in East Los Angeles. How did Sommers become an activist? What factors led her to political organizing? Like many feminists, I hunted for foremothers; like many social historians, I was convinced that the lives of "ordinary" women deserved a hearing. As a child of the "apolitical" 1950s, later politicized by the civil rights and feminist movements, I also idealized the fervor of radicals in the 1930s and 1940s, even when I criticized the staleness of Old Left ideas.

Alita Letwin's interest also lay in Tish's past, particularly the period when they were both raising young children and struggling to shape new political directions for themselves. She and Tish reconstructed the context of their political involvement, affirmed their commitment, explored their common ground. Alita empathized with Tish's struggle as a mother and soothed her pain, reaching for understanding. We all returned again and again to questions about what makes a meaningful life, what message might be found in the past to guide action today.

Our commonalities included being white, relatively privileged economically, and well-educated women. Alita and Tish shared a common political history and developed their family-based friendship in the 1950s, when each had a two-year old son. Tish and I shared feminist politics and worked together in Seattle's black community. Tish was twenty-three years older but seemed an age peer to me during the late 1960s, the time of her divorce and when we both started new lives in California. But she and I were also quite different. My own class background was closer to that of Laurie Shields—hers as the Irish Catholic daughter of a candy maker and a housewife from Chicago, and mine as the Irish, formerly Catholic daughter of a tanner and a housewife from Delaware. Tish started her divorced life with a substantial independent income; I was then a female head of household living on a secretary's wages with minimal child-care support. During most of the 1970s I saw little of Tish, perhaps one or two visits a year. We saw one another more often after her cancer recurrence in 1979. I invited her to speak at San Diego State University's conference on women and the future in 1981, but I was only vaguely aware of her growing national reputation. Ageist myself then, I saw her work as interesting but peripheral.

When the three of us began, no one was the detached observer. The only guide we used in the beginning was Sherna Gluck's outline for oral history interviewing.[1] We were clumsy at first, beginning chronologically but jumping back and forth over time. Initially we focused on the past, chatting incidentally over meals about Tish's work with OWL. We met in Alita and Leon Letwin's 1930s Los Angeles Spanish–style house. We ate chocolate-chip coffee cake and bagels in the morning and had cheerful borscht dinners with earnest yelling conversations over the blue-tiled table—jokes and politics and friendship. Whether it was Leon's colleagues and students from the law school or student friends of their three sons, the house was often very full. Music, probably Bach and Vivaldi, quietly spilled into the corners. At the Letwin parties we all attended there were robust sing-alongs, old labor chants, action songs, often both loud and sweet— "Which side are you on . . . ," "There once was a union maid. . . ."

Tish was at first reluctant to participate in telling her story.

She preferred to focus on the present and her work with the Older Women's League rather than her history. As the first weekend became two, then a series, she began to justify the exercise. Her story could become part of her legacy as an organizer. Her voice would be heard, her lessons could be set out, she could influence others to take a similar path.

Within six months the idea of a book surfaced, though our process was still very informal. We came together exhausted, resistant, too preoccupied with other parts of our lives to pay attention, too busy to have done any study of what we had talked about the time before. Friday nights we were worn out, but we persisted because we were old friends, because we had promised to be there, because the story was getting interesting. By Sunday we were stimulated and refreshed, laughing and excited. We had the feeling described by Carol Heilbrun in *Writing Women's Lives*: "Women laugh together only in freedom, in the recognition of independence and female bonding."[2]

At some point the process wasn't an oral history anymore; it was part of Tish's healing. As her health declined and work was less satisfying, the reviewing and reshaping of her past revived her. It wasn't only that she began to use her own stories as material for her current speeches, though she did that too. She sought control over her life, going over and over events for their significance, tying past and present together. Each time she reviewed events, she saw something a bit different, reached for a new synthesis. She distilled the lessons she felt she had learned, crystallized her understanding.

As we groped toward shaping a book, Tish sought themes for each chapter, analyzed how it was to be an organizer, how to live the good life. During this phase it was her story, her control, her vision. I was the instrument of her autobiography, guided by her will. At one Los Angeles taping session, she stood, braced against the living-room sofa, and made me promise to finish the book. Made me swear to do it, "or I'll haunt you," she joked. It did not feel like a joke.

There comes a point of separation in creating a biography,

and for me it came after Tish died. At that point the collaborative effort, the process of feminist biography as friendship, transformed. Now it was my research, my voice, which would generate a different story. Out of the more than one hundred hours of tape; three thousand pages of transcript; additional interviews; extensive reading; and review of Tish's files, diaries, and date books I had to find a more balanced perspective, a more distanced retelling of the life of an activist. I began to select, to edit for better flow, to counter her vision with the complexities of implementation.[3]

Our friendship had meant more openness initially, as the barriers of reserve between strangers did not exist. I had no sense of awe about her public stature, and I had a sense of her frailties and limits. Aware of the dangers of familiarity to a fair presentation, I sought balance. Some of that came as I checked facts against written records or sought other opinions. My separation from her influence also developed over the five years since her death, so that I took a more critical stance, one that acknowledged both our common celebration of activism and our differences in style and substance. As I did this, Tish's final years with OWL and her struggle with death and dying came forward as increasingly important aspects of her life.

This shift was intensified when I interviewed her co-workers and friends and read the letters generated by her media appearances. She had touched many lives, and talking about her seemed part of their grieving. Many who knew only her public role saw her with reverence, near adoration. While I was often impatient with what I saw as their sentimentality and over-idealization of a complex, fallible woman, I came to understand the sense of loss, the need for a positive role model who aged gracefully and was brave in her dying.

Again, a quotation from Carol Heilbrun seems apt: "few women think of old age and power as compatible ideas for them."[4] The final structure evolved from rethinking the centrality of Tish's power in her old age and the value of activist connections. Clearly her last decade was dynamic, her political skills most actualized in her work with OWL. New questions emerged. What does it mean to "be in control," particularly for those in support roles? What components of death with dignity are most attainable or desirable—and at what cost?

The book begins and ends with Tish's dying and her struggle to stay in control. Chapters weave together the present and the past, leading from her strengths as an activist who cared about aging and pushed all of us to understand age and death as women's issues.

Acknowledgments

There are several people who lived with this project from the beginning and for whom I will always be grateful. Alita Letwin and I began taping in 1982, and her probing intelligence generated many of the most dynamic interviews and helped shape the book. We developed an intense friendship, full of loud laughter and grand, insignificant arguments (the sushi stays in!). In a similar way, Tanis Walters has read and re-read, pushed and encouraged this work. Laurie Shields constantly urged me to move on, even when she was not sure of the outcome. We grieved together, shared wine and memories, and she opened her home and heart to me. These special friendships, and our ongoing political and personal dialogues, are the best of fringe benefits. I could not have finished without them. At the center has been Roy Miles, my life partner who, cheerfully for the most part, tolerated mental and physical absences and comforted my heartaches.

SDSU colleague and historian Dr. Susan Cayleff joined me in the last year in work on the book, agreed to write a historical essay, and gave me the benefit of her sharp editorial mind. Susan cajoled more effort from me than I thought was possible, took my fears seriously, and kindly extended to me some of her own enthusiasm. Others who affected the texture of this experience are Jayne Brown and Judy MacLean, who read and commented on early versions of the manuscript. My thanks to readers for the University of Tennessee Press, Elise Boulding and Emily Abel, as well as Carol Orr, the Press's director, and Stan Ivester, manuscript editor. Bonnie Zimmerman and Mary Alcock commiserated, bolstered, and cheered me on. Victoria Brown, Fran Foster,

Carol Perkins, and Ted Warren provided endless hours of friendship, moral support, and encouragement.

Mary Kollmeyer and Denise Hollis shepherded the final versions with overwhelming goodwill and endless patience. Lynda Hamilton, Sharon McMahon, and Mary Pederson provided clean copy on transcripts and early drafts, along with tender regard and lemon lozenges. Students Sally Hewitt and Regina Kerns helped with research and typing. My thanks also to Annie Cheatham, who reminded me that books birth in their own time, and to Tom Henchy, who helped promote its growth and mine. Rhonda Henderson and Susan Edenborough of the Oakland Alta Bates hospice program generously shared their companionship, comfort, and insights about death and dying.

For their time and candor, my thanks to all those who wrote letters or agreed to be interviewed. Tish spent the most hours, on and off tape, sharing her life, trying to shape her legacy. Others included, on Tish's childhood: Murray and Jean Innes, Paula Krotser, and Leona Ludwig; on the 1930s and 1940s: Florrie Gordon Thunen, Sidney Burkette, Bella Lewitsky, Sidney Green, Sy Kaplan, Paul Joseph, Frank Wilkinson, Bari Hardwick Rolfe, Annette Hazen, and Carl and Sylvia; on the 1950s: Anita Gurian (Joe Sommers's sister), Alita Letwin, Doris Notestein, and Leon Wofsy; on the 1960s: W. Ivan King, Walter J. Hundley, James Washington, Vivian Caver, Roberta Byrd Barr, and Bill Sommers; on the 1970s: Tanis Walters, Spring Friedlander, Genny Guracar (bülbul), Barbara Dudley, Toni Carabillo, Aileen Hernandez, and Judith Meuli; and on the Older Women's League and the 1980s: Lou Glasse, Vicki Jaycox, Alice Quinlan, Cindy Marano, Betsy Blakeslee, Bari Hardwick Rolfe, Fran Leonard, Margaret Malberti, Laurie Shields, Dorothy Pitts, Jeanne Saletan, Lena Friedman, Diana Wolman, Tracy Gary, Joyce Klein, Gloria Duckworth, and Jean Stern.

Institutional support for this project included time and/or money from the College of Arts and Letters at San Diego State University and the SDSU Foundation. I'm grateful also for the

SDSU Love Library Special Collections (Ruth Leerhoff and Lyn Olsen); SDSU Interlibrary Loan; Bonnie Biggs at SDSU North County Library; the USC School of Social Work Library; the Urban Archives at CSU Northridge; the Los Angeles County's East Side Library newspaper collection; and the UCLA Special Collections Library.

"Go On and Organize!"

The most constructive thing that I've done is probably
show to people that you can have a life-threatening
disease, a death-sentence disease, and not only carry
on but flower.

Me retire? I've just begun to fly!

No amount of planning and readiness buffers the visual impact of
disease taking over. Tish's hospital bed was a surprise, as was the
size of her swollen leg and belly. Her hug was still strong, although her arms and face had become very thin. In the sun-
washed room, stacks of books and medication journals crowded
the table and chairs. Roses bloomed by the driveway across the
street, next to the house with the tattered roof. Tish Sommers's
agenda has been full, and she continued to push pain away with
work, but by September 1985, her energy was flagging.

The old house was quiet, though on most days there were at
least a half dozen volunteers and Older Women's League (OWL)
staff working at desks in what used to be the living room. They
wrote fund-raising proposals, or developed legislative projects, or
helped edit the *OWL Observer* newspaper. The group that col-
lected care-giving stories for *Women Take Care* met around an old
dining-room table.[1] Tish spent part of each day at work, meeting
with foundations to raise money, dictating farewell letters, filming
interviews about hospices and about death and dying as well as a
video message for the next year's OWL convention and a final set

of instructions for OWL's board members. She retained her intense focus in spite of terminal illness, inspiring and sometimes intimidating her supporters.

Friends and co-workers in New York and Washington as well as in Oakland were called to last meetings with her. They were amused by her apparently endless lists and touched by her gifts and encouragement. Some gifts were just personal; others were designed to reward and stimulate continued involvement. The Tiffany silver strawberry bowl that belonged to Tish's grandmother went to the woman who developed OWL's national ad campaign, Chinese crane silk paintings to a corporate sponsor and friend; each close friend received a memento. Tish urged co-workers to keep up the Older Women's League they started together. She told them how much they meant to her and helped them accept her coming death. Each session ended with an upbeat exhortation. Tish joked that she planned to live until the turn of the year, "for tax reasons, of course." Or until her favorite holiday, Halloween, a marker since the time her business card identified her as a "freelance agitator," complete with witch on broom and the slogan, "Me Retire? I've just begun to fly!"

Soft-spoken Tish Sommers became a vibrant voice on behalf of older women in the early 1970s. Identifying common bonds, she first talked about her own loss of health insurance after divorce and her growing awareness of barriers against older women. She "named the problem" and made divorced or widowed "displaced homemakers" visible nationally. As her political sophistication and ability to identify timely issues grew, she symbolized women's fight against inequality and age discrimination. Thousands continue to respond to both the displaced-homemaker movement and the Older Women's League (OWL) that she and Laurie Shields generated and nurtured from the mid–1970s to the mid–1980s.[2]

Tish, who once spoke so convincingly for women with limited job options or self-confidence, now spoke of death and dying. She recorded media interviews from her bedroom urging greater openness about care giving and death. She wrote to OWL's fifteen thousand members,

> Death, I am learning through my own experience, need not be frightening. After all, we are all born terminal cases. . . . Death is part of life. I have lived life fully and enjoyed it greatly, which makes it easier to consider bowing out than if you feel that you have missed out on a lot. I had already received the word of incurable cancer before OWL was founded. I moved forward in part because I wanted the work I had done on older women's issues to continue after I was gone. And the growth of OWL has been enormously rewarding. In fact I do believe that OWL has kept me alive. These last few years have been the most fulfilling of my entire life.[3]

Her prominence intensified after her testimony on staying in control to the end of life at OWL's national forum, her National Public Radio interview following a Hemlock Society conference on the policy implications of euthanasia, her support for legislation recognizing living wills, and her identification of care giving as a women's issue. Tish encouraged others to speak frankly, deal with fear, and prepare for what cannot be avoided.

Mixing the personal and the political as she often did, Tish addressed OWL members about her will: "I do have some assets which I inherited from my mother and these have grown in value over the years because I have always lived frugally. It is a joy . . . to have something to leave for those closest to me. And in this painful period of approaching death it is reassuring to know that I can leave a sizable sum to OWL to make certain the organization for which I've worked so hard these past years will continue when I'm no longer around."[4]

Extending the political hook, Tish went on to suggest, "Perhaps other members would like to do the same," and concluded with her own motif: "One way we have worked in OWL is to take our experience—some of it bitter—and turn it into good energy to make this a better society for ourselves and those who will follow us. 'We build a new road to aging and the road builds us.' Facing death and planning for it, squeezing the sweet juice out of adversity, is part of what OWL is all about. I hope that my experience and what I've learned from it can be helpful to others."[5]

That was her public posture. One September weekend she made private time for old friends. Japanese food from a nearby restaurant included six kinds of sushi, curled ginger, tuna in seaweed, and crab with avocado. Tish loved the lightness, sea-saltiness, and precise designs. Her housemate was indifferent to the food. Hair out like curled straw, OWL sweatshirt smeared with ashes, Laurie Shields, co-founder of OWL and now Tish's primary care giver, was too exhausted with worry and responsibility. Besides, if it's green, forget it, was her approach. Meat and potatoes, that was it for her. Smoke and fat and protein and some wine for good measure. In contrast, slender Tish was on a mostly holistic diet for the past few years as part of her cancer therapy.

Arranging the food on blue Mexican plates, Laurie turned the kitchen table, moved a stack of newspapers and magazines, and shoved a cat to the floor. Tish still came downstairs. That night she wore a long white robe, an early holiday gift from Laurie. She lowered herself cautiously into the aluminum lawn chair, grimacing. She had seemed tired earlier, but by evening the sharp pain and her struggle to hold on were much more evident.

The next day she shared her latest brainstorm. Often in the past a new project allowed her to "claim Victory and move on." Even though there would not be a new organization or project this time, she was still excited about the planning. As she started to talk, she sat up more, stretched her arms for emphasis, quickened her tone and pace. The paisley scarf over her thin hair was a bit askew, but her smile was broad.

Tish, from her sick bed, plotted an OWL campaign for the next year. Her theme was "Health Care Is a Right, Not a Privilege." Moved by the creative use of protest ribbons around the Pentagon, she envisioned a massive banner project. She wanted OWL chapters to work with other local women's groups to generate imaginative and colorful political banners. Convinced that the timing was right and that the project would build toward the 1988 election campaign, she saw a potential mushrooming effect. "It's grass-rootsy, geared to women's skills and interest, and it helps create climate." The United Methodists, who might extend the project to their own women's groups, liked the idea. And she asked old friends Genny Guracar (the cartoonist known as bülbul, who illustrated Tish's first book and later worked on one of the peace quilts displayed at the International Decade for Women conference in Nairobi), and mask maker and mime instructor Bari Rolfe to head a local committee to make sample banners. She paused, aware that: "I'll never see the project, but I know there's a likelihood it will go on. It's a legacy. I feel I'm throwing the ball for the next period."

This dream ultimately reached limited fruition. There was never the national banner-making coalition among hundreds of organizations that Tish hoped for, but the committee did develop twenty samples, which were paraded fashion-show style at the 1986 OWL convention in Oakland. Slogans like "Give 'Em Health!" "Needle the Government for Better Health Care," and "Health Care—a Right Not a Privilege" were embroidered or painted on costumes and banners. These and others were later displayed at a press conference on the Capitol steps in Washington, for OWL's Mother's Day campaign in 1987.[6]

Tish saw herself as a "shameless role model" for those facing the personal and legal aspects of dying. As she once urged women to take pride in physical signs of aging by overturning negative attitudes, she now claimed awareness of death as a political virtue. One OWL member wrote, "You are wonderful. When disappointments happen to other people they bemoan their fate. When they happen to you, you set up an institution to solve the problems raised." Tish, in turn, was affected by these expressions of support and appreciation. The outpouring of love broke some long-standing barriers of reserve in her. She responded to friends with increasing candor and acknowledged her own feelings more openly. She talked often about reciprocal needs and giving.

Mother's Day card from 1987 OWL campaign. Courtesy of OWL.

Health Care is a Right, Not a Privilege!

Honor your mother by voting for

- Protection against the catastrophic cost of chronic health problems
- No more cuts in Medicare and Medicaid
- Income security for spouses of nursing home patients
- Action on the special health needs of women

Happy Mother's Day!

Her son Bill, down from Seattle recently, was told of her plan to die at home, supported by hospice and friends. Their relationship was often problematic and painful for Tish, and she had only recently come to terms with letting her son find his own way. Their final visit was a good one, with time for warm good-byes. Political allies and old friends had also rallied during those past two months, bringing food and seeking one last meeting. Many were currently involved in OWL's projects, but some were part of the 1970s' Jobs for Older Women project, or the NOW Task Force on Older Women, or Displaced Homemaker activism; a few had been part of her life even longer.

Reflecting on her rekindled relationships, she discussed her niece Gail, someone she'd previously been too busy for. "I think

I'm for her like Persis, my cousin, was for me—a maverick relative she can identify with, someone who has also broken the family mold." Tish also talked about her deepening bonds with Laurie. They had built the Displaced Homemaker movement a decade before, becoming political allies and then housemates here on Harrison Street, with offices downstairs and each with her own room upstairs. They co-founded OWLEF (Older Women's League Education Fund) in 1978 and the Older Women's League in 1980. In a decade of partnership, they generated two national organizations: OWL, with more than fifteen thousand members and close to one hundred chapters; and the Displaced Homemakers Network, a coalition of more than one thousand service centers in all fifty states.[7]

Illness intensified their personal bond as well. While OWL continued to grow, Laurie was more and more consumed with the care and self-giving invested in protecting Tish. Less able to do for herself, Tish resisted dependency but increasingly needed help. Part of that resistance showed in her irritation with Laurie, who had a tendency to hover. She was also concerned about the potential effect of the care-giving burden on Laurie's health.

For the next night's dinner, Laurie made her famous mashed potatoes, with both sour cream and swirls of butter. Conversation roamed pleasantly from teasing about dietary lapses to chatter about the new television series "Golden Girls" to Tish and Laurie's hopes for the new OWL director and the plan to relocate the *OWL Observer* to the national (Washington, D.C.) office. During a pause, Tish turned slightly, looked over her shoulder, and suggested that other people could be asked to help Laurie with chores—particularly the hospice volunteers. Tish wanted some relief for (and from) Laurie, but Laurie wanted to do all the care giving. They had obviously been over this ground before, and Tish used the presence of others to mediate this sore point. Laurie bristled, pushed back from the table, and, after a few joking exchanges, ended the conversation sharply and left the room.

Downstairs the cats wandered in and out. Kic, an orange butterball, finished the chicken livers left by fussy grey Fookie and hissed at bowling-ball calico Poppy, whose favorite path was from eating dish to the top of the copy machine. There was a strong ammonia smell from the litter box near Laurie's desk in the old dining room. The cats sat on the kitchen table oilcloth while she read adventure novels and listened to Mozart. Late one night nearly a month later, when Tish was dying, Fookie startled and scattered a basket of butterscotch candies all over the floor, everywhere. It seemed a deliberate craziness, a confusing distraction.

Sunday morning was another warm day, and Tish's cancer support group, that day three younger and five older women, met outside in the backyard. They gathered at one another's homes about once a month, health permitting, to talk over their struggles with the disease. In late morning they took a break for oranges and cheese, snacks and herbal tea—how much sharing food is a base note in the interaction of women. In the kitchen one lovely young woman, thin and dark haired, told Laurie she had shadow pain, had pain where there shouldn't be any, and was afraid to have more tests. She didn't want Tish or the others to know but felt safe enough to tell Laurie. With a gruff cough, Laurie hugged her.

Laurie wasn't always part of the support group. She criticized Tish: "I still think you were exclusionary in your whole approach. I suggested more than once a separate meeting of the essential persons for people involved in the group. . . . But that end you let down. You didn't do it. But that's me putting the blame on you. Maybe what I should have done was said, 'OK, why have them organize us, why don't we organize ourselves.' I think it could have been useful and helpful." With evident irony, Laurie went on, "Okay, so I got cancer and got in the goddamn group!" They all laughed. "I hate being left out."[8]

These exchanges capture their different styles. Tish used the personal concerns to draw a larger lesson, emotionally detached and grounded in rational analysis. Nothing was impersonal for Laurie, and when tensions rose, she used laughter to clear the air.

Generally, Tish set a positive tone for the group, responded to
complaints, then prodded, "What can you do about it, what will
make a difference, what can you turn around to help yourself?"
She relaxed in her bailiwick, gave and got reinforcement, control-
ling the flow of energy.

Tish once wrote less patiently to a woman who had just had
breast surgery:

> It's OK to mourn the loss of a boob for awhile, but the time
> comes—as in any mourning—when you have to get on with your
> life. . . . Life is too precious. Stop doing penance and look around.
> Millions of women are in the same predicament, and they can't
> have all done wrong. Cancer has no favorites. Since I have had
> fairly widespread metastases, I find these years more precious than
> ever. Precisely because my life is shortened, I am goaded into ac-
> tivity to make the most of these precious days. Use me as a role
> model if you are looking for one. Say Tish overcame, and she's in
> worse shape than I am, so why am I feeling sorry for myself.[9]

This was Tish's way of being in the world. She described it as
"making lemonade from life's lemons," using experience as opportunity and emotional pain as the basis for advocacy. Seldom
sentimental, she would listen to others' troubles for awhile but
then suggest motion. "Action solves problems" was almost always her response. She was more comfortable translating the personal into manageable goals. It worked for her, and she insisted
that it could work for anyone. And she felt more in control: "organizing, not agonizing," was the touchstone of Tish's philoso-
phy.

In her final months, she was bolstered by her hospice experience. "When I decided to take a final trip to New York last
month, there might have been criticism or questioning from traditional medical people. But the nurse, Lily, knew it was important to me, and whether it shortened my days or not, it was
important in completing my life pattern. She was completely
supportive." Tish also used her work to manage her pain. "Since
I'm going through this experience, I'll turn it into energy for
positive change. Of course that energizes me. . . . I go in daytime

on adrenalin and at night on sleeping pills. I now find it's hard to meditate. When I relax and go blank, I'm so aware of physical discomfort. Meditation no longer works for me, while action does."

One of her action projects was this book about her life. Most people did not know that Tish was an organizer all during her twenties and thirties, long before she was a homemaker. She also had extensive organizing experience during World War II.

At seventy-one, she was struck by something about her younger self during the 1940s: "How arrogant I was! I ran my own show. I worked for these agencies, but in my opinion *I* initiated the work I did. . . . Sometimes I shared information with the staff or director, or wrote reports, but I had no feeling for working within any bureaucratic structure." She smiled, dark eyes twinkling, and shook her head. "How naive I was! It never occurred to me that things couldn't be done, or that those institutions weren't ready to change with the times."

In reviewing her past, Tish most remembered her friends' youthful high spirits, their idealistic quest for unity as a way of winning World War II, and their incredible energies. In particular she reveled in her own "can do" attitude. "There was a nuttiness, a flying off in many directions. Like that first dance production with teenagers in East Los Angeles in spring 1942. I convinced a sidewalk chalk artist, Leo Politi, to do the sets. Then I found someone to write original music, and recruited a whole chamber orchestra to play for us. And this was all for *one* "ladies'" luncheon downtown, one performance only!"[10] Seeing herself then and in the present, she realized she hadn't changed. "I'm more sophisticated, more effective, and the work is more on target. But it's the same pattern." She carried that "freelance" attitude and energy into OWL, where she *was* in the center of an organization. She continued to be enthusiastic and independent. Her resistance to bureaucratic structure and limited capacity for shared decision making were not appreciated by everyone. The resulting tensions are part of this book as well.

Later, Tish talked about striking the book from her list. When her last tasks were done, she intended to take pain medication and accept death. She reflected, "When we first talked about a book I was uncomfortable. All this focus on me didn't feel right. There was always the sense of not wanting to put myself forward, partly a woman's thing, but also part of my leadership style." She felt that, over time, particularly as she neared death, her reservations seemed less important. "To provide leadership you have to put yourself forward. Perhaps the fact that I'm terminally ill allows me certain freedoms or eccentricities. It's a kind of 'deathbed power.' It's OK to be a shameless role model. The trick is to bring others along, to say 'Let's open a new door, take a risk and go in here.'"

"Well," she concluded, arms wide and with a big smile, "Enough. There's the first chapter—'Go On and Organize!'"

Beginnings

With the cry of "DON'T AGONIZE, ORGANIZE," she changed the world for a host of women who will pass it on to their children.

—Dorothy W. Pitts to author, 1988

I look forward to the time when we can merchandise a cosmetic line to make youth look older—a special crow's foot pencil, the silver bleaches, the stick to make those delicious brown spots on the hands, eyeliner under the eye for that sexy mature look. Let the young ones eat their hearts out!

—Sommers, "Growing Older Female," 1973

"We were pioneers," Tish told a reporter who asked about OWL's beginnings, "speaking for the aged to feminist groups, and calling attention to women's concerns in groups focused on aging."[1] The Older Women's League was established in 1980 but was rooted in the 1970s turmoil of Tish's mid-life years.[2] Divorced at fifty-seven, she immersed herself in feminism and transformed her experiences into political strategy. She struggled with her own aging, identified it as a social issue for women, and in so doing drew others to her. While she built a name for herself, she shaped a new political agenda for feminists and gerontologists. Her last fifteen years contradicted the stereotype of divorced aging women living spiritually impoverished lives and were a tribute to the potential for a rich life through activism.

Ira Hirschfield, foundation executive, was a friend and political ally who observed Tish's growth as a leader. Involved in the study of aging, he first became aware of her work during the Displaced Homemaker campaign and brought her to teach a summer institute at the University of Southern California Gerontology Center in 1977. She geared her presentation for each audience, speaking softly and with empathy to grass-roots women ("to the festered silence in their souls," as Ira put it), then with clarity and force to traditional students and middle-class, more conventional "ladies' groups." She learned to use the media effectively and polished her style for prosperous foundations. "Tish was clearly one of the finest charismatic leaders I have ever known. . . . She had the gift of vision, articulating and packaging ideas, . . . but was also very much a 'nuts and boltser.' She wasn't afraid to do any mundane task."

He also admired her capacity for hard work. When Tish wanted money for OWL from businesses and large corporations, she came to Ira. "We would scheme up a list of twenty-four things she needed to do, and the next time I saw her in a couple of weeks she would say, 'I want to report on twenty-two of the twenty-four.'" He went on, "Tish was professional in the finest sense. She was always prepared, serious. She looked you square in the eye, and spoke from facts. It didn't matter what it was or who the audience, she took it seriously and people knew that."[3]

She began to make older women's issues her own in the early 1970s, when she was in her late fifties. Infected with feminist fervor, she joined the National Organization for Women (NOW) and chaired their Task Force on Older Women from 1971 to 1978. Tish also addressed problems of aging women through the Bay Area Jobs for Older Women Project (1973–75) and then the Displaced Homemaker movement (1975–80). The NOW task force gave Tish a national base and recognition that grew as a result of the Alliance for Displaced Homemakers and its push for state and federal legislation. Wilma Scott Heide, former NOW president, called Tish "one of the too unsung heroes of feminism"

for instigating "creative and organized attention" to the displace-
ment of homemakers.[4] By the 1980s, with the passage of twenty-
six state laws and the inclusion of displaced homemakers in the
federal Comprehensive Employment and Training Act, Tish was
ready to build a new grass-roots organization which could lobby
on the full range of interests of older women.[5]

When the federal legislation passed in 1978, the Alliance for
Displaced Homemakers was dissolved, and others took on the
new Displaced Homemaker Network. Tish and Laurie Shields set
up the Older Women's League Education Fund to publish educational materials as groundwork for a broadly based, grass-roots
organization. As more and more requests for information and support came in, Tish realized that the issue of aging and women was
ripe. Late in 1979 she reviewed someone else's proposal for federal
funding to start a Center on Older Women and reacted in her
journal: "It had a great deal of breadth and not much depth, and I
resented the negation of years of substantive work I've done on
issues of older women."[6] Why should others capitalize on the
efforts she'd already made? She had defined the issue and saw it as
rightfully her own political arena.

Word spread that there was to be funding for a mini-conference on older women a year prior to the 1981 White House
Conference on Aging. Tish alerted her contacts. OWLEF wasn't
part of the aging establishment, so they needed a coalition and
soon found one with the Western Gerontological Society (WGS).[7]
They agreed to co-sponsorship. Tish and Laurie then planned both
the conference and the birth of the Older Women's League.

First displaced homemakers, then the Older Women's League,
an organizational evolution from 1975 to 1980. Retrospective
outlines are deceptively simplified, covering false starts and dis-
tracting personal issues. This transition to OWL, like others in
her life, was not a smooth one, in part because Tish was not
absolutely sure of her own direction. She was also coping with a
recurrence of cancer (in 1979), and her energies were focused on
self-healing. At the end of January 1980 she still wavered, caught

by ambivalence and depression, and wrote in her journal: "No
enthusiasm for work today—or yesterday—or the day before.
Don't know exactly why. Probably multiple reasons: not sure
where I'm really going these days; too many diverse projects with
deadlines, creating pressure; and I just don't feel too energetic."

She was pulled by three possible alternatives. Should she continue OWLEF and launch OWL? Perhaps it would be in her best
interest to continue freelance selection of projects. Or should she
put her whole attention on cancer, write a book, make a mark in
this most personal area? "I guess I want all three, and it can't be
done, especially with my lowered level of energy and restricted
time. The result—pressure and frustration."

Tish started the new year thinking she would most prefer to
continue research on being a cancer patient. "If I could write the
script, . . . I would (1) find the right person(s) to take on the
OWLEF/OWL leadership and be a supporter, (2) phase out of the
freelance agitator role, and (3) starting in May, concentrate on
cancer with the book as the focus."

That's not how it worked out. Tish's ambivalence dissolved as
the funding came for the mini-conference on older women. She
and Laurie celebrated with a trip to Ireland. They planned as they
and Barbara Dudley, who had drafted the first displaced-homemaker legislation, visited with Laurie's family and wandered
through wet green lanes on the southern Irish coast.

The October 1980 mini-conference in Des Moines, Iowa, on
women's issues was to close with an extra day set aside to birth
the new organization. Delegates were invited to stay over to
launch OWL. The fact that their super-saver plane fares required
them to stay until Sunday anyway was a planned enticement.
Tish and Laurie used their extensive contacts across the country
to select potential board members. They sought minority repre-
sentation, geographical diversity, and potential clout in the policy arena, bringing in old friends and newly identified allies. Their
vision of a national voice for older women was beginning to
solidify.

The timing was right. Hundreds who had worked on women's

issues were becoming conscious of problems related to aging. "I was primed for it," said one delegate, "since other organizations just weren't paying attention to older women."[8] And having the meeting in Iowa was also a smart decision. The grass-roots origins proved to be an asset. Media sympathy coalesced, prodded by constant organizing and soliciting of interviews. Older women were "hot copy," and the enthusiasm of conference attendees speaking out on the plight and hopes of older women was spread across the country by newspapers and magazines.[9]

The Older Women's League signed up the first three hundred members that day: a new movement officially began. They started with three core issues: access to health care insurance, Social Security reform, and pension rights—issues that Tish saw as timely for older women and "manageable" for a fledgling organization. OWL's founding conference report, "Growing Numbers, Growing Force," stated their purpose: "These issues can forge a link between the women's movement and aging activism. They can provide the common agenda to make OWL fly."[10]

Sure enough, women were ready. An item planted in Sylvia Porter's syndicated financial column reported on the conference and drew forty-five hundred letters.[11] The first local chapters were Louisville-Kentuckiana (October 1980) and Seattle–King County (1980). In early 1982, Laurie joyously proclaimed: "OWL really has grown by leaps and bounds—over seventy chapters across the country and nearly five thousand members since [its founding on] October 11, 1980!"[12]

OWL was thriving by 1982 when Tish, slowed by her cancer, agreed to record her activist origins. She resisted at first but, over the next three years used the process to set her life in perspective, identifying her own sources of inspiration and obstacles to fulfillment. The more she went over her own history, the more she drew on images from her past as sources for her contemporary activism. Reflecting on her early years and familial relationships had an exhilarating and contemplative effect on her.

She began this exploration with reflections on childhood. Her

OWL's first board of directors, 1982. *First row, left to right,* Eleanor Perez, Ruth Pauly, Dorothy Pitts, Tish Sommers, Eugenia Hickman, Cindy Marano. *Back row, left to right,* Mary Charles, Jo Turner, Ruth Marcus, Bonnie Genevay, Margaret Clemons, Allie Hixson. (Missing are Shirley Sandage, Martha Gresham, and Executive Director Laurie Shields.) Photograph courtesy of OWL.

OWL Mother's Day campaign on Capitol Hill, 1982. *Left to right*, Sylvia Brown, Tish, "Tip" O'Neill, Elsie Frank, Mary Alice Jackson. Photograph courtesy of OWL.

Murray Innes, Tish's father, ca. 1895.

own picture of herself was as a shy loner who became a "good-
girl" intermediary between her parents. A self-described "bluestocking" in high school, she remembered vividly the turmoil of
family life and her adolescent conflicts with her mother. Although
many viewed Tish as an upper-class woman of patrician origins,
she actually came from two distinct backgrounds: one of privilege
and the consequent belief that you have the right and ability to
do what you please as well as an obligation to serve others; the
other a far humbler background, one built upon hard work, honest dealings, and simple yearnings.

"I didn't like my paternal grandmother," she recalled. Mrs.

Catherine (Kate) Dorsch Innes, Tish's mother, ca. 1904.

Innes was stiff, formal, and always wore a white lace high-neck blouse. She and her unmarried daughter Clara lived elegantly at the Vendome Hotel in San Jose, where Tish's family traveled by train about once a month. To the young Tish "it was both scary and kind of pleasant to visit." Children were to be seen and not heard, and no conflict was to be expressed in public. Restraint and good manners were expected at all times. Social standing was important, and her father was proud to be able to trace his Scotch-Irish genealogy to a wealthy and distinguished family descended from the great seventeenth-century architect, Inigo Jones.[13]

Dr. John Miller, cousin to Tish's father, encouraged his daugh-

ters to become involved in philanthropy befitting their class background: Diantha and Sally in San Jose and Persis Miller in England were exemplary models. Tish's father, Murray Innes, as executive of several mining companies, enjoyed upper middle-class
status in elite men's organizations such as the Manhattan Club in
New York, the Family Club in San Francisco, and the Jonathan
Club in Los Angeles.[14]

Tish's mother, Catherine (Kate) Dorsch, in contrast, came
from the town of Quincy, California, where her family owned a
small hardware store. Tish recalled only its dusty darkness and
kegs of nails. Her Dorsch aunts were kind to the young Tish on
summer visits, but her mother had been glad to escape the small-
town, lower middle-class atmosphere in which she was reared.
She was twenty-two and teaching school in 1904 when she married Murray, a thirty-five-year-old mining engineer.

They had been married ten years when Letitia Gail Innes was
born on 8 September 1914 in Cambria, California. There were
two brothers: Bill, just a year old, and Murray, Jr., nine years
older than Tish. Another brother, Gordon, had died two years
before she was born. Her father was then working at the Oceanic
quicksilver mine, most prosperous since its ore was essential to
the World War I munitions industry.

Distinct images returned to Tish: chasing cows with her
brother Bill, and the chalky smell of their one-room schoolhouse.
And moving around. For awhile they lived at the Oak Hill mine
in the Sierra Nevada, where they had a nurse (a widow they called
Nana) who walked them to school and cared for them. Tish's
mother fretted from the isolation, despite frequent visitors, and
often left for San Francisco. Her father, never a demonstrative
man, was more relaxed in the outdoors, walking with the children through the old apple orchard, giving them fresh warm
milk under the fig tree. Tish also recalled neighborhood cookouts
with immigrant Italian families. Most of the miners were single
men, and Tish and her brothers sometimes shared their meals in
the bunkhouse, where pancakes with molasses and cook-house
beans were considered a great treat.

My father made a lot of money during that time, through the mines and his business speculation. He would come and go. We moved an awful lot, about an average of once a year, from one furnished house to another. It was partly my father's history, with his fortunes up and down, but it also had to do with certain preconceptions he had. My mother used to complain because he never wanted to have a home, and always wanted to be free to move.

The warm and carefree mining-town era ended for Tish at age five. With her father's fortunes on the rise, they moved into San Francisco. That shift from the freedom of the country school to the elegant kindergarten at the Fairmont Hotel was a cultural shock she never forgot. "I don't know what it was, I just felt inadequate. They pushed kids to read and write. There was a piece of paper, it said 'name,' and instead of putting down my name, I wrote 'name.' They laughed at me. Those are the things you remember. You remember the humiliations and the inadequacies. I was always very shy. Very, very shy. That was one of the problems I had as a youngster. I was kind of a loner."

Things were better during the summers when they moved up to the mountains. Through a relative, her father had purchased federal land in the Feather River area in the Sierra Nevada. A few properties had been set aside where people could build cottages, and they built theirs at Long Lake. Tish loved the remote wilderness, where the family first took a train, then a motor coach to approach the lake, then used donkeys or horses to pack in food, supplies, and the cook. People and supplies then had to be rowed across the lake. It was from this experience that Tish gained her lifelong pleasure in the outdoors. "Fishing was great. There was a mountain range. Wolves howled at night. There were bats, lots of them in the evening." With fewer formal social events, Tish's mother was relaxed enough to enjoy picnics with the children. They had a lot of company, and Tish joked about the caches of liquor buried in various places with a map left for guests to use.

Sometimes they rode horses into the mountains. On one trip Tish's mother wore a rubber corset, a mistake in the hot Sierra afternoon. Within an hour she was overcome by the heat. Every-

Beveridge (Bill) Innes and Tish, ca. 1918.

Tish with Bill and Kate at Long Lake, ca. 1922.

Kate Innes, *at left in carriage,* on 1922 trip to Egypt.

thing came to a stop while she got rid of the cumbersome gar-
ment, but it was too late to prevent a rash of blisters. She was
miserable for days. It wasn't that she was a chronic dieter, Tish
thought, looking back, but rather that her mother had just
reached her forties and was somewhat vain about her figure. Kate
was the life of the party in her daughter's eyes, a saucy woman
who joked and did slightly outrageous things. "She bobbed her
hair, and smoked earlier than most women, had the first permanent when they came out. I'd say she was an independent spirit.
And I think she was a very creative person. She had a strong
feeling for independence, and if she had lived in a different period
would have been a really liberated woman." Tish's mother served
as a dual model in Tish's life: one vain, frivolous, and self-centered,
the other a vibrant individualist.

   Mountains and water were a magnet for Tish throughout her

life, providing enrichment and stimulation. But their solace could not balance the instability in her young life. In addition to the frequent household moves, her father was often absent on trips to various mines. Then, in 1922, Tish and her brothers were left at home with their father while her mother was taken on a trip to Egypt by affluent friends. The travelers were photographed in front of the pyramids, as was fashionable, dressed in full San Francisco regalia, seated at a tea table with Oriental rug spread, servants on each side, and of course local camels. Her mother was gone several months, and Tish remembered little in the way of celebration that Christmas.

Tish first realized that her parents' marriage was in trouble when she was about ten years old. She, her brothers, and her mother were staying at their Long Lake cabin. Her father had been gone for a long time, checking his Mexican mining interests. On previous trips, there had been excitement when he returned—a child's anticipation of presents and tales. Once he brought her a bracelet of Mexican gold pieces. He bragged about the pyramids there, which he said were much better than the ones her mother had gone to see in Egypt. This time he didn't come up to Long Lake when he got back. Worried, her mother finally went in to San Francisco to see him.

> The three of us went to pick her up with the boat. She was in my older brother's arms, weeping. She got into the boat and he was rowing across. No one was telling me what it was all about. And then, suddenly, she tried to jump in the water. My brothers struggled with her and got her back in the boat. I remember wandering around once we were on shore, trying to figure it out. The word divorce came up. I knew we had to go home earlier than originally planned. And I knew things were not going to be the same, I did know that.

Tish's bedroom overlooked the garden of their narrow, brown-shingled house on San Francisco's Nob Hill. Her very proper and reserved parents screamed and yelled in the room below. Before she knew it, her father packed and was gone. "I remember asking what is divorce, what is it about, what does it mean? I had never known about it. After all, divorce wasn't that common, none of the kids I knew had ever experienced it. I remember asking one childhood friend did she know what it was about and why had it happened, and why me."

Her narrative evoked her youthful pain and confusion. Tish's father left in October 1925, and the divorce was granted the next spring. Personal pain was joined with public embarrassment. The *San Francisco Chronicle* reported: "Bachelor Joys Revive after 19 Years and Wreck Home."[15] The report went on: "The freedom which Murray Innes, mining engineer, experienced while his wife was absent in Europe for several months convinced him he was a bachelor at heart and should never have married." The public story was that their parting was precipitated by Murray selling the mountain cabin at Long Lake without Kate's consent. Kate was awarded custody of the children and three hundred dollars per month in support.

Years later Tish learned more intimate details. Her father had given her mother gonorrhea. That day when Kate tried to throw herself into the lake, she had just learned about the disease. Before the era of antibiotics, gonorrhea was serious indeed. With medical complications, Kate was in and out of hospitals for a year. During one particularly gruesome bout she almost died.

While the children were unaware of the publicity surrounding the divorce, their lives were disrupted. Their whole economic situation had changed; there were no servants anymore. A bewildered Tish understood little except that her mother was desperately unhappy. About a month after her father left, Tish was sitting in front of the fireplace doing some kind of handwork. Her mother, suddenly enraged, hit her. Tish ran to her room and sobbed. She had never been struck before. Her mother later apologized and they cried together, but the outburst unsettled and frightened Tish.

During the time her mother was in the hospital and recovering, Tish and her brothers were sent to live with Nana in Sacra-

Tish, ca. 1924.

mento. Her older brother graduated from high school there, and Tish remembered vaguely pleasant days. The separation lasted more than a year, and they were only reunited when her mother recovered. Friends came to her mother's aid, including her father's straight-laced relatives who felt he had been a cad. They sent money for Tish's summer camp and helped with expenses. Tish and her family were now the poor relations.

Her father, who claimed he was nearly bankrupt at the time of the divorce, had moved to San Diego and said he had not even been represented in the court.[16] Tish didn't see him for more than a year after the separation—until her mother first used her to pry funds from him. She then gained a very practical understanding of the economic vulnerability of divorced women.

Tish was forced to be the classic go-between for two feuding parents. "She wanted me to be very nice to my father, so he would pay up the alimony, pay for support." Being nice to him and asking for money created a major dilemma for Tish because her mother had been so hostile about him. "She had been bad-mouthing him so much in my presence. She began to talk about men, how you could never trust them." It was a very confusing and emotionally disturbing time for Tish. At the time of the separation, her mother was forty-two and her father fifty-five. Her mother became a displaced homemaker, the precise condition to which Tish would later devote herself.

Reunited with her children, Kate had to earn her own living. She was articulate and lively, had many social contacts, and at first did well selling insurance. Then security waned: she lost confidence in insurance, or perhaps in herself, and moved on to sell high-fashion clothing, for which she had a flair and was relatively successful.

Most contacts between the parents revolved around the children and finances. Her father received money from a distant relative in 1929 and passed some on to Kate, who responded flirtatiously, "Good night, old dear—and thanks a lot for being sweet to your ex-wife—funny isn't it—because I don't really feel ex- a bit."[17] But the contributions were uneven, and in 1933 she took him back to court. By then he argued that he'd lost his monies on the stock market and was virtually broke.

Kate knew Murray would inherit more money after the death of this wealthy relative for whom he had handled some business. She was willing to wait. And, from time to time, she wrote him very fondly. The letters were oddly romantic, as she called on old feelings to elicit as much support as possible for her children:

> Murray dear—you are so close to me—and so far away—a part of me that is always here—a dull and constant ache. Tonight I am so lonely—I wonder—do you remember the many times I have put my head on your shoulder for comfort—and always found it. Tonight I should like to do just that—to see your eyes get tender and feel your hand on my head—telling me to cheer up. . . . I am a fool to write you this—and yet somehow I want you to know—perhaps there are times you miss me too—memories that are not all unhappy—perhaps the knowing that I have and always will love you will be comforting to you. Goodbye ole dear—thanks for the check and make a million—somehow. I am surely going to need a lot for the children from now on. Sister is almost a young lady and they will both be in college soon. love, K.[18]

The quality of Kate's and the children's lives had changed so drastically that they took rooms at a genteel boardinghouse. Ironically, they had once leased the same entire building when Tish's father was most prosperous. When the older brother, Murray, married and left, her mother decided to move with Tish and brother Bill into an apartment of their own. Now all the cooking, cleaning, and chores became theirs. Tish, called "Sister" in the family, was responsible for the shopping. "This was in the Depression, and I could buy enough food for dinner with one dollar, including the meat and some vegetables." She did the preliminary preparations; then her mother, who liked cooking, finished the meal. These lean times created an adult later in life teasingly called "Frugal Fanny."[19]

At first brought closer by their new situation, Kate and her daughter came to experience more and more friction. Tish was annoyed by her mother's partying amidst the family's scrimping. Still, when there were contract-bridge parties, Sister was the one who made the gin. "I was pretty good at chemistry, and my mother thought I would probably be better at making it. It was a simple recipe, so much juniper berries, so much raw alcohol, so much water. It wasn't very complicated, and aged about a half hour."

Looking back on herself as a young woman, Tish noted how critical she was of everybody—particularly her mother. Once, she confronted her mother with her adolescent insight that love was just self-interest, and that it was best to have no illusions. Her mother criticized her in return and accused her of sticking pins in people's bubbles. Reflecting on their conflicts, Tish realized, "I think I resented her having sent me down to get money from my father. I was a bright, thinking child, and used to read a lot, novels, Dickens and stuff like that. And I was analytical." She was also in adolescent rebellion.

Amid this familial turmoil there were two close friends in Tish's life during high school and again decades later, Paula Krotser and Leona Ludwig.[20] They were counterbalances for her. Leona lived across the street and recalls that they saw themselves as "bluestockings," interested in ideas and serious thoughts. She admired Tish's mother and kept in touch with her after Tish left home. Paula's Jewish family was artistic, warm, and "bohemian"; they exposed Tish to music and culture she had not known existed. Tish's mother felt Paula was not the "right kind" of friend for Tish, meaning at least in part too vulgar, or as she stereotypically saw it, too "Jewish." Kate tried to end their friendship but relented when confronted by the irate Paula.

Tish occasionally saw her father in San Diego during her last two years of high school. He was remarried—to a gushy, dramatic woman. Tish felt pushed to choose between her parents. "But I was my mother's partisan. By this time, I had a strong feeling that despite all her difficulties and the differences we had between us, she had been done wrong by. There was definitely a feeling of protectiveness."

When she was seventeen, another experience marked a turning point for Tish. It was a warm September day when she and some friends cut classes to go swimming at Half Moon Bay. Tish was in the water with another girl and two boys when she noticed one of the boys being swept out by a riptide. They swam out to try to rescue him and were caught themselves. Tish was a strong swimmer from her days as a Campfire Girl, but she felt suddenly overpowered. She turned back, swimming hard. She was afraid she, too, would be swept away, and only just managed to reach shore.

Despite her unsuccessful attempt, Tish was written up as a heroine in the *San Francisco Chronicle*, her picture appearing under the headline, "Boy Drowns in Rip Tide Battling Aid of Girl Rescuers."[21] She also received a commendation from the governor. But Tish felt like a fraud. She believed she had not gone far enough to try to save her friend. She felt so guilty she burned the award in the wastebasket. Her guilt lingered for a long time, and the experience affected her sense of self. "I felt I had to make my life meaningful, particularly for myself, that somehow I owed that. In other words, I had to give it back."

Lauded as a heroine for trying to save her high-school friend from drowning, Tish later became determined to be worthy of praise. She held herself to a high level of expectations for the rest of her life, and in her last years was sometimes exhausted by the tasks she set for herself. Momentarily frustrated, she wrote in the 1980s, "Every involvement leads to future commitments. Every exposure opens up new responsibilities. And none of this action has lasting value without following through. An organizer's life is not a free one."

Intermittently she tried for balance in her life, setting limits on how much she took on and encouraging others to assume more responsibility. She criticized her own behavior, scolded herself.

Tish at Yosemite in the 1980s.
Photograph by Bari Rolfe, used with permission.

"Reject 'ambition,'" she wrote in her journal, and "give up the desire to be in the forefront, the 'leader.' I know I'm respected, 'loved' in the broad sense, admired and used as a role model. That's *enough*. I don't have to rescue the world or older women as a category. . . . Give a paddle here and there but let others negotiate the rapids."[22]

Relief from these internal admonitions came with her return to the mountains. The painful memories of her mother's attempt to jump into the lake and Tish's feelings of helplessness about her friend's drowning were mitigated for her as an adult by positive experiences with water and the wilderness. She was most relaxed and self-confident in the Sierra Nevada. After one hike of fourteen miles up to Yosemite's North Dome, she wrote, "I come closest to religious feeling in this magnificent setting. I may not succeed in overcoming my cancer, but my 'wellness' has a better chance when identifying with the sublime."[23] And in the last period of her life, Tish took up white-water rafting as challenge and solace.

The rafting trips were adventures in which she could conquer something that threatened to conquer her, as well as unwind while planning new projects—very special times. During one she wrote lyrically: "The water was very high, flowers were magnificent, vegetation was lush, and the creeks rushed into the Salmon River pure white with the fullness of their water, like Yosemite in the spring. Each creek was more beautiful than the rest. And the multitude of butterflies!"[24]

She was full of energy, despite the cold dunkings in the river. Always a self-critical observer, she analyzed in her journal. "I was afraid of falling and many banks were made up of loose boulders. My balance was sometimes uncertain. [Although] at times I forgot my fear and recovered my former ease in rock climbing, I was actually very cautious—perhaps too much so." She pointed out the lesson to be learned: "Fear is such an inhibitor. To be fearless means to take risks but to achieve more, and to function with greater ease and better balance—in every facet of our lives. Fear holds back cancer patients, but we of all people have the least to lose. . . . I was at least twenty-five years older than anyone else, but I felt no generation gap, except in myself at times. Holding back."

The summer trips restored Tish and provided lively images for her political speeches:

> For me, rivers are a symbol of an activist's life. Last year our little raft was dashing down this churning cauldron, the young boatsperson yelling directions, the river about to make a figure S, and right in the middle was a big rock. Will we wrap around it or whoosh on through? We did flash by, but another boat wasn't so lucky. No one was hurt. But those few days, when the only concerns are the next rocks ahead, make us realize how lucky we all are to be testing our strength and skill against the raging river of this period we live in. There are lots of rocks and plenty of danger—and it's very difficult to row upstream. That's what this is all about. Learn to read the river, scout the rocks ahead. Find the eddies where the water moves upstream, learn how to throw a line out if things go wrong. Wouldn't you rather be in there with all the excitement than moping on the bank?[25]

Cindy Marano grew close to Tish through the Displaced Homemakers movement and these summer trips. These were times to plan on a large scale, chew over philosophical issues, but most of all to enjoy themselves. Cindy fondly recalled one rough and rocky Salmon River excursion in 1983.[26] Several women were rowing a small raft when a huge wave swooped over the front, where Tish sat. They were terrified. Instantly, Tish leaped into the middle of the raft, yelling with laughter, "My will's drawn up—what about the rest of you? My affairs are in order! Are yours?"

She was no longer shy, nor a bluestocking loner. Nearly seventy years old, Tish was exuberant, self-confident, and established as a leader. She relished her rafting personally but also loved to counter stereotypes. She believed OWL and its lively activists could provide an example for the next generation. "Any older woman who comes out and does things and is a strong advocate and is public about it, and walks or runs or whatever she does that breaks the traditional image, is going to get a terrific amount of positive feedback. She knows that people are saying, 'I applaud you, I wish my mother were doing that, it's just so great, now I'm not afraid of growing old.'"

Birthing a Political Self

Frequently the networks of love and support that enable politically and professionally active women to function independently and intensively consist largely of other women.
—Cook, *Women and Support Networks*

The striving for perfection is innate with every artistically creative person.
—Wigman, *The Language of Dance*

By the 1980s Tish knew that she was admired and that she served to inspire many women. She liked being a catalyst, nurturing potential talent. Acting as a role model became her strongest organizing tool, one with which she could blend personal needs with political achievements. With older women she emphasized common experiences, arguing that, if she could be an activist at her age, so could they. She listened to the hopes of the young and spurred them to take control of their own future. Tish accepted admiration if it was accompanied by dedication to work, but she had little patience or apparent need for adoration. For this trait, some found her cold and nonresponsive. She was, however, willing to spend time to find and develop useful talent. This was less a "mothering" quality (in fact many younger women admired Tish precisely because she seemed so *unlike* their own mothers) than it was organizational acumen. It was a purposeful nurturing, and not at all unconditional. As a charismatic leader, she aroused potential members/workers. She then transformed their initial personal allegiance into energy for the Older Women's League.[1]

Laurie Shields was one older woman drawn to Tish. When they met, Laurie was a fifty-five-year-old widow who had experienced discrimination on the basis of both sex and age. In 1975, through friends of her daughter Christine, Laurie attended a meeting led by Tish. They struck a spark, and Laurie was launched on a new career as an unpaid grass-roots organizer. Her background in advertising, her buoyant energy and quick wit complemented Tish's vision and analysis. Tish's encouragement brought out the latent politician. Their collaboration on the displaced-homemaker legislation brought together the "freelance agitator" with the "footloose organizer," Tish to develop strategy and Laurie to travel across the country making allies. The blend was so successful that they eventually moved into a house together and became co-founders of OWL.

Other older women joined Tish's efforts through similar routes. Margaret Malberti, a middle-years displaced homemaker who came to work at the first Displaced Homemaker center, was drawn by Tish's energy and upbeat approach, and eventually became OWL's office manager.[2] Martha Gresham, retired cryptoanalyst, moved to California, worked with the displaced-homemaker movement, became a founding OWL member, and volunteered at the Oakland office until her death in 1983. These and other older women felt empowered by Tish and remained loyal to her goals and projects.

Tish also touched the lives of much younger women. When she met them, Tish was in her sixties and they were in their twenties and thirties. They saw her, as did many older women, as an enabler. She nurtured their ambitions, encouraged them to grow in their own lives, and shared some of her private dreams and intellectual visions. Closest to Tish were Barbara Dudley, the attorney who drafted the displaced-homemaker legislation, and Cindy Marano, director of the Baltimore Displaced Homemakers Center. Barbara and Tish learned the ropes of the legislative arena

Laurie Shields at her Harrison Street desk, ca. 1983.
Photograph courtesy of OWL.

together, and Tish helped her think through how to use her inheritance to meet social goals. They also shared concerns about how to balance motherhood and activism. Cindy found in Tish an intellectual and spiritual role model as well as a rafting companion. Over time, she challenged Tish's reticence and broke the barriers between mentor and protégé to build a more complex friendship. Cynthia Gorney was a college student when she met Tish in the early 1970s through Jobs for Older Women. Gorney helped spur national interest in the plight of displaced homemakers through her journalism, and they remained close even when Cynthia's career took her away from California.

There was also Alice Quinlan, a former nun who left her graduate studies to join the Displaced Homemaker Network. At Tish's initiative and with the support of independent lobbyist Fran Butler, Quinlan opened the OWL office in Washington, D.C., and went on to become a respected legislative analyst. There was also Fran Leonard, legal counsel to OWL, who shared with Tish and Laurie the organizational growing pains of the transition to a national office and welcomed Tish to her family's Sierra mountain haven.

Fran never experienced a personal generation gap but felt that Tish helped her see the potential of older women. In particular, Fran learned to reconsider her own biases against traditional, middle-class women's groups. In the 1970s, many young feminists dismissed mainstream religious and social organizations. Tish had a wider perspective and urged the younger women to seek potential allies throughout society. When OWL decided to use mass mailings to solicit funds, the young consultant, Diane Benjamin, identified *Ms.* magazine and the Gray Panthers as sources. Tish pushed her, "Don't forget the *Ladies Home Journal, Good Housekeeping, Family Circle*—good and intelligent, feminist women read these magazines."[3] "She taught me to take the long view," said another younger friend, "not to be too caught by current political setbacks, to take a breath and keep on."

Not all these or other women stayed with Tish. The emotion-

Tish Sommers
Freelance Agitator

Coordinator, Task Force on Older Women
National Organization for Women (NOW)
3800 Harrison St., Oakland, CA 94611
Tel. (415) 653-1435

Me retire?
I've just begun
to fly!

Tish's business card, ca. 1972. Designed by bülbül (Genny Guracar), used with permission.

ally needy ones were not satisfied by Tish's rational focus and intense dedication to OWL's goals. They also found her personal reserve intimidating. Several older women like Martha Gresham died before Tish did. Sometimes the women's own ambitions led them to other organizations or cities. For some, like Milo Smith (of Jobs for Older Women and first director of Alameda County Displaced Homemaker Center) and Shirley Sandage (former executive director of OWL), the differences in personal style or goals were greater than the bonds that initially united them; either Tish moved on or they did.

Women went in and out of Tish's inner circle—a small group sharing the rafting trips or holidays in Yosemite as well as the organizing work. There were a few companions from earlier eras and political campaigns who shared time as their lives crossed hers. Part of the richness of Tish's last decade was the texture of her woman-centered environment—a weaving of women through her work, through the core of her life. They sustained her; she gave them her perspective and support.

Tish herself was affected by strong role models. Three women, with three distinct modes of action, stand out. One was her mother, an often negative model in the young Tish's mind. The others were Mary Wigman, modern dancer, and Persis Miller, her father's cousin and Tish's intellectual catalyst. As she reviewed how she came to be an activist, Tish reflected on her late teens and early twenties and the impact these women had on her life. Their influence as she became an adult combined with a pre–World War II historical climate which stimulated her political awareness and growth.

It was in the 1930s that Tish discovered dance. First she became a dancer; then she was an organizer—one led to the other. Dance gave her personal focus, discipline, patience, and contact with her inner feelings. It also required intense concentration. Another thread of her life is the way she came to dance and how that transformed her.

Her earliest memories of dance were from about age ten, in 1924, when her family lived in the small house in San Francisco where her parents fought and separated. It was a confusing and painful period for Tish, and the moments when she could play music and dance in her room seemed the only peaceful ones. Then, during her teens, Tish found herself in growing conflict with her mother. As an idealist, Tish disapproved of her mother's extravagant socializing. While she loved borrowing pretty dresses for special occasions, she rebelled against what she saw as frivolous standards. Tish wanted to be away, on her own. She was relieved when cousin Diantha Miller provided the fifty dollars per month it took to enroll at Berkeley in 1932.

Not quite the total rebel, Tish joined a sorority at her mother's urging. It was hard for Tish to remember names, and the weekly meetings were painfully embarrassing. She had little in common with the "sisters" and was awkward at their social events. She was no more at ease on the campus. The sheer size awed her, and the science classes weren't what she had expected from her reading of the popular history book *The Microbe Hunters*. Initially she commuted across the bay on the old ferry, but by spring she found a rooming house not far from campus.

Before long, Tish discovered Orchesis, the campus dance group. She brought to it all her energies, learning movement and performance skills. Although she had no formal training, just ballroom dance classes and her own solitary turning, Tish did have a very long and limber back, expressive arms, and intense concentration. In Orchesis she found a home and, without regret, dropped her sorority.

The world of dance seemed pure because there seemed no room for pretense, none of the hypocrisy she saw and hated in her mother's life. Tish no longer felt so shy and lonely. She was warmed by the friendliness of the dancers and excited by the sense of freedom she experienced. Within a few months Tish was a central dancer for Orchesis performances. Bernice van Gelder was Tish's instructor and inspiration. She encouraged Tish, calling her at home after rehearsal to praise her work, and was the first to suggest that Tish consider a professional dance career. Heartened by the attention, Tish was excited by the idea of following her dynamic instructor in dedication to the arts. After her first performance, Tish's mother was also enthusiastic but jokingly suggested that a real dancer should have red hair.

Tish recalled shrugging it off at the time but fifty years later smiled ruefully at the memory. Young Tish took herself very seriously in her choreographic journal, where the dancer (herself) is described as "a central figure . . . fighting with little pests, like insincerity, materialisms, and human weaknesses. This person is striving to create . . . the Perfect Soul."

When the Mary Wigman free-expressionist dance company made its second U.S. tour in 1933, Bernice van Gelder got tickets for Orchesis members. Although her reputation had diminished some in her native Germany, Americans responded enthusiastically. *New York Times* critic John Martin praised Wigman for "her heroic stature, her great sculptures of antiquity suddenly breathed into movement."[4] Hanya Holm, later known for her Broadway choreography of "Kiss Me Kate" and "My Fair Lady," described Wigman's stage presence: "Her predominantly dark images of life, the world of her inmost experiences, her danced confessions, bore testimony to her own being, and beyond that, to mankind as reflected in her dance . . . . [She was] the Eleanora Duse of dance."[5]

Tish was overwhelmed. The Orchesis students saw two performances and sent flowers backstage. After seeing Wigman, they found it hard to practice, feeling comparatively superficial and inept. Here was the *Truth* Tish sought. She spent hours on the sun porch at her boardinghouse, seeking a trancelike state to elicit movement from her emotions, not her head. Wigman had made a deep impression on Tish, one that was to frame the next several years.

When her mother proposed a mother-daughter trip to Italy, to be paid for by Kate's bridge-playing skills, Tish was at first excited. Her father objected strenuously, however, and eventually Tish shifted her goal and chose instead to attend Mary Wigman's school in Dresden. Never adept at learning languages, she took German that spring term, in 1933, at Berkeley. That July she, Bernice van Gelder, and a group from Orchesis sailed from New York to Hamburg. Tish was ecstatic: "I was determined I would stay once I got there. Bernice was my dream and star, I idolized her. We stood at the rail of the ship holding hands, and it was all wonderful." Tish was a very starry-eyed, naive nineteen-year-old. When friends asked about Hitler, she told them art had nothing to do with politics. She didn't believe in politics and didn't care who was in power. Politicians were corrupt. Truth was to be sought elsewhere.[6]

She knew little about the burning of the Reichstag and the March 1933 Enabling Act which gave power to Hitler and the National Socialists. She didn't know about the dismissal of non-Aryans from the professional civil service, or that the first ten concentration camps had been established, with twenty-five thousand prisoners by 1933.[7] She wasn't aware of the abolition of trade unions or the violent boycott of Jewish businesses. Neither these facts nor their implications were understood by most people in the United States or in Germany at that time.

Everybody knew times were hard, unemployment high. In a worldwide Depression many proposals for improvement were generated, and the fascism represented by Mussolini, for example, seemed to be bringing about economic recovery for Italy. None of this concerned Tish. For her this was a grand adventure, away from home and the fights with her mother. She focused on the excitement of the dance.

At the time of Tish's arrival, students came to study at the Dresden school from all over Europe and the United States.[8] While Wigman was on her frequent performing tours, her sister Elizabeth directed the school, located in an old-fashioned villa. Most of the major free-expressionist dancers of the period worked with Wigman. Visitors included well-known artists and performers, like Uday-Shankar who had developed a new form based on traditional Indian folk dances. Wigman commented to her biographer: "What went on behind the facade of this solid bourgeois building looked like the life in an anthill. From early morning until late at night dancing feet thumped and clattered through the entire house. In the studios hammered and sighed the pianos, thundered and rattled the rhythms of the drums."[9]

Tish loved Dresden's natural beauty, the Elbe River and lush green linden trees. But perhaps with echoes of her mother's values she thought it "notably the dullest town in Europe. . . . Never in my life have I seen worse dressed people . . . and strict—they object to lipstick, to stockings and smoking in public."[10] This is the same Dresden that had been an artistic center in the 1920s, where the first exhibitions of abstract paintings by Klee, Kandinsky, Feininger, and many others shocked and moved people.[11] In 1933 Tish saw a different city, one still in the middle of economic depression, where public attitudes reflected the growth of Nazi conservatism.

When Tish and the tour group first moved into their Dresden boardinghouse, newspaper reports of the Reichstag trials were discussed at the dinner table by their pro-Hitler landlords. Their children were members of the Hitler Youth, and the oldest son had joined the SS. They talked positively about Hitler and the wonderful things the Hitler Youth were doing. Discounting the Nazi fervor, the Americans thought the young man was pompous and silly. They laughed about his uniform and agreed it really wasn't their business.

Bernice van Gelder and the group enjoyed their stay at the Wigman school. July and August were filled with dance classes, visits to regional castles, and weekend excursions. Tish treasured a blouse she bought one Sunday in Prague, a lovely one, hand embroidered with caramel and gold thread, which brought back pleasant memories of strolling by the Elbe River in the evening, flirting with the young men. One Austrian friend drove Tish to the nearby mountains and to Moritzburg. "It's a beautiful little town," she wrote her mother, "and there August der Starke built a huge castle with lakes on both sides. It's wonderful from the outside, strong simple lines, but inside! How would you like to have your bedroom entirely papered in pheasant feathers or have sixty-nine stag heads on a wall?"

As much as Tish and the other visitors enjoyed the sight-seeing and social evenings, they were most excited by Mary Wigman's presence. They thought mainly of the school and their lessons with her. Tish wrote, "I have never in my life felt a personality like that before. . . . You couldn't be superficial with a person like that." This was an observation others would make about Tish in her later life. Wigman entertained them with stories of her American tours, leafing through her photo albums. The dancers were impressed and touched to see a photo of their roses and the card from the Orchesis group. Tish was enthralled and commented in a letter to her mother: "What a face that woman has! I've never seen such vital power in my life. You should be flattered when I say she reminds me of you. She is about your age, her hair is the same, and something else, too is similar."

At the end of the summer, the other American students and Bernice van Gelder returned to the United States. When they left, Tish wrote, "Now I have to make my own way. She [Bernice] has been friend and mother to me. I owe her a debt of gratitude I can never repay." Bernice, who headed the dance department at Berkeley, later married and lived in New York.[12] There had been teasing about Tish's adoration of the teacher, with the hint of a lesbian interest on Tish's part. Embarrassed, she did not want to see her again. And she didn't: Tish never made contact with her after Germany.

When her companions left, Tish was lonely but plunged into routine at the Wigman school. Whatever tensions there had been before, she felt beholden to her mother, and so wrote often. At first, Tish was homesick and critical: "They speak a very bad dialect and don't know anything about cooking. Oh, for some boiled eggs, Campbell's baked beans, corn flakes, or for a good American milk-shake. Even their ice cream is terrible here. . . . Your style-hungry taste would wither up and die. . . . My delirious thoughts float back to steam heat, lamb chops, fog, small keys and American uniforms."

Tish, reflecting her self-involvement and American naïveté, also reassured her mother: "Believe me there is no danger as far as I am concerned. They treat strangers very, very well, and try to make them Hitlerites. . . . Everything is very much under control here, and under the official eye. Nazis march continually on the streets and shake cans for money."

In fact, by this time the Nazi party had been declared the only legal party in Germany. Allegiance to Nazi organizations was considered essential, and women's groups, including feminists, were urged to subsume their interests in National Socialism. Jews were not allowed to be tax assessors, jurors, or commercial judges, and quotas were established in education. From 1933 to 1935, the Nazis also began to limit access of women to universities and encouraged women's education to center on "female" subjects.[13] No artists could perform unless they were members of the Reich Chamber of Culture guilds—organizations which excluded Jews. Ruth Sorel (Abramowitsch), premiere dancer with the Berlin Municipal Opera Company and a former Wigman student, was forced to resign. Lewitan, editor of *Der Tanz* (The Dance), noted: "Due to the new formation of German life, Miss Sorel had to resign. . . . As a non-Aryan she has no prospects in Germany anymore." Himself a non-Aryan under the new legal definitions, Lewitan was shortly forced to resign as well.[14]

Theirs were not the only careers affected by the growing Nazi power. While Tish was beginning her professional studies at the Wigman school, unemployment among dancers and artists accelerated, and the political pressures grew. Kurt Jooss, director of the main dance company in Essen, had refused to fire Jewish employees. He escaped across the border eighteen hours before the police came to arrest him.[15]

Although Tish wasn't aware of it, 1933 was also the year the Wigman school teachers joined the Reich Chamber of Culture unit and automatically became members of the National Socialist Teachers' League (NSLB).[16] Like other teachers and civil servants, whether they believed in the ideology of National Socialism or not, they joined. After the war, some critics felt it was for many "a step dictated by opportunism and the need for economic survival rather than by political conviction." Whatever Wigman's motive or level of understanding, her school came increasingly to reflect the political realities in Germany.

Still, Dresden was one hundred miles from Berlin, the center of Nazi politics and rhetoric, and the school was a small, insulated world. Banners proclaiming "Joy through Work" appeared on the streets, but for Tish life centered upon dance. Like the other students, she was living on limited funds, from fifty to seventy-five dollars a month provided mostly by her father's wealthy and generous cousin, Diantha Miller. This was supplemented by money from her mother or gifts of socks and clothes. She described her typical day: "half past seven . . . go out and get the milk and szwieback for breakfast. Clean up, sew, wash, write or any odds and ends that have to be done. At ten-thirty, a nice walk. Classes until one, luncheon at two (at home), then rest, read, write, draw, etc., until four-thirty and back to school to practice dancing until six." Tish conquered any embarrassment about her body in the friendly, casual exhaustion they all shared as they bathed in the six-by-six tiled tub after classes. Her main complaint (aside from the food) was the chill in her unheated room in town: one clear advantage of the school was that it was warmer.

Tish was frustrated and conscious of her body's limits as she began more intensive work in technique, gymnastics, and composition. Her letters to her mother reflected her impatience. "I smile looking back on my naive ideas about how long it would take to make me a dancer, and realize that I have a long hard grind ahead of me. There is a rather nice balance between encouragement and despair." Wigman's words about her own artistic struggle echo what Tish experienced: "One doubts and despairs of everything, even at last of oneself, and in the end one carried it off nevertheless. For there is a power which does not cease to urge one, and there is a voice that cannot be quieted. . . . The striving for perfection is innate with every artistically creative person."[17]

Tish learned to discipline her body, to reach for ways to communicate her internal feelings. She began to develop patience to match her enthusiasm. She was deeply affected by the intensity of Wigman's dedication, her perceptiveness about students, and her slogan, "service to art, service to humanity."

Although Tish was still somewhat shy and reserved, she did make friends, particularly with Florrie Gordon, an American student who had already been at the Wigman school more than a year. Somewhat older, she came from a politically active Jewish family in the United States and was more sophisticated than Tish. She was also sharply critical of the Nazis. The two women spent time together though they were in different levels of classes. When a room became available, Florrie asked Tish to join her in renting attic space from the Jacoby family. Tish agreed, pleased with the prospect of steady companionship. They had their main meal of the day at noon with the family and the two German maids. They were often hungry from exercising, and Tish never had quite enough to eat, though there were plenty of potatoes. To staunch their appetites, they often picked up an apple strudel or sweet roll.

Florrie remembered Tish as beautiful, diffident, and extremely appealing in her performances at the school. They were close for about a year, until Florrie left in 1934. Her graduation performance, based on traditional Jewish dybbuk themes, was applauded by Wigman, though by this time Jewish culture was condemned as decadent by the Nazis.

Like other German families, the Jacobys took in students because times were hard, and the house was large. Half of Tish's monthly fifty to seventy-five dollars went to the school for tui-

Tish in Dresden, ca. 1934. Photograph taken by Tish's lover, Heinz.

tion, the rest to the Jacobys for housing. Mr. Jacoby's family had been court jewelers going back to the eighteenth-century reign of Augustus the Strong (der Stärke), and like many German Jews, they were Christianized. His wife, now deceased, had been a Lutheran, and their daughter Irena had been brought up in the church. When Tish first lived with them, Mr. Jacoby believed he was secure because of the long history of his family in Germany and his status as a decorated war veteran. In the spring 1933 Nazi boycott of Jewish businesses, his establishment had been immune. He had not lost any business, and old customers remained faithful. The family discussed the Nazis, and while an SS officer came each week to collect the donation for the Nazi Relief Fund, Tish sensed no major concern. She reassured her mother. "Any picture you may have of Germany as lawless, wild or dangerous is absolutely unfounded. Control and more control is the big principle. I am safer here than in any second country and particularly so as a foreigner."

The months passed, and at the pre-Lenten carnival Tish met Heinz, her first lover, who worked as an assistant to a local photographer. Retrospectively she was amused by her own response: "I went to a dance, he gave me a rush and so forth, dated me a couple of times, eventually got me into bed. It was of course very scary and not particularly pleasing. Well, it was and wasn't. There was both guilt and pleasure." Tish's face was round, her full-bosomed body in good condition from all the exercise. Her hair was parted in the middle and fell straight to the collar without bangs, in the same style as the celebrated dancer Pavlova. For the sepia-toned portrait Heinz composed, she wore a soft, flowered kimono, her dark hair fanned on pillows. Tish and Heinz went on trips, he taught her to ski, and she became familiar with and fond of sex.

"Contraception?" She laughed, "I didn't know anything about it, and I don't think Heinz did either. He didn't even use a condom." Not surprisingly, she got pregnant. "It was just about a year after I'd been there and I was terribly scared. God was that scary. I went from one doctor to see somebody else who recommended somebody else and nobody would touch me." Finally, Heinz found the name of an abortionist in Prague. Tish went alone on the train. She remembered being scared and having little money.

She knew nothing about her body: "I don't know how pregnant I was, but it must have been close to three months, because there was concern to find somebody quickly. Of course, I also did the jumping up and down, and I took some medicine Heinz brought—nothing." The German doctors treated her as if she had a pestilence. They didn't want to know, weren't interested because they were protecting themselves. "I told them I was a dancer and not married and didn't want to have a baby. They moralized: 'You shouldn't have gotten into this!' 'It's your fault.' I don't remember the exact words but that was the message." She remembered going to Prague on the train, being scared to death and having just enough money to pay. "He was not a doctor. It was a family home, because I stayed in bed for a period of about five days afterwards. There was probably some complication. He said that the baby wouldn't have been born right anyway. Who knows. But it was done without any anesthetic, and it was very painful." Stuffed with vaginal padding and put to bed, she had two very difficult days. Looking back, she also noted how quickly she recovered, so that within a short time she was on a skiing trip.

Her speedy recovery was attributable to her youth, and to her attachment to her work and to Heinz. Without mentioning the abortion, she told her mother about Heinz. Her mother was alarmed, but Tish assured her she had no intention to marry, and, again responding to her mother, confirmed that Heinz was not Jewish. "That problem makes many long fights—he is, in fact, Nazi. I rather think he would make a good husband if I wanted one, but that would only be in America." No one Tish knew expected the Nazis or Hitler to last.[18] She recalled only one troubling episode from her first two years in Germany. On a summer hiking trip in the Alps with Austrian friends, they heard a rumor that the chancellor had been assassinated. Convinced their country would be overrun by the Nazis, her friends rushed home. The political climate was increasingly tense.

The household she lived in soon began to feel the change. Irena Jacoby, who was about Tish's age, was studying for a technical degree but, under the new educational quotas, was not permitted to graduate. She was also affected by general restrictions on Jews and by pressure to purge women from higher education (this changed later for Aryan women as economic times improved and war preparations accelerated). Eventually, Irena's non-Jewish boyfriend broke off their relationship because he was worried about losing his job. While Tish's opportunities expanded, Irena's world became more and more restricted by increased Nazi control.

The ability to see the contrast between her own and Irena's choices came much later for Tish. At the time she was still focused on herself and dance. In her first organizing effort, she persuaded a group of students to contribute a few *Pfennigs* for a rehearsal pianist. "Imagine having a composer play for you his own music for seventy-five cents an hour!" she wrote. This was also her first experience with group choreography, a sign of unusual initiative praised by Wigman.

Tish often went off by herself to a park along the Elbe River. There she danced among the birch trees, playing her newly learned recorder, dressed in a long grey princess-style dress. Once an old man caught sight of her and she played a game, disappearing and reappearing in the trees. It was a playful self-image she created for herself, and a romantic vision of the solitary nymph who charms and eludes others.

Her dances at the Wigman school showed another, not so whimsical, side. Her mood was much more somber, and intensely expressive. In one performance Tish wore a shapeless, drab olive costume that hung to the floor, concealing all but her hands and bare feet. Her movements were solemn, soulful, and mournful, fraught with tension. Afterward, Wigman was kind but critical. She commended Tish on her total concentration and immersion in the emotional content of the dance. However, Wigman made it clear that too much was internal, not enough shared. Tish had not communicated at all with the audience.[19]

Wounded, but believing Wigman correct, Tish searched for a form that better fit her body and style. Visitors to the Wigman School had talked about the work that Kurt Jooss, now a refugee, was doing at Dartington Hall in England. Well known for his celebrated masterpiece, "The Green Table" (1932), a bitter satire on diplomacy as practiced at the Versailles Conference after World War I, Jooss incorporated elements of classical ballet into the free-dance compositions.[20] This approach appealed to Tish, and besides, after a year and a half in Germany, she was ready for a change.

She was no longer so enthralled by Wigman's personality as she developed a stronger sense of her own needs. And though she continued to see Heinz, the urgency had gone from the relationship. She wrote to her father's cousin, Persis Miller, that she would visit her in London on her way to spring term at Dartington Hall.

Persis Miller was to become her most cherished role model. Then in her early thirties, about ten years older than Tish, Persis glowed with energy and warmth—although she was not beautiful in a conventional way. She had left San Jose and her socially prominent family for a career as a translator of Italian poetry. Persis lived in the center of London's pre–World War II socialist intelligentsia. She lived modestly and graciously, in an apartment filled with books and artworks.

They had met at family gatherings in California, but Tish didn't know her well. The week in Persis's London flat was a revelation to the young dancer. They did some sight-seeing, but it was the after-dinner company that most intrigued Tish. A distant cousin from the Irish branch of Persis's family, J. Desmond Bernal, brought in John Strachey, author and social critic, and J. B. S. Haldane, Marxist scientist.[21] These friends of Persis were knowledgeable, interested in socialism, and concerned about the fate of Communists under Hitler. All were passionately concerned about the role of scientists in society and wanted to hear about Tish's experiences in Germany.

Embarrassed by their penetrating questions, Tish responded defensively about the situation. Though she realized there was pressure on German Jews, she still had no overall understanding of politics. She was not, she reminded them, in the industrial Ruhr or in Berlin. Persis and the others wanted to hear about the worst; they knew about the camps, the terrorism, the racist ideology. Tish became upset—after all, she was living there and they were not. While Tish was against the Nazis, from her perspective as a twenty-year-old dancer the situation just wasn't as bad as they described. Fascism was there, but she didn't see the threat they did.

Tish was treated kindly by Persis's guests but sensed she was out of her depth. Her embarrassment led to greater introspection. She was encouraged by long talks with Persis, who urged her to be more aware and to see what the changes in Germany might mean. They also discussed a socialist vision and the experiments going on in the Soviet Union. Tish was attracted to the independent life Persis led amidst culture, art, and the world of ideas. The visit was exciting, stimulating, and a little confusing for her.

Tish went right from Persis to three months in the whirl of Dartington Hall. Founded in 1925 by Leonard and Dorothy Whitney Elmhirst as an experiment in progressive education, Dartington evolved by the mid–1930s into an unconventional progressive school, developed a series of small industries, and expanded its professional performing arts center. It became a sanctuary for European artists escaping Hitler.

Dartington Hall's approach to education was novel, and the massive reconstruction of the fourteenth-century manor disrupted the local community. Because of this it was controversial. Lavishly funded by Dorothy Whitney Elmhirst's inheritance, the school attracted innovators, intellectuals, and artists who sought an alternative to the traditional school system. Professional artists gave performance and art classes and mixed socially with the regular staff and older students. Students were deemed independent learners who could develop their own interests and their own curriculum. Students were also encouraged to do practical labor in Dartington's many enterprises. These included "a textile mill, a glass factory, a furniture and joinery works, a number of shops, a substantial share in a large building contractor, farms, woodlands, [and] a horticultural department."[22]

By local standards the atmosphere was heady and bohemian. That spring there was a large gathering in the Grand Hall to discuss local complaints about nude bathing in the river, which ran by the train tracks. The representative of the train authority said he didn't really mind, as the sight of the nude bathers was probably good for business. The locals continued to be shocked by the school's apparent defiance of convention. Michael Young, who was a lower-school pupil at the time of Tish's stay, later described the ambiance: "For a few years the courtyard, itself a cross between a theatre and a Court, was teeming with young Germans, young Hollanders, young Americans. . . . There were sixty dancers to add to the score or more of actors and actresses, . . . the singers and other musicians, . . . and the painters or sculptors, . . . the whole courtyard abuzz with talk, people standing on the grass arguing or flirting, others hanging out of the windows, . . . There were endless parties."[23]

For Tish this was in sharp contrast to the cold and hunger of Dresden. The rooms each had steam heat, and the food was plentiful, if institutional. The Grand Hall was magnificently restored, with great wooden beams and a fireplace big enough to roast an ox. There were large open areas, and masses of spring daffodils carpeted the sloping front lawn. Construction had begun for the theater to be directed by Anton Chekov's nephew, Michael.

Instructors offered special classes in music, art, and scenic design. Tish chose painting lessons with Mark Tobey, just back from a year in Japan. He was compelling, attractive, and a spiritual leader for her because of his interest in Baha'i. Their ideas, as expressed by Tobey, appealed to Tish: "Baha'i humanism . . . opposes all social divisions and barriers which can engender hostility, injustice, or strife, whether personal, national, or religious; and it advocates an auxiliary international language, international mediation, world peace, and the ultimate unification of peoples in a single world state . . . for we are all waves of one sea."[24] At age twenty, Tish still sought absolute truth. Baha'i seemed to offer her the equality emphasized by Strachey and others of Persis's circle, plus the warmth and unity she yearned for. For a few weeks she considered herself converted. Then a Baha'i speaker came to the school, and Tish saw her as a "typical club woman." That was that. There were too many echoes of her mother's social pretensions, and the bubble burst. The creed still appealed to her, but after that experience Tish was no longer a disciple.

The time at Dartington was exciting for Tish. She was challenged and stimulated by the bohemian atmosphere, a romance with a very attractive Austrian sculptor, and most importantly a new, more formalized dance discipline provided by the Jooss training. Day and night there were rehearsals, concerts, and intense discussions about art and its role in society. She felt nearly smothered. To escape the Dartington intensity, which she likened to having too much whipped cream, Tish and a few companions sought Saturday movies and drinking at a nearby Totnes pub. As the term ended, Tish was ready to leave.

Tish returned to Dresden and the Wigman school. She was affected both by her increased dance discipline and by the ideas discussed with Persis. The latter made being in Germany harder this time. Tish saw things differently and began to ask more questions. Why did the Jacobys have to donate the cost of one meal a week to the Nazis? Where did that money really go? Why couldn't people vote, as in a democracy? What happened to people who protested? When she asked questions at the school, she was told to keep quiet. Still the picture was not complete for her. When the indoctrination classes on *Mein Kampf* were added to the school curriculum, Tish and others laughed, considering it a passing nuisance. While she objected to the Nazis' treatment of Jews, she made light of other changes. This view was encouraged by what she saw around her. The students and teachers presented a compliant facade, performing obligatory Nazi salutes before classes only when visitors were present.

Although the school still operated, things had changed drastically by 1935. Hitler Youth groups were offered more and more classes on racial ideology and physical conditioning. One Wigman teacher who had distributed anti-Nazi literature disappeared. It was said she returned to her native Bavaria.[25]

There had been Jewish instructors, performers, and students at the Wigman school. No more. Students gossiped about Wigman's revised "Women's Dances," a cycle including five roles for women: the bride, the mother, the custodian of human dignity, the prophetess, and the demon.[26] The last, "Witches Dance," had been revised over the years and seemed to observers much less frenzied and demonic than earlier versions. All the dances seemed softer and conformed to the Nazi model for the new German woman. Some felt this represented Wigman's capitulation to the new regime. The school's gradual reshaping came into focus for Tish, in part because she couldn't avoid it, and because of her contacts with Persis and her friends.

"I was aware and oblivious all at once," Tish commented. At dinner one evening, she told the Jacobys that she and Heinz took a weekend trip out of town on his motorcycle. As they registered at the inn, they turned in their identity papers. Since they didn't have quite enough money to pay the bill, they sneaked out early in the morning and sent payment later from Dresden. In the meantime the inn reported them, and a warrant for their arrest was issued. Drinking the last of her ersatz coffee, she gleefully told the Jacobys about the two of them at the police station. She was laughing about the silly moment when Heinz had to show his certificate of Aryanship. How pompous and officious these Nazis were. There was quiet in the room when she finished.

"What if he hadn't had that certificate?" Mr. Jacoby asked. Now Tish was silent and ashamed of her own self-absorption.

More ominous signs were seen by others. Violent hate articles against the Jews were published, demanding total exclusion of Jews from German life. Jewish shops in Berlin were destroyed in July 1935, and in September the Nuremberg laws were passed prohibiting intermarriage and extramarital intercourse.[27] And, bringing the sweeping change home, Jews were no longer permitted to employ Aryan women under the age of forty-five as domestic workers: the two German maids in the Jacoby household were gone.

This personal manifestation of Nazi rule shocked the Jacoby family and made Tish sharply aware of their distress. Restrictions increased: Jews were no longer permitted into public swimming pools or theaters, so daughter Irena and her friends had to sneak into the movies. Irena quickly joined the steady stream of young Jews who emigrated.[28] First she went to Poland (1936) and later moved on to Bolivia. But her father stayed, convinced the Nazis were just part of a difficult political period. He felt sure the Germans would come to their senses. He continued to talk about support from his loyal customers. He was then in his fifties. Where could he go? His business was still in Germany, his life was German.[29]

That summer of 1935 was also a time of personal change for Tish. First, she received her certificate as a Mary Wigman teacher. Second, her mother, having received a small inheritance from Tish's Aunt Clara's estate, decided to tour Europe with her daughter.

They were both unpleasantly startled by their reunion. The warm chattiness of their letters, the idealized mother-daughter bond, did not match their face-to-face conflicts. "It was clear that I'd built my mother up in my mind the way I wanted her to be. While we had differences, at least there seemed to be this basic core. But from the moment we got together that summer there were such basic differences that we couldn't communicate at all.

She was unhappy and I was unhappy." Kate wanted to travel graciously through Budapest and Vienna, meeting socially acceptable people. Her daughter was more comfortable in third class. "I was a different person and had been living very frugally, extremely frugally. And the students I knew were worse off than I. Most of them at the school were having a hard time getting enough to eat so they had strength to dance." Her mother's values and aspirations displeased and alienated Tish even more than they had earlier. After Vienna they parted, and twenty-one-year-old Tish went off to find adventure on her own.

Two more incidents crystallized German political reality for her. On a walking trip on the Rhine after she left her mother, Tish met a young German police cadet who deepened her political awareness. He was handsome and full of himself. His explanation about the troubles in Germany was that the Jews had copulated with apes in Africa. Tish found his assumptions not only absurd but deeply troubling.

A final clarification occurred early in 1936, when Mary Wigman offered Tish a place in her professional dance group. As Germany prepared to host the Summer Olympics that year, there was widespread excitement at the school and elsewhere. Germany and the Nazis planned to show their best to the outside world: their pride in the nation's economic and social recovery and the glory of the Third Reich. As part of the celebrations, dancers from around the world were invited to attend an International Dance Festival in Berlin just prior to the opening of the Olympics. The Wigman dancers were among those expected to participate in the pre-Olympic spectacular with ten thousand dancers and Hitler Youth members.[30]

Things did not turn out as planned. Wigman's troupe did perform, but most well-known dancers from the United States, including Martha Graham, were urged to boycott the festival and did.[31] Hanya Holm, a former student of Wigman's, responded to the general anti-Nazi feelings by dropping the Mary Wigman name from her New York dance school.

For Tish the time had come to make a choice. She yearned to join the Wigman troupe, and the invitation was the culmination of her years of effort. But she could not support the festival or the facade of Nazi society by agreeing to dance. She could no longer couple her love of dance with her knowledge of what was right. She informed the school that she was returning to the United States.

Tish had been in Germany nearly four years and retrospectively wondered why she and so many thought fascism a temporary aberration. That illusion was sustained by the incremental and cumulative shifts in German society, the press of everyday life and isolation at the school, the lack of apparent alternatives, and the reluctance to see. Tish's immaturity also contributed to slowing her awareness. Denial and positivism affected many others: even when the household maids were forced to leave and Irena Jacoby had to end her education, her father still held illusions of safety.

Tish learned in the spring of 1936 that Persis also planned to return to the United States and arranged to sail from Hamburg to Southampton to join her. On the boat to Germany, Tish had held hands with her dance teacher and dreamed of an artistic utopia. Going home, she had become less self-involved and cared more about ideas. She and Persis had an intense five days together. They strolled on the windy decks for hours, discussing Tish's experiences in Germany, the increased persecution of Jews, and the likelihood of war in Spain. Persis gave her John Strachey's popular book about the failures of capitalism and the connection to fascism, *The Coming Struggle for Power*. His arguments were convincing and gave Tish a much-needed intellectual framework. The book crystallized for her what she had seen in Germany and expanded her vision. Her involvement with dance had been an artist's individual expression of freedom and equality, but Strachey's socialist vision and Persis's encouragement to work against fascism broadened her perceptions. A socialist future with freedom and equality for all now seemed worth working toward.

Mary Wigman, however, chose a different life-course. Although the Dresden school was finally closed in 1943, the year she choreographed the premiere of Carl Orff's *Carmina Burana*, Wigman continued to teach throughout the war at the Leipzig Academy of Music in Germany.[32] Early on, she—like others—chose to conform to the Nazi expectations. Her awakening came too late. Wigman's biographer, Walter Sorrell, explained her probable motives:

> She was a German who had grown up and risen to fame in her country. She felt she had no right to leave her native soil and her contemporaries at a time of their greatest and gravest trial. She did not think of saving herself, not even when she was denounced as a leftist and Jew lover by the Nazi. . . . But the pressures of the National Socialist party grew stronger, and the party took control of her school. . . . She undoubtedly underestimated the horror that was to come. Like her compatriot, the great sculptor Ernst Barlac, ... she woke up too late to the demonic and tragic furor of Nazism.[33]

Mary Wigman gave Tish dance, artistic discipline and inspiration, as well as a technique for expressing deep feeling through movement. That mentor relationship ceased when Wigman put her art before her politics. Her posture of collaboration with the Nazis was disillusioning. Tish had in many ways outgrown Wigman's influence. From her mother Tish learned to persevere, to make do under difficult circumstances. Tish initially rejected what she saw as her mother's superficial mode and only much later recognized her mother as courageous in her own right.

Tish perceived Persis as her most lasting intellectual and ethical role model, though they never spent much time together. Tish admired Persis's serious concern with ideas and issues as well as her integrity. She remembered gratefully that Persis exposed her to the world of politics, and her conceptualization of Persis as an ideal sustained her own direction over the years. Persis devoted the later part of her life to refugee work in southern France. This, too, inspired Tish.

Persis also provided a financial model for Tish. She was very frugal in her expenditures but generous in applying her inherited funds to support causes. For example, Tish knew that Persis supported a worker in the English birth-control movement. In another instance, Heinz, her former lover, asked Tish for money to leave Germany. Tish turned to Persis for two thousand dollars to help him start over in South America, and Persis provided the funds, pointing out that she had also helped others more at risk than Heinz to leave Germany. Tish was later guided by this attitude toward money. She frequently used her own inheritance to support organizations and political workers while living at the most modest level herself.

Tish drew a sense of revulsion and a fear of political tyranny and racist ideology from her experience in Germany that motivated her the rest of her life. She explained her transition from dancer to political adulthood: "I don't recall ever believing that I could be a prima ballerina. . . . It was a drive for expression of understanding, of selfhood, whatever. . . . I was looking for *deeper* meanings. The things that happened to me as a child—the Depression, the experience with Germany . . . plus the experience with Heinz were disturbing and confusing. That's why Persis was so important. She gave me a path to follow."

Dreams and Reality

My own cancer seems to be moving ahead much faster, the tempo is speeded, so that I'm trying as much as possible to bring things together.

Radicals were much more common then than they are now. They were equivalent to liberals today in terms of numbers and influence.

Throughout her life, Tish's struggle for self-knowledge and moral codes permeated her more immediate concerns. While there were frivolous moments and detours in her emotional search, there was always an urge toward understanding and a drive to give form to her own destiny. And, after Germany, Tish was much more likely to see her own experiences in a political context. In 1983, two forces vied for dominance: her own terminal illness and OWL's blossoming as a national organization.

Both Laurie and Tish experienced illness and hospital stays in 1983. And so, while the intense, enthusiastic response to OWL's media campaign across the country was heartening, it was also draining. Tish was conscious of the burdens generated by OWL: "I just realized I'm trying to raise a $315,000 OWL budget—a non-governmental budget." They had already raised $140,000 and were about to start a direct-mail campaign with a list of fifty thousand. "A proposal a week feeds OWL's hungry beak," she laughed wryly.

These and other OWL efforts were advanced by a public-service ad campaign designed and donated by an advertising firm.[1] Young & Rubicam created three black-and-white ads. The first showed a tearful Statue of Liberty with the statement, "When it comes to the treatment of Older Women, we take a lot of liberties." The second ad said, "For men, they created retirement plans, medical benefits, profit sharing and gold watches. For women, they created Mother's Day." The third was similarly striking, "When my husband was here, we had his pension, his medical benefits and his profit sharing. Unfortunately, they left when he did." The ads appeared in *Women's Day*, *Newsweek*, and *Time* magazines. Tish was on the "Today" and "Phil Donahue" shows as a result. She was also interviewed by several newspapers. That ad campaign led to a story in *Family Circle,* which pulled about one hundred letters a day from women all over the country, most telling their own problem stories, some enclosing money.[2]

OWL also opened its Washington, D.C., office in 1983. Alice Quinlan, from the Displaced Homemakers Network, was already working on OWL's legislative issues, and Shirley Sandage—from the Iowa "Door Opener" center—joined her to serve as OWL's executive director. The next few months were a whirlwind.

Tish's other battle, with cancer, was equally consuming. She noted, "From a personal point of view, my own cancer seems to be moving ahead much faster. The tempo is speeded so that I'm trying as much as possible to bring things together, to tie the knots." One thread being tied was OWL's transition from a locally to a nationally based office. OWL was no longer a small organization run from the kitchen table in Oakland.

That earlier Oakland style is itself valuable women's history. It was captured in a 1987 *OWL Observer* article. Reporter Susan Bales wrote about Tish and Laurie's house at 3800 Harrison Street "to capture some of the magic before its special spirit of place was lost to memory."[3] This upbeat article captured the warm memories of volunteer and paid staff. There is a line drawing of the old house, with the bay window, leaded glass fanlight, and second-story windows of Tish's room. The lines are straighter than the actual house, tilted and cracked as it was by earthquake damage. The retold stories of lunches on the patio and around the kitchen table leave out the sticking door and peeling linoleum. The remembered camaraderie de-emphasizes any struggles.

Margaret Malberti, the artist of the sketch, worked as office manager with Tish and Laurie for twelve years. She had been a displaced homemaker, one of their first successful trainees at the Alameda County Displaced Homemaker Center—the first such center in the nation to be state funded—which was established through the efforts of Tish and Laurie. Margaret joined them when Tish left the center, and she and Laurie first conceptualized the Older Women's League Education Fund (OWLEF), the precursor to OWL. Later, Margaret managed OWL's Oakland office and helped produce the *OWL Observer*. She recalled those days fondly: "There was always laughter. And a wonderful freedom to be critical. This was largely established by Tish and Laurie's relationship. They would meet to discuss an issue, and you would hear them going back and forth, trying it this way, trying it another way, disagreeing and then bursting into laughter. This wonderful sisterly spirit set the tone for all of us."

Tish excelled at drawing people to her and eliciting their best efforts. Consequently the bonds among the Oakland crew were strong, particularly for those who had been with Laurie and Tish for years. Good memories: cat stories, pastries from Ladyfingers bakery, joy and good humor—"homeyness." But this idyllic version is also myth making. It paints a lovely picture that is not so much inaccurate as incomplete. There *was* a genuine sharing of ideas, and much playing with possible approaches, but deference to Tish's vision and judgment prevailed. Most "shared" decisions were directed by Tish's will. It was equal and not, according to Fran Leonard, OWL's legal counsel, because of Tish's acknowledged leadership ability and years of experience. "Besides," laughed Fran, "her ideas were such good ones. It was hard to disagree when she articulated ideas so well."[4]

Tish also romanticized when she looked back, and she per-

When it comes to the treatment of older women, we take a lot of liberties.

In a country that prides itself on equality and humanity, it's frightening that older women are so deprived.

- 2.8 million women over 65 live in poverty, compared to less than a million men.
- 12.2 million retirement age women have no access whatsoever to pensions.
- 60% of women over 65 living alone have social security as their only income.
- 4 million women between 45-65 have no health insurance at all.

A new nationwide organization is fighting to change these facts of life. The Older Women's League ("OWL") is helping women, on a national and personal level, to prepare and deal with the problems of growing old. For information, write to: OWL National Headquarters, P.O. Box 11450, Wash., D.C. 20008.

Older Women's League

Advertisement from OWL's 1983 campaign.
Courtesy of Young & Rubicam, San Francisco.

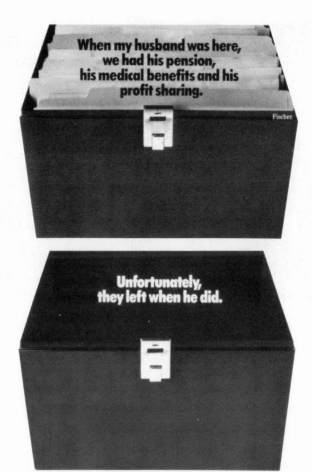

Whether you lose your husband through divorce or death, chances are you'll lose a lot more than just a mate. For while you were once able to benefit from your husband's medical coverage, pension plan and other schemes as a spouse, they can all end abruptly when you're no longer together.

The Older Women's League ("OWL") is a national organization that's helping women to prepare for the devastating losses that separation can bring. And more than that, OWL chapters nationwide are working to change the harsh facts of life that older women inevitably face. For more information, write to: OWL National Headquarters, P.O. Box 11450, Washington D.C. 20008.

Older Women's League

Advertisement from OWL's 1983 campaign.
Courtesy of Young & Rubicam, San Francisco.

sisted in wanting to replicate her ideal of OWL as a "kitchen table" organization. Since she stressed the folksy harmony, she wanted the national office to run the same way. She often mused, "Why can't they be more like us?" Differences in style and approach generated new problems and complicated the shift from Oakland to the national office.

One issue that was particularly divisive was the pay scale. The debate over egalitarian structure and salaries has plagued the women's movement and other radical organizations over the decades, and it thrived in OWL. Tish's utopian model was one where all workers committed themselves to fight for the cause. Her view was that they should also accept economic sacrifice. Others agreed with her about commitment but felt the need to validate their worth as "professionals" by adequate pay.

Tish took no salary and worked seven days a week. Laurie got half Margaret's modest salary (twelve thousand dollars in 1983) for full-time editing of the *OWL Observer* and free living space in the house. Attorney Fran Leonard accepted the same wages for her half-time legal and proposal-writing work as Margaret did for running the office. The only full-time paid staff member in Oakland was Margaret, who served as office manager and general ground controller. The other part-timers were subsidized by Tish until grant proposals yielded funding. Most had additional sources of income, even if slight. The "professional" and the "volunteer" got the same low wages.

Tish's desire that OWL's Oakland and national offices be structured alike was unrealistic. Tish was an atypical model for the others: she lived modestly, was compulsively frugal, and had always had an independent income as a cushion. She was also reluctant to build in fringe benefits for employees, including a retirement plan, and had to be convinced that the principle was essential for an organization that lobbied for these benefits for all older women. On this issue, funds were eventually found.

As some in Washington saw it, they were trying to combine commitment to OWL with making a living. Further, several on the board and staff felt that women's work needed to be validated by professional wage levels since it was historically underpaid. This ideological conflict continued. Thus, Tish's voice and agenda generated and shaped OWL, but she never accepted or approved of the more professional, hierarchically based Washington structure.

She was very frustrated by the end of 1983, tired and irritated by the friction. Internal conflict could lead to fragmentation, and she was concerned that the organization would be sidetracked from its primary goals. She also understood that she tended to keep to her own agenda and was at times disinclined to hear the views of others. She generally avoided conflict, and was willing to confront directly only as a last resort.

Two potential conflicts were on the November board meeting agenda. The first was whether to raise OWL's annual dues from five to ten dollars. It seemed simple but had been a burning issue for some time. Tish had the staff list the arguments pro and con, and the vote went the way she hoped it would: dues would be kept low to include the poor and appeal to the broadest possible base.[5]

The second issue was raising the staff's salaries. The executive director studied how OWL compared with other organizations and found that her own salary was much lower than the going rate. Also, in other local nonprofit organizations the bottom layer of salaries, for clerks and secretaries, was higher than at OWL. The board's budget committee proposed to raise the upper-level salary by three thousand dollars a year, other "professionals" by two thousand, and leave the lowest salaries as they were. A tremendous blowup ensued with Tish leading the opposition. "I used two arguments. First, can a social change organization have comparable salaries with other lobbying groups, or is it pricing itself out of existence, is it jeopardizing its own future?" Her second concern was the unfairness of the range of salaries. "The first thing off the bat, one of the other board members said, we're not increasing it *enough*, we ought to raise the executive director's

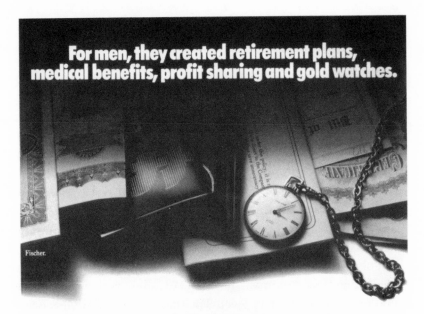

For men, they created retirement plans, medical benefits, profit sharing and gold watches.

Fischer.

For women, they created Mother's Day.

Millions of midlife and older women in America are trying to survive on a fraction of the benefits and income men receive. If you're a woman in this category, it's a fact of life you know all too well.

But now, there's the Older Women's League ("OWL"), a national organization that's working to change these facts of life. OWL chapters nationwide are helping women on a national and personal level. But we need your help to aid the cause of older women everywhere, many of whom live in poverty, without medical benefits, without pensions. Your ideas, your energy and your commitment are valuable resources that the Older Women's League needs. If you want to help, or if you want information on the OWL chapter nearest you, write to: OWL National Headquarters, P.O. Box 11450, Washington, D.C. 20008.

Older Women's League

Advertisement from OWL's 1983 campaign.
Courtesy of Young & Rubicam, San Francisco.

salary even more, she is doing all this fine work and so on." Other board members felt that few professional women in Washington, D.C., could afford the salaries Tish thought reasonable.[6]

Tish lost that battle, and it hurt. She was concerned about costs and what these increases could mean. "How the hell are we going to raise a $600,000 budget for 1984? That's a lot of money." She again emphasized that they all got the same pay in Oakland, what she considered a full living wage based on the principle that the organizer lives on the same scale as the workers. She believed that salary gaps created problems and generated power inequities since paid staff accrued more power with higher pay while non-paid people or those at the bottom of the scale had no clout. The board overruled her.

She turned the problems over in her mind, reviewing this defeat. The basic argument in this OWL fight was: we can't get good people at that salary level. The theory was that professionals couldn't live on that lower salary in Washington, D.C., yet it wasn't questioned whether the person on the lower level could. "With this particular leadership it's a losing battle, I'm not going to convince them." She felt bruised by their apparent failure to understand. Used to a compliant board, Tish was also surprised and wounded by their refusal to accept her will on a major issue.

The struggle within the organization was demoralizing. By the beginning of 1984, Tish had turned her attention to the telling of her personal story since it reduced her level of frustration and emphasized a more positive legacy. Thinking about how she learned to organize reaffirmed her desire to educate others. She also sought to fulfill her "role model" responsibilities by tracing her activist history and explaining how organizing enriched her life. During this period, she stressed a "common bonds" theme, asserting that almost anyone can do something to bring about change. She emphasized that she was not so exceptional, that what worked for her could work for others.

She had turned to the evolution of her organizing efforts as early as her return from Germany in May 1936, when she was attempting to blend her new political awareness with her dance aesthetic. By this time, Mary Wigman's fame had definitely lessened because of her assumed collaboration with the Nazis. When Tish attended a major dance concert in New York, featuring such great dancers as Martha Graham, Jose Limon, and Doris Humphrey, she felt very intimidated. "I sensed New York was not for me, but felt I'll be back to show you all."[7]

She returned to San Francisco and shared her mother's apartment for a predictably short time. Her mother finally received money from her former husband, who had, as anticipated, inherited a substantial sum. Kate could now afford a more luxurious lifestyle, one that contrasted sharply with Tish's frugal standards. Tish decided to move on. Shortly after that, her mother decided to go to China. Kate enjoyed herself, spent much time with Russian émigrés, played bridge constantly, and bought superb art from people fleeing the Japanese invasion. Some of this art was given to and later went from home to home with Tish. Mother and daughter visited after this, but they neither lived together nor were close again.

Tish moved next to Los Angeles and went back to school at UCLA in January 1937. She bounced from one major to another. "At first I started out as an economics major because at this time I was truly into Marx. But I found my economics didn't agree with the professors'. In the first paper I wrote, I straightened them out." She laughed, "It was clear we were not going to see eye to eye. Then I decided that physical education would obviously be the thing, since the dance program was part of physical education." She was scared off by the strenuous athletics on the hockey field. "So I switched my major to history. I've forgotten what the problem was there. Within three months I went through three or four majors and finally ended up in psychology. Why psychology? Because they had a couple of left-wing professors. I thought I could do better there, so I got my degree in psychology."[8]

Tish in Los Angeles, ca. 1937.

She also worked as a dancer and choreographer for the successful Dance Recital programs at UCLA. The programs were
presented from 1936 to 1941 and were well received by Los Angeles dance enthusiasts and critics. Martha Deane, department
head for many years, described the jubilance and eagerness with
which the students put in long hours.[9] Much creativity was generated by musicians, dancers, and artists from all over campus.
Though they had few financial resources and their facilities were
rugged, there was great camaraderie. They rehearsed in a rough,
open-air shed—where the flies stuck to their sweaty arms and
legs—and dyed their own costumes, dipping the muslin in the
sinks. Their arms were multicolored as they swirled around the
floor.

Deane remembered and praised Tish's contributions as a
dancer and choreographer. One program lists her as Letitia Innes,
designer of the section, "Of Us, Americans" by (Gertrude) Stein.
She was also named, with Robert Lee and Deane, as co-director

for the entire 1940 Dance Recital. Forty were on that production crew, with eighty-six dancers performing. Among them was Yuriko Ameniuja who later danced with Tish in San Francisco. After World War II, Yuriko became a leading dancer with the Martha Graham dance group in New York.

Tish worked with the Dance Recital for two or three years, primarily on choreography. She came to know composer John Cage, who wrote a dance piece for her. She also helped design a dance based on Archibald MacLeish's poetic *Land of the Free*.[10] Tish earned money by teaching dance classes for fifty cents an hour, sponsored by a National Recovery program. "Well, they didn't pay me for a full hour. Twenty-five minutes to dress and undress, so they only paid twenty-five cents a class." She also did historical research on dance, building the department's small library. It was a diverse and challenging time, which Tish remembered fondly: "I loved going back to school, I really did."

At the same time, Tish was also pleased to reestablish an old friendship. Her former housemate in Germany, Florrie Gordon, had married John Thunen and was involved with the Lester Horton Dance Theater. Through Florrie, Tish joined Horton's group. Horton had captured the imagination of California audiences by the late 1930s with his bold works.[11] His was one of the first multi-ethnic dance groups in the country as well as a West Coast center for iconoclastic modern dancers. They rehearsed in his large, airy, terra-cotta and blue studio, where Tish felt at home, though she knew she didn't quite have a "Lester Horton" dancer's body.

She also felt comfortable with the group's socially conscious dances. Horton's biographer characterized their content this way: "The intense commitment of [Communist] party workers in his group and the strength of his belief that the central humanistic ideas were morally correct had led to a radical perspective. . . . Not only did the works tell what was wrong, but often they suggested some fairly specific mode of action as a remedy, i.e., unite, rebel, strike."[12] Tish recalled performing in at least two

Horton ballets: *Ku Klux Klan* and *Prologue to an Earth Celebration*, described as "a primitive spring ceremonial."[13]

Lester Horton's star dancer in the 1930s was Bella Lewitsky, who remembered Tish as "a very lovely person, committed, caring, warm." Though she hesitated to comment after so many years, she did recall that Tish wasn't the most gifted of the Horton dancers: "Her body was not terribly flexible, and there was no brilliance to her style. She did interesting choreographic work, and was at her best form then. She was a wonderful member of the company, truthful, honest, hardworking." Lewitsky also felt Tish was very shy. "One had to work at becoming her friend, as she was a bit retiring." She added, "There were no pretensions, no subterfuge, no clouded inferences—a direct and honest person."[14]

Dance was still at the center of Tish's life during this period, but she began shifting toward organizational work as better suited to her own talents. Mary Wigman's assessment had been that Tish would probably never be a famous solo dancer but would make an excellent teacher. Similarly kind, Lewitsky emphasized Tish's contributions to the company, not her dance abilities.

Tish found new direction as an organizer during Horton's production of *Le Sacre du printemps* at the Hollywood Bowl in August 1937. The grim conditions the dance troupe endured sparked protest and collective action. Tish recalled, "We had augmented the group with other students because we needed a large crowd for the space. And costumes were made with absolutely minimum cost. We weren't getting paid a cent. I was getting madder and madder, and other dancers were griping about it too." She realized others were organizing, so why shouldn't they? As their first action, they planned a picket line around the Hollywood Bowl. "We got leaflets made, but the printer was Lester Horton's printer and told him what we planned. Horton pleaded with us not to protest, that this was his big chance. People liked him so much, we decided we couldn't let him down and went ahead with the show." Once that performance was over, they moved to organize a Dancers' Federation. "I was pretty much the instigator of it, but I wasn't the president because I wasn't enough of a recognized dancer." At a rally the following year Lester Horton joined other well-known dancers and professional performers in support for the resident Hollywood Bowl ballet company called for by the federation.[15]

Their organizing efforts brought the Horton dancers to the attention of the Tenney committee, the panel investigating "subversives" in California. Testifying in 1943, a witness said, "Dancers formed a separate unit with other Communist party dancers in Los Angeles County, some of whom were said to compose the Horton Dance Group, among whom were Letitia Innes, . . . whom I met as a Communist comrade."[16] There were no direct consequences, but the secretary of the northern Dance Federation wrote a letter asking if the southern organization had been infiltrated by "Reds." That 1943 hearing testimony was repeated in 1947 California hearings and eventually went into Tish's FBI record, which also picked up a *People's World* news item about a "Committee for Correspondence" social event from that period. According to the FBI, this was a "Communist infiltrated organization," and Letitia Innes "would lead the Conga and other dances at the party."[17]

An interesting series of events preceded Tish's decision to join the Communist party in 1936. Not long after she arrived in Los Angeles, she was invited to attend a meeting by a young man interested in her experiences in Germany. "It turned out to be a Communist party meeting. I told what I could of my experiences there. Of course I was given the usual criticism." The same criticism she had received in London. "People who hadn't been there just looked at it differently. It wasn't that I wasn't critical, and wasn't beginning to see the context. I was reading political analysis by this time. But I would tell factually what I had seen. And it wasn't what they expected to hear." In spite of this awkward session, Tish was drawn to them, and believed the Communist party was fighting against the fascism she hated.[18]

This was the Popular Front period of the late 1930s. The

American Communist party expanded rapidly, choosing to emphasize their support for general American values rather than the
party's ideological differences from the mainstream. Tish, like
thousands of others, was captivated by what seemed a major historical force. Discussing the phenomenon in Southern California,
historians Ceplair and Englund pointed out, "Most mid- and late-
decade joiners enrolled in the rush of great emotion aroused by
the wave of fascist aggression. . . . [They] were not ideologues
but idealists, propelled far more by their liberal temperament and
an emotional commitment to dramatic causes than by any medi-
ated engagement to communism, the social revolution or the Soviet Union."[19] Tish certainly fit this description.

Sid Burke invited Tish to that first meeting, and they soon
began to date. Simultaneously Tish was seeing a young man from
San Diego "whom I had met on a visit to my father's. . . . My
stepmother was quite pretentious, she loved to have 'do's.' She
decided to promote her stepdaughter socially by having me dance
in front of a lawn party. This resulted in an invitation to dance at
some charity ball, at the elegant, Victorian Del Coronado Hotel.
I'm sure it went over big. I did it to Bach, all dressed up in a
lovely white satin gown." That's where she met this young man
from a wealthy department store family. There she was, dating
these two men. Both were beginning to push her toward marriage. "I could see myself being corrupted by wealth. That was
really the reason I think that I chose Sid. I don't think I was in
love with Sid, but it seemed 'right.' He was a radical, and was
guilt-tripping me a lot too."

Before Sid and Tish married, Sid was invited by Tish's father
to the exclusive Jonathan Club in Los Angeles to discuss Sid's
future. Jews (as well as other minorities and women) weren't
admitted to club membership, and Sid felt her father saw the
marriage as beneath her. This Jewish radical had no future in the
eyes of Murray Innes. Despite this familial reception, they soon
got married at City Hall. It was 1938. When her mother returned from China, Tish and Sid had settled in. Kate was ap-

palled at the way they were living. "She didn't like Sid and he didn't like her. They had nothing in common and he didn't put himself out." Their marriage reinforced Tish's break from her family background.

It was not, however, a particularly happy marriage. Often unemployed during the Depression, Sid reported on the arts and general political activities and eventually became editor of a newspaper for longshoremen. He was also an intellectual, devoted to classical music and poetry. Tish was impressed with his good mind and his full revolt against his parents' middle-class lifestyle. He pushed her political development, but they were temperamentally mismatched. They broke up several times and then came back together over four or five years.

They lived very cheaply. Tish relished the memory: "I had a cookbook, get the most for your money sort, and I could squeeze my funds, like making soup from pea pods. We used to go out to a place where you could get a six-course meal with wine for about thirty-nine cents. It was cheap even for its time, one of those family-style bargain places." Everybody they knew managed on little money, went to free concerts, and met at cheap restaurants where the talk was more important than the cuisine.

Bella Lewitsky, Tish's friend, insisted Tish was too submissive in the relationship. She viewed it as a "terribly mis-matched marriage." Lewitsky acknowledged Sid's charm, intelligence, interest in culture, and considerable writing skills, but disdained his rudeness and self-involvement. She also felt Tish was cowed by him. She wanted to say to Tish, "You're so much better than he is."

Tish returned to her studies a married woman, an atypical undergraduate experience for that time. She was also a bit older than the other students and certainly had more life experience. She joined the Young Communist League (YCL) but couldn't stand it. To her, "It seemed like a fraternity/sorority with boys and girls trying to date." Being older and married also made a difference. She had trouble fitting in and became critical when she couldn't adapt. Many of the YCL members had been brought up in left-wing households. She felt they hadn't had to work out their radical identity on their own. "They just took it for granted," she recalled, "they didn't question." She found a new small Communist group of age peers, primarily graduate students. "Because of the dance and being in Europe for three years, I thought of myself as somewhat superior. There was a kind of intellectual elitism there."

Tish reviewed her joining the Communist party in 1936 as the turning point in her life: "It just seemed a huge click. The Communist theory opened up and explained my experiences in Germany, and it gave hope for a new kind of society." She remembered hearing Elizabeth Gurley Flynn say she would see socialism in her lifetime. "I recall later sitting on a beach in Santa Monica, re-reading Strachey's *The Coming Struggle for Power*, and being impatient just sitting in the sun, waiting and feeling here was a whole new world to be built—how would I go about doing it?"

Joining the party was an answer to the uncertainties she experienced. It provided guidance and leadership, the direction in which she should move. For almost two decades the party provided her with a home, cultural support, and a tight network of friends. Personal and political blended; a world view and code of behavior provided direction. The theory she read in those early years also made sense to her, particularly the idea of democratic centralism. "To me it meant the greatest possible democracy on the one hand, input from the grass roots so to speak. Then, once a decision is agreed upon, everybody adheres to it, and you move as one force."

The theme of democratic centralism stayed with Tish and informed much of her later work: "The greater the participation from the bottom in making decisions, the greater likelihood that people will have the willingness, the drive, the commitment to carry on." She was convinced this was the core of grass-roots organizing. It became her central guiding principle.

She recognized that in the party it was mostly theory. "In practice it was pure manipulation. You had a course of action decided by the top leadership, and then you got people to accept it by making them think they were taking part and having real debate." She saw her own approach differently. "Now I feel the likelihood to reach effective decisions is greater when you can really get the maximum participation." Close observers of her leadership style with OWL challenged the reality of this claim. While members were indeed presented with alternative proposals, and asked to decide on issues or strategies, the rationale for decision-making was weighted in the direction Tish wanted to move. She controlled OWL's agenda; they ratified her strategies. Her theory of decision-making often did not match their experience working with her.

Even though she became a dedicated party member in the 1930s, Tish saw herself as an outsider once again. She had experienced this previously in her family, in Germany, in professional dance—and now with the Communist party. Tish claimed it as a positive attribute, signaling her independence. She was far from being sad about it. As she saw it, she was almost always a cultural worker, or "mass worker," and not inside policy circles. "One reason I didn't like the internal party stuff was the dogma. Most meetings were very rigid in format. You had a very tight agenda: you did the world, the national, regional, then local, and set tasks and so on. It was static, cut and dried and boring."

But Tish found tremendous satisfaction in her own cultural tasks. "Mass work was something else! Without the Communist label, you helped people work toward broad, humanistic goals. I was good at it, and because I was, the party accepted me as a mass worker. Also, because I was in the arts that set me apart a little." Her recollection was that she generally acted on her own, without much party guidance. "Later, in San Francisco for example, I don't even remember going to meetings. I remember going to parties, fund raisers, but not doing much but teaching dance."

Retrospectively, her link to communism was primarily ideological and intellectual. She loved being part of a world-wide movement. She also absorbed a dialectical method, focused on constant change to prevent disillusionment. That sense of the continuity of struggle stayed with her and enabled her to see disappointments or failures from a positive point of view. She learned to be patient about political change.

A trade union celebration in Tijuana, attended by hundreds of leftists from Southern California, epitomized the dynamic context Tish valued. The Mexican government opened the Aguas Calientes Racetrack to accommodate celebrants, and visitors slept on cots or the floor. There were demonstrations, and visits to a local commune. For Tish, singing the "Internationale" in Spanish, with thousands of enthusiasts joining in, was a thrilling moment.

The memory of that dynamic moment drew her back to Mexico in 1940. She and Sid weren't getting along that summer—sexually or any other way. Without much hesitation she left him and their friction to join friends in Mexico City. These comrades shared a three-bedroom apartment in a newer section of the city. After her friends went back to Los Angeles, Tish stayed on. She witnessed huge public parades prior to the elections and the revolutionary fervor that filled the city.

There was a large group of American radicals, significant in numbers and influence, in Mexico City at that time. To Tish, "Those three months were singularly exciting. They really showed me a way to go during revolutionary periods, what can be accomplished. You had the sense of the potential for social change when a people is in motion, even though this one was past its zenith and on its way down." There was violence surrounding the election, and considerable shooting. Tish heard loud shouts, watched the ambulances, and saw the raw violence.[20]

Moving around the countryside by bus, Tish was befriended by a member of a cultural education team. He took her to a rural community where they were conducting health care education and literacy training. She watched as the team met with local peasants, organizing to solve community problems. Finding it extremely creative and exciting, she felt this was the way to build a new world.

She decided to return to Sid; whatever problems they had seemed insignificant next to the shared political vision. She rejoined him in San Francisco, where they lived in a small apartment in a converted whorehouse. Their reconciliation didn't last long—just long enough for Tish to get pregnant and have another abortion. Tish reminisced about their marriage and the climate of the times: "It was more than common political concerns that the marriage was based on. Sid was an intellectual, and I was really strong on intellectual mentors. I learned some basic philosophical concepts from him." It was a carryover from Persis, like carrying on to learn further of the wonders and mysteries she had first introduced. "You know, I really did respect him, he was a nice guy, but it just wasn't right for us."

Sid still seemed pained in 1985 when he talked about their marriage. Like Tish, he felt the marriage had foundered over sex. He attributed the breakup to Tish, who (in his view) had "a lot of sexual hangups" and sought relationships with other men. He recalled she always selected "interesting" partners, perhaps some consolation for him. He didn't remember Tish's abortion, but she said she probably didn't tell him. When they separated for good, Tish took an apartment with a friend from her high-school days. Never very worried about managing financially, she made a little money teaching dance classes.[21]

Tish revelled in her autonomy. She soon found a way to bring together her interests in organizing and choreography. The next summer she embarked on an ambitious program for the Stern Grove Music Festival in Golden Gate Park. She envisioned a series of dances performed in the open air. The Festival Committee approved the project, with a hundred-dollar budget, setting the date for August 24, 1941.[22]

Tish savored the memory of the energies poured into preparation. She and her friends called themselves the Modern Ballet Group of San Francisco. Each of the three directors designed a dance, Tish's based on the novel *Green Mansions*. Yuriko agreed to come up from Los Angeles to dance Rima, the bird girl, and Lou Harrison wrote new music for the piece. Tish recruited the other dancers, arranged funding, and molded the production. Much later, she laughed remembering the limits of her choreography, since each section had to start with the right foot to keep the amateur dancers together.

As Tish said, "Why not reach for the moon?" They worked day and night, laughing and complaining of weary bones. Tish's old friend, Leona, stitched and sewed, surrounded by the friendly—if frantic—group. One night she went to fix dinner, and as she opened the oven door, bloomers and a skirt fell out. Somehow in the chaos it all came together. The large crowd at Stern Grove that Sunday in August was enthusiastic, particularly about Yuriko's beautiful performance as child of the lost race. The reviewers agreed about Yuriko's special talent, but were critical overall: "[the choreography] will need a lot of work before it lives up to its setting and its music. It is slow in spots and in spots it dies altogether."[23]

Stern Grove was an example of something that plagued, encouraged, and spurred Tish on for the rest of her life. That is, "dreaming up things which are too big and then *almost* making them work. Sometimes, rarely, rarely do they come off as the dream because it's impossible to begin with. But I certainly have never been daunted!"

Inspired by her near-victory, she was ready for change, and a new relationship provided the opportunity. She had fallen in love with a man twenty years her senior, who had designed the house she lived in. He came around often, continuing to remodel the building. He was a womanizer as well, and she was susceptible. At the time Tish had no awareness of his wife's vulnerability, though she realized the wife was bitter toward her. But in reconstructing this story, she was sensitive to her earlier opportunism and selfishness. "That was a rather bohemian time, you could pretty well do what you wanted if you were both on the left and an artist. She was an older woman, and it was a typical example of an older man picking up a younger woman, going off trying to rejuvenate." She was twenty-seven and he was forty-seven.

Tish in San Francisco, ca. 1941.

"Through me, he was getting youth, he was getting energy, and he was getting the belief in himself that he could start again."

Tish wanted to go back to Los Angeles, and he wanted to write for the movies, so before long they established themselves in a collective household in Hollywood. Given the housing shortage, other dancers and artists were happy to share chores and space for reasonable rent. Tish made a dance studio out of the large living room. She printed up flyers with a busy schedule of classes: folk dancing on Sundays; modern dance on Monday evenings and Wednesday mornings; dance workshops on Wednesday evenings, private lessons by appointment; and "special classes for young screen artists." Her fees ranged from twenty-five cents for folk dancing to fifteen dollars per month for screen artists. For a short time, Katherine Dunham's group prepared for their next tour in the living room. Tish was fascinated by Dunham and particularly liked her combination of African and modern dance movements, which she later incorporated in her own work.[24] House and life established, she turned her attention once again to politics.

Tish had only been back in Los Angeles a few months when the whole atmosphere was dramatically changed by the bombing of Pearl Harbor. "Now everybody was thrown into the anti-Nazi war effort. I was feeling very guilty, what am I doing for the war effort, having these classes? Dancing with servicemen at USO parties hardly seemed enough." Women were urged to go into war work, so she decided to put aside her art and make armaments. She applied at Lockheed but flunked the hand-eye coordination test.

"Feeling rather unwanted," she went on, "I let my imagination begin to stir. I decided that what was needed was some kind of daycare for kids of women who were going to work." By 1942, magazines and newspapers were reporting on the patriotic acts of women and the related lack of adequate child care facilities. She went to a community center and asked about using the facilities for children. Assembling a group of volunteers, she convinced them of the project's importance to the war effort. Here again, Tish's enthusiasm exceeded her skills. "We then brought in this mob of children," she recalled, laughing, "and of course I knew absolutely nothing about kids! It was a madhouse! Finally we got some movies, and found some art materials. Eventually it led toward the development of pretty good child care because people who knew what they were doing got into it, and I got out."[25]

Tish also worked with the Joint Anti-Fascist Refugee Committee on a benefit for Spanish refugee children who had been sent to Mexico. A local art teacher encouraged young people to create prints and drawings to raise money. Tish organized the event, which was mounted in her living room, and was covered by *California Arts and Architecture* as the "Children's Fair for Refugee Youth."[26] She kept a print called "Three Marias," later proudly displayed in her Oakland bedroom. Not until 1985 did she learn that at that same time her cousin Persis was also working with Spanish refugee children, in the south of France.[27] Tish liked the coincidence, the commonality unknown at the time.

Tish's work on the art fair kept her busy, but her relationship with her older lover was not going well. The collective house disbanded when they began to have difficulties. He couldn't sell his work, and he wanted her to give him ideas for films. "I didn't think he had very sharp ideas, and his writing wasn't very good. He was very frustrated and bitter because it wasn't working out like his dreams. It also wasn't working out like *my* dreams, but I was doing better than he was. I couldn't stand it and walked out."

During this era, the early 1940s, Tish saw art *as* politics. "It was all part of the creative struggle to live poor but with a rich mental, intellectual and spiritual life. It was a time of great excitement, of people going to huge mass meetings and talking about socialism in their time—a vision shared by millions, of making a new society, working together toward it."

Tish committed herself throughout this period to combining ideology and art. As she absorbed the ideas, she translated them into dances that made a political statement. For example, she choreographed a dance for UCLA grounded in the Spanish Civil War. They opened with a gay, lively scene, people exuberant, skirts whirling. Then Tish, dressed in black as the cry of doom or the prophetess, entered. As she danced through, people drew back. She represented a crying out of the Spanish soul in sorrow for their land and people. The dance closed with a reenacted air raid. Only her figure was left, standing in sorrow over the devastation. Tish recalled that powerful moment: "That's one example of trying to mold the political and aesthetic."

For Tish this was "a period of moving, going forward on this vision of the future, and integrating. Political artist, political activist, wife." Pausing, Tish noted with some irony the least smooth part of her life: "Actually, what I wasn't integrating very well was 'wife.'"

Harmony in A-flat

And it was fun, it was creative, it was culturally exciting and politically stimulating. . . . I remember those years as being joyous ones apart from everything else.

It's never easy, the struggle to fit together what you believe in with what you're doing.

Tish's struggle forty years later was to integrate the political with a rapidly declining, weakened body. In her last years cancer dominated, and in the process of coping, she achieved a measure of personal balance. She brought to the experience of illness the same skills and strategies that had informed and guided her earlier political life.

Tish was stunned when she learned about the recurrence of her cancer in 1979. At first she saw it as a death sentence. It didn't take long, however, for her to transform despair into energy for a new task. Her response was consistent. First the diagnosis forced her into introspection, and a certain amount of self-recrimination. She did not have health insurance and was a few months short of Medicare eligibility. She had gambled by letting her insurance lapse. "I thought I could beat the percentages." She wondered whether the DES she had taken in 1951 or the estrogen she was prescribed in the mid–1960s for menopause might have stimulated the cancer. She fretted over the possibility that something in her personality made a difference.

After some brooding over whether she might be to blame for

her own disease because of stresses in her life (overwork? expecting too much of herself? reaching beyond her own self image?), Tish began to approach cancer differently. She started a journal, planning to use it as the basis for a book. Thinking strategically, she knew "the health care cost question is hot. I could make a significant statement. Maybe sell it and recoup the expenses—for the movement. If I live, it can be an example of politicalizing a personal struggle as well as a human document to draw attention to the issues. If I die, a model of going down fighting." With this decision, she felt renewed, "my own sense of life expectancy was suddenly enhanced."

As was her habit, she began to make lists. She also developed healing visualizations. Some were abstract (cancer cells are "bad" ideas like racism, ageism, sexism, while white cells are humanist ideas or organizers), others concrete (cancer cells are dandelions, weeds, and she was the gardener). Another image she used was of a Northwest Indian ritual, a dancer with an owl mask magically banishing disease. Later she used a beach image. Here debris was destroyed and the shore cleansed. "When at last I see the beach clean, I am well again."

Tish worked with traditional physicians and a nontraditional health counselor, Betsy Blakeslee. She tried radiation and chemotherapy as well as biofeedback, visualization, meditation, and diet therapy. She attended sessions of I Can Cope (the American Cancer Society support group), went to cancer conferences, and read voraciously as bibliotherapy. She found comfort and a sense of control in her plan for herself. Before long she moved away from "digging in the dark recesses for *causes* of cancer" and became more focused on discipline and balance. Elements of her plan included discipline in every area:

> 1. work, in moderation, but continuing along the course already established; 2. the special goal or project [at this point her book on cancer]; 3. ordered recreation; 4. adequate personal-social relationships; 5. exercise, nutrition, sleep—all given attention; 6. medical

assistance as needed; 7. a peer support group; 8. faith in myself and my plan.[1]

She was "in training" for life, dedicating her tremendous drive and will to her program. She coached herself like an athlete, kept records, boosted her spirits with upbeat self-admonitions. Like other cancer patients, she reported uneven results. "Some days are just not as great as others. . . . Wondered as I did my walk/run and anticipated the cycling why I put myself through all this. The discomfort can be intense." At times she felt unable to work, exhausted or distracted by overcommitments. But then there were the good periods as well. "A complete change of mood!" she reported, "Why? The 'natural' permanent [hair-do] for one. It looks *great* and I'm having a rare attack of vanity." She was preparing for Hugh Downs's "Over Easy" television special on older women, and the professional makeup session made her "feel gorgeous, comparatively speaking."[2]

One of her most satisfying efforts was pulling together a support group. "From my experience with the women's movement, I knew that when you are going through a real crisis, a significant transition in your life, you can learn more from those who have been through it than anyone else."[3]

The friends who formed the group decided they wanted positively oriented people, those who were fighting against cancer. "We didn't want to take on other people's problems, we had enough of our own. Also, we wanted to admit there were limits. That we would help if we could, but if we couldn't, that should not be taken personally."

Tish remembered how close she felt to one early member. She was impressed by the woman's leadership skills and personal warmth. Then, "Jean had a very sudden recurrence. She came home [from folk dancing] and felt this pain, recognized it as the same as an earlier bone involvement." Its growth was rapid. Within three or four months from that point she was completely bedridden.

Tish experienced Jean's rapid decline and death as a personal blow. "In a sense I lost faith. Jean's death was such a surprise because she did everything right. She did those things so much better than any of us, the diet, exercise, the visualization, the positive attitude. She was the first member of our group who did die. I think we had had a sense that together we had immortality if we held on to each other."

Tish became even more introspective upon Jean's death. "For me it was also the fact that her cancer seemed to mirror mine. The symptoms were very similar. I identified so strongly with her that her death was a real threat to me, apart from the loss of her person." The bonds of support were tempered by the loss of several members over the years, a bittersweet reminder of the limits of such groups.

Since cancer was their primary connection, they were sometimes surprised to discover just how different they were from one another. One woman talked about Linda: "By the time she came into our group she was already in pain, and refusing any of the traditional medical cures. I did think Linda was nuts not to go to doctors. And she was on stuff I'd always thought weird. The support that Linda got from this group for her wheat grass diet or whatever the hell else it was she wanted to do for the last part of her life was the best thing any group could ever have given."

Tish was well aware of the empowerment. "A support group provides information about options. It also gives the perspective that there's a whole spectrum of responses to being a cancer patient, from being a pawn of the medical profession down to the other extreme of doing only the alternatives." She liked the group support for individual decisions and the honest feedback. "If a person is talking about, or is scared to death about cancer, sometimes there is a very distorted perception. I've found that I've been encouraged, bolstered, been goosed or whatever. There's another thing it does for us—it helps us get on with our lives."

Despite the support group, by early 1984 Tish was dismayed on two fronts: she was concerned about recent bleeding episodes and her overcommitments at work. And she was continually frustrated by the national OWL office's direction. She and the director were not in harmony.

To minimize irritation, Tish was now "willing to give up the 100 percent gung ho approach to OWL. That's a bit tough." She meant to change her lifestyle in a fundamental way. "The old way was to make my life as useful as possible, even if it shortened my time. Now I've changed. If I can get well, what a role model! I've always said I wanted to have a proper balance between being a cancer patient and being Tish Sommers, activist, so that one didn't dominate. . . . Now I'm trying to integrate the two. In other words, Tish Sommers, Activist Beating Cancer!"

To Tish, achieving balance did not mean being idle. She planned her seventieth birthday party for September 1984 at the neighborhood church in Oakland. Old friends and co-workers were asked to bring a potluck dish for what she considered a victory celebration. During that birthday month, she also attended OWL's national convention in Washington, D.C., where she rested in her hotel room much of the time. She was still at odds with OWL's executive director but pleased that she had identified a potential successor to herself as president.[4] She also managed to attend the San Francisco OWL Development Council fund-raiser, where Jane Fonda brought in a good crowd of potential donors. She continued to write OWL funding proposals and completed projects, including the last of some organizing workbooks for local chapters.[5]

To manage her response to stress, Tish met with health counselor Betsy Blakeslee. At her advice, she did visualizations more often and went back to a simple diet. She talked herself into spending money on a VCR because it would give her access to healing films. "After all, it's cheaper than being in the hospital!"

At the Western Gerontology Society[6] meetings in Anaheim, Tish reveled in recruiting OWL members. She was tickled to make a good showing in her age-group footrace. "Well, second of two is terrific, after all!" She looked well, the facial puffiness from

Jane Fonda with Tish at OWL fund-raiser, 1984. Photograph courtesy of OWL.

medication gone. She was still uncomfortable from her bladder catheter but seemed more at ease.

Tish's other primary concern was the future leadership of OWL. She saw the loss of the battle over salaries the previous fall as a bad sign. She feared the move from political dynamism to static administrative management. "Keeping the vision, the excitement, the sense of direct involvement of all those who are responsible, especially staff people, is something people who have not been activists don't understand. I don't know whether you can communicate that need to somebody who doesn't have the feel for it."

Tish downplayed her own charisma and talent as well as her decades of experience. "I have positive features which an awful lot of people share. I've just honed them and applied them a little bit more thoroughly to my life, but there's nothing new." Her view was that she had no special magic, nor did people need a lot of training or skill to become organizers. "People have to get over the fear of the experts and have more confidence in their own commonsense. We know a hell of a lot more than we think we know, if we only apply it." Many responded positively to her humility, her conviction that anyone can (and should) act, even when they did not quite accept Tish's admonition that "anybody can do it." Her sincerity helped her connect, enabled her to lead without seeming "above" others. But her vision was blurred when it came to the limits of amateurs, or the problems facing simultaneous visionaries and implementors. The qualities that made OWL so attractive as the "new kid on the block" politically were not necessarily the skills needed to sustain a growing organization.

Tish pondered which of three ways OWL might go. She saw that it might fizzle for lack of initiative and money. Or it could become like other traditional women's organizations, conservative with some liberal interests. She preferred the third option: "OWL stays in the forefront of . . . the women's movement and pushes forward with a more militant leadership, seeing the broader context and working in alliance with other groups." This was consonant with her own vision, although she acknowledged the possible negative outcome of the organization's disharmony. Awaiting the outcome was an unfamiliar and uncomfortable role for Tish.

But, less than a year after the opening of the national OWL office, Tish started to pull back. Her political/ideological frustration prompted her to lower the level of her direct participation with staff. As she did, her attention turned to this book on her life. She saw it as a legacy in the making, and an important self-motivator. "This started off as an oral history—'Quick, before Sommers kicks the bucket.' Now it's a much larger project in which I'm a very active participant. In a sense I'm using it as a way of tying my life together." She believed it would reaffirm political strategies under fire. She also felt more in control of her own life story than of OWL. Tish talked moderation and balance but then dove into the book.

Her new focus triggered an exploration of the period when her own political vision and practical organizing skills matured. She was personally ready, and the World War II upheaval provided opportunities for growth. By 1942, Los Angeles was jammed with new immigrants. Families poured in from everywhere to take jobs in the war industries, and wives moved to be near spouses bound for the Pacific. Reports of battles lost and territory gained filled the newspapers as fear of invasion by the Japanese blended with anti-Nazi fervor.

Upbeat patriotism was tinged with wartime tensions. Soldiers and sailors on weekend leave crowded into buses and streetcars, spending their last hours before shipping out in the busy night spots of Los Angeles. They were instant heroes—defenders of national honor. Newspapers contrasted "our boys in uniform" with arrogant civilian troublemakers whose uniform was the "zoot suit," with the "reet pleat" and "drape shape" made popular by jazz musician Cab Calloway. In Los Angeles the zoot suit became linked in the public mind with "pachucos," Mexican-American "delinquents," though it was often worn by nondelinquent teens. The mainstream press focused on arrests of these "pachucos," decrying the "villainous" zoot-suiters who threatened the city.[7]

On the night of 7 June, racial tensions erupted. Sailors and soldiers swarmed into the downtown area and then into East Los Angeles. Beatrice Winston Griffith's sociological and literary portrait of East Los Angeles, *American Me,* reported they were "halting street cars and breaking into theaters, dragging pachucos out into the streets, stripping them naked and beating them senseless." She captured the climate: "It was like the sailors and marines were taking over the whole city. . . . They had bottles and belts, clubs and iron pipes in their hands. . . . The people were filling the streets . . . like they were drunk or crazy. . . . Hell man, this is a street in Germany tonight. This isn't Los Angeles, this is a street in Germany."[8]

Life and *Time* carried stories on the riots as did newspapers across the country. The military declared Los Angeles off-limits to servicemen, and the City Council passed an ordinance banning the wearing of "zoot suits."[9] Tish saw racism as the root cause. She, too, saw the connection with the streets of Germany. The riots convinced her that Mexican-Americans were being singled out for the kind of treatment she had seen Jews experience in the 1930s.

She looked for ways to contribute her talents and energies in East Los Angeles. Thus she applied for a newly opened job with the Park Department. "I went through the civil service exam. For the practical part, I dropped the baseball, dislocating my finger. I think they felt sorry for me so they passed me! They were amazed that I would want to work at Aliso Village because that was almost the worst part of town. But I was out to change the world."

In fact, Aliso Village, Pico Gardens, and Ramona Gardens—built in the early 1940s—were among the first racially integrated housing projects in the country. Run by the City of Los Angeles Housing Authority, they mixed poor whites from the South,

Mexican-Americans, and blacks—most of them workers in nearby war industries. A traditional port of entry for Jews, Armenians, and Japanese, Boyle Heights and Lincoln Heights residents were increasingly Mexican-American. The changes disturbed some long-term residents and merchants for whom "cross-cultural" had meant European.[10]

When Tish first went to East Los Angeles, Frank Wilkinson was managing the Ramona Gardens project. He was one of a group of whites attracted to the community with whom Tish developed a close friendship. "You should have seen her before a crowd," he recounted, "How electric she was, so full of energy. . . . There was a lot of body movement, hand movement, an intensely expressive face. . . . She excited people with ideas she had." He stressed that the focus of Tish's work was "establishing cultural unity as a necessity of winning the war." Speaking of his own role, he said, "We brought the first black families into the housing projects. . . . We had child care, we took four or eight units and broke them up into two child care units by cutting out the walls. The work in the housing projects *was* war work. They were called war-worker housing projects."[11]

In late summer East Los Angeles was hot. Palm fronds and dead bougainvillea blossoms scattered the dusty sidewalks. Tish walked by old women dressed in black as they watered geraniums in the bright light. Food smells, spiced apple from the bakery and the tang of scorched tomatoes, followed her down Brooklyn Avenue. She passed barbershops, cleaners, small dry goods stores, and of course the corner groceries and bars.

Tish often saw young people hanging out by the grocery store, savoring the cherry and lemon *raspadas* (ice cones). Some of the boys wore the triple-soled shoes, slicked-back hair, and fingertip coats of the pachucos. Their girls, known as "slick chicks," smiled and moved slowly by. As Griffith wrote, "Rosie was all pretty in a big purple skirt and pink blouse, with gold beads on her neck and arms. Fifteen bracelets she had, one for each year of her living; . . . all beautiful and jingly she was, swinging her silk skirt down the street."[12] There were sedate homes down one street, small furniture factories and businesses at the intersections. Jewish delicatessens were sometimes next-door to tortillerias.

Tish once again moved with enthusiasm that exceeded her abilities. "I had no experience at all in working with poor, tough teenagers of another culture. I came in with my enthusiasm and my creative ideas. If they were going to write graffiti on the walls, I just covered the walls with paper so we could make it art. If they wanted to carve things because they had knives, I brought some balsa wood so they could do sculpture contests." The young people loved her ideas. But they also loved to do things like steal her keys. It was all too much for her, and she was happy to create a different job for herself fairly quickly.

When Tish first volunteered her services in 1943, the Los Angeles International Institute was a busy place, housed in a lovely old Spanish Colonial style mansion, on a street of fading but gracious homes. The International Institute was part of a national network of helping agencies, first established at Ellis Island by the YWCA in 1913 to prevent victimization of young women immigrants.[13] Meeting rooms and offices surrounded the brick courtyard, where groups met for refreshments and social activities. The social workers helped immigrants fill out papers, locate friends and relatives, and find work and housing. The institute's double focus was on making the transition to a new land easier while preserving the culture of the homeland.

Institute-sponsored events featured the costumes, music, and food of Scandinavia, China, and Russia. Daily, the social workers helped individuals and families adjust. Until the war the clientele was primarily former European refugees, mostly Jewish. Because of the new housing projects, the changing composition of the neighborhood, and the out-migration of Jews, the institute's clientele gradually included more Mexicans and fewer European or Asian immigrants.[14] Miss Newton, the director since 1919, was trained in the Progressive Era settlement-house tradition and delighted that Tish wanted to teach dance to the small group of

Mexican girls who came to the institute. "This was just their cup of tea, nice young girls and cultural preservation. Little did they know!"

The director encouraged Tish to design a spring dance program. Tish didn't know much about Mexican or other Latin dances, but she figured it shouldn't be too hard to learn. She knew a woman who had been with the Padua Hills folk dance company, and she could use the new downtown library, or go to Tijuana for help. The girls were enthusiastic and quickly got some boys to join the group. Within weeks the International Institute was allocated funds from the Los Angeles Youth Project. This allowed Tish to leave her Park Department job and be paid for what was known as "antidelinquency" work.[15]

Tish recruited help from among her own dance students. Bari Rolfe Hardwick, formerly a dancer, was now an office worker taking classes to strengthen her injured back. They became friends, and soon Bari volunteered to drive Tish over to the East Side in the late afternoons. She and Tish shopped at thrift shops for the full petticoats they later dyed at home, creating as best they could authentic Latin American costumes. For the next few years she supported Tish's cultural work, pleased with their goal of presenting elements from the Mexican culture to non-Mexicans. Bari and Tish worked hard with the youngsters and celebrated hard too. They made friends with staff from the housing projects; spent much of their free time together discussing the war, politics, and themselves; and shared meals at nearby restaurants.

The first appearance of the Pan American Dance Group ("PADG," as Tish called it), was probably at Ramona Gardens, on a night when Orson Welles and Rita Hayworth appeared at a fund-raiser where seven hundred dinners were served.[16] The girls were Mexican but had to be taught the few steps Tish had just learned. Bari recalled the girls' modesty and nervousness about changing costumes behind a makeshift barrier near the dance platform.

It didn't take too long to decide on a more ambitious project, "Call Me California." Tish plunged in. This was to be their first downtown appearance, a brief, after-lunch performance for a group of society matrons. But it had at least the ambitions of the UCLA Dance Recitals. Of course there were the Mexican dances, but Tish also outlined the story of California, including the Russian fur traders ("we left the bloody parts out," she noted), the Gold Rush, a whole historic panorama. And for scenery, Tish persuaded illustrator and sidewalk chalk artist Leo Politi to design simple sets the dancers could move on and off. There was original music and a small chamber orchestra organized by friends. Ambitious, yes. Slightly oversized—well, that too. But consistent with Tish's tremendous enthusiasm.

One bittersweet episode connected to that first performance was symptomatic of the frustrations of antidelinquency work. Tish and Bari felt that handsome and charming Tiny was the most talented of the amateur dancers. They agreed that he had the charisma and talent to make a career in films, and they had already talked with friends in the industry about his potential. He was beautiful to watch—his energy and skill lifted the whole group. However, in the final days of rehearsal, his older brother came home from prison and took Tiny with him on a burglary. The police waited until after the performance but then took the young man away. Tiny's dance career was over.[17]

Tish's group was a hit, and she took on new territory. Before long the PADG was booked all over the city in USOs, churches, and community centers, for two or three performances a week. It was a frenzied time for Tish, booking new dates, rehearsing new dances, adding more young people, enjoying the applause. She was moving faster and faster. For Cinco de Mayo and other holidays they performed with other groups from the East Side. At the curtain call of their show, "Let's Sing Together," the Pan American Dance Group was presented a Brotherhood Week award by Frank Sinatra. To coincide with the United Nations organizing meetings in San Francisco, Tish set up a United Nations Rally

(Festival) in Hollenbeck Park built around the theme of peace and unity.[18]

Unbelievably, Tish's work expanded. Under the umbrella of the Hollenbeck Youth Theater she brought together youngsters from the housing projects, the Soto-Michigan Jewish Community Center, and the International Institute. The racially integrated group was received with cheers for their VE (Victory in Europe) Day performance of "Hello Neighbor Hello" at Theodore Roosevelt High School. That June 1945 performance also marked the end of Tish's association with the International Institute. The Pan American Dance Group had been designed to provide cultural support and generate self-confidence and pride for the young people. It certainly was doing that. But Tish's underlying goal was to show the value of racial integration in the local community—a problem for the International Institute.

The post-rehearsal visits and socializing upset the institute staff. Preserving Mexican-American culture was an approved goal, but bringing black youngsters into the institute was not. Across the country, other inner-city institutes were experiencing similar "discomforts." They, too, were undergoing dramatic shifts in population. Their National Board agenda for fall 1945 addressed postwar issues such as resettlement of returning Japanese. They also faced increasing community pressure to work with minority groups as well as the foreign-born. The National Board concluded that, while they were aware of the "Negro problem," the institutes' initial focus was on the foreign-born; therefore, their traditional role should be continued.[19]

The institute's director, in a diplomatic letter to the national office, noted that Tish and the institute had agreed to go separate ways. She summed up the problem: "Her [Tish's] burning desire to draw Negroes and Jewish youngsters into the group has completely changed its character and it no longer can do the interpretive work that it originally was able to do." In short, the director believed "her work with the children of the housing projects is responsible for the difficulty that has arisen."[20]

actors. To top it off, the unpaid writer had to be ready for continual changes, such as the last-minute omission of a number or a leading character.[22]

The story line reflected a simple political perspective. The central problem was housing; the solution was the young people working together in harmony to solve their own problems. The themes of unity and self-help appeared throughout, even in the flashback to "the good old days," the modern dance (à la Katherine Dunham) set in "primitive" times which was the hit of the show. The twenty production numbers, the costumes, sets, music, and scripts reflected the work of hundreds of volunteers and young participants. Funding came from ticket sales and a small grant from the Youth Project leadership budget. Total expenses were $594.48, including $40.00 to replace two pairs of rented boots stolen by backstage visitors. It was a tremendously complex, ambitious, and successful project.

From fall 1943 until after the production of "Harmony in A-flat" in 1947, Tish concentrated on organizing young people. Beginning with the original five teenagers at the International Institute, Tish developed the Pan American Dance Group and Hollenbeck Theater Group into racially integrated social and performing entities. With constant turnover, the group averaged about thirty members, nearly half of whom were black, a third Mexican-American, and a fifth Jewish youth from the Soto-Michigan Jewish Community Center. At one reunion, nearly a hundred showed up to share their memories. Still tied by the discipline and fervor of the dance experiences, their pride was evident.

In the late 1960s, Bari spoke to a group on Catalina Island, off the coast of Los Angeles. When she finished, a young woman rose and said, "Let me tell you about this woman. She and Tish organized a dance group and I was part of it." She then testified to the activity and the effect it had on her and the other youngsters. By the time she stopped, there were tears in many eyes. Bari recalled, "Tish and I used to say that whatever else came out of that experience, there are going to be thirty kids on the East Side in brotherhood activity for the rest of their lives. This was the quality coming from her work."[23]

By 1947, Tish's life was very busy and demanding. She lived simply in a tiny studio apartment in the Silverlake district near downtown, managing well on her modest paychecks. She dressed in ballet slippers, plain full skirts and leotards, and still wore her straight brown hair at shoulder length. Expanding her arena, she chaired a citywide youth festival sponsored by the Los Angeles Youth Council at the Hotel Embassy in the spring. She continued her work with neighborhood teen clubs, Li'l First and Pico Girls, as well as the Pan American Dance Group and a modern dance group. She also helped develop the Eastside Youth Council for Brotherhood at the Soto-Michigan Jewish Community Center. Her leadership abilities were extensive, and she responded to new opportunities.

But the harmony embodied in her musical productions eluded her personally. She was busy but very lonely. Concerned, she saw a psychologist who focused on what to do about her intimate life, especially her sex life. There were lovers in Tish's life, but there were also guilt feelings. She had an intense relationship with a married man. She broke with him because she felt guilty and didn't want to be responsible for breaking up another marriage. Another lover was a close friend of this man, but she thought he had problems of his own. As she scathingly indicted herself, "I was thinking that I was probably a slut."

Retrospectively, Tish found many contemporary parallels in her personal situation. "Probably it was quite similar to what it is for women today—the uncertainty and bad feelings, the lack of satisfaction because the relationship was not a complete one. I was yearning for a solid relationship rather than pieces of one. I didn't want the off and ons, the broken-offs, the I-gotta-have-yous and the having to put people aside. It was too emotionally draining. I thought that I was screwed up as a woman. That somehow or other I missed the boat. I just hadn't gotten it together, I was already thirty-three and didn't have a partner. What was the matter? Where had I gone wrong?"

She didn't see then that these were societal problems, pressures related to her assumed role as a young woman. Her male psychologist, true to the general approach of the period, told her she was an "unfulfilled" woman. She already knew that, but she felt psychological solutions weren't helping. As Tish saw it, "What I was interested in was a permanent relationship, both for moral reasons, because I felt that was the only *right* kind of relationship, but also to finally put all of these problems with guilt to rest."[24]

She met with the psychologist for several months but was soon distracted by new work-related opportunities. Her passport application to travel to Yugoslavia "to work on the Youth Railway" and to help plan the upcoming World Youth Festival to be held in Prague was denied, though she was given no reason. Since she couldn't get to the planning sessions, she devoted herself to lobbying until selected the next year (1947) by the Los Angeles Youth Council as its delegate to the festival. This time the passport application was approved, and she set off. On board the ocean liner, Tish was asked to be the cultural director of the American delegation: "After all, I *was* cultured," she laughed. "So, says I, let's put on a show!" They rehearsed every morning on the ship, developing the broad message, "American young people want peace and freedom." She merged songs from the Northeast and the South to show the cultural mix.

For Tish, "It was a marvelous trip. There was a sense among the youth groups that the world was going to be different and they were going to make sure that it would be. I was a little intimidated when we got to Prague and saw some of the state-sponsored, professional programs, but we put on our little amateur show anyway, and it was very well received."

"We Build the Road, the Road Builds Us," was the slogan Tish brought back with her. She used it often in her later organizing work. "The World Youth Festival was one of those marvelous highs in your life that you remember forever. There were thousands of people. Huge delegations, of course, from socialist countries. There was tremendous camaraderie among the different groups, an exchange of national pins, all that goes with it."[25] There was also the exhilaration that working together can produce. Groups of delegates were sent out to work in the country on a local road-building project. "It was very symbolic. We spent a week, I mean how much work can you do in a week with pick and shovel?" What endured for Tish was the sense of building, coming together to construct a better future.

Others in her festival group recognized Tish's leadership potential. When the head of the delegation decided to take a trip to the Soviet Union instead of returning to the United States, Tish was selected as his replacement. She knew she was a unity figure for the group. She was a good "translator," avoiding the weighty Communist party jargon. Her emphasis on broadly based democratic themes may also have appeased those who feared a left-dominated delegation.

Her good feelings about herself were bolstered even more by a romantic encounter. She traveled alone before she joined the returning ship in Venice and ran into an English architecture student who showed her around Italy. "It was a funny episode—sex in return for this wonderful tour. It was romantic, I got wonderful letters after and all that. It was just right for the time." She enjoyed this fleeting episode, so removed from her ongoing life, without guilt.

Tish returned that fall to the U.S. House Un-American Activities Committee investigations of Hollywood. This time she possessed none of the naïveté that so characterized her time in Germany. She knew instantly that the days of cooperation and tolerance for progressives and radicals of any brand were over. Despite obvious risks, she assembled a slide show of the festival and trip and made over a hundred speeches at churches, schools, and organizations. "There was only one red-baiting moment. I went to a church to give my little pitch, and somebody who was very right wing came out with a story of it in a local paper, including a sneering reference to the fact that when I'd gone back across the street I'd lit a cigarette."

Tish's FBI file was started in 1946, probably after her Yugoslavian passport request was denied. Although Sid and Tish were divorced in 1942, the FBI erroneously noted on her Security Index card (kept for "those individuals who can be considered to be a threat to the internal security of this country") that "subject is married to Sidney Burke, present Los Angeles editor of *The People's World.*" It took them another two years to correct the record on that point. In developing the file, the FBI used informers, public records, and newspaper items from *The People's World* or *The Daily Worker.* They also recorded the 1943 testimony from California's anti-Communist Tenney committee. The FBI file, though it contains errors, helps in corroborating chronology and addresses. It is replete with miscues. For example, the FBI knew Tish had a "sister" (her father's stepdaughter), but it took several years before they noted Tish had one brother. They never seemed to realize there were two.[26]

In her own circle the political climate changed quickly. At the center, one staff member urged Tish's firing: she was obviously too radical, and all her talks about the festival distracted from her assigned work. The press kept the national anti-Communist purges on the front page, and the Hollywood investigations continued. Although she did not lose her job, Tish felt it was time to move on from the Jewish Community Center. Personal disquietude absorbed her only temporarily. She felt much better about herself, more confident in her organizing abilities, less troubled about personal relationships.

The moment ripe for change, Tish went to work full-time in Henry Wallace's third-party presidential campaign in Los Angeles. She was asked to head the Southern California Youth for Wallace office as national enthusiasm for his campaign grew. Harvesting her earlier experience, she drew on her East Los Angeles network of groups and individuals to bring out the crowds for Wallace's Los Angeles appearances.

Youngsters from the Jewish Community Center ran off flyers and cruised the neighborhoods in old trucks with banners. One

Young Progressives reception to honor Tish as new director, June
1948. *Left to right,* Charlotte Kanter, Martin Kanter, Tish, Claire
Perry, and Helen Lewis.

political co-worker from those days commented on Tish's creativity: "She used balloons, and once wanted to find some Chinese
hoops like those she had seen at the Youth Festival. There was an
air of celebration. . . . I remember going to all these Wallace ral-
lies and being one of the 'lieutenants,' in the chain of command.
And being all excited about going to the office and cranking the
mimeo machine, stuffing envelopes. There were big festivals,
youth festivals out in the fields with lots of folk dancing and
marching."[27]

    As excitement grew, the potential seemed limitless. There
were massive, colorful political events in fields on the East Side.

Families worked together to make tacos, beans, enchiladas, and various other dishes, sold to raise money. Girls told Tish how many hours they spent taking seeds out of the chilis, how that made their fingers burn. The events were always noisy, with sound systems on the trucks and much singing.

Tish was identified as regional director of Wallace's campaign in a *People's World* story on his Los Angeles appearance in October 1948: "Young Progressives signed up 1,147 new members at the rally. . . . A selling point was their float depicting young house-wives sweeping and doing household chores and at the same time phoning neighbors about election issues. . . . [They] were cheered as they burned up the cinders [on the Coliseum track,] bringing in $1,000 in contributions."[28]

Tish moved into decision-making circles at this point. She was respected as an outstanding worker for the party as well as for the campaign. In her new role, she was asked to book speaking engagements for a New York Wallace enthusiast. Despite her frantic schedule, she agreed to meet Joe Sommers at the Soto-Michigan Jewish Community Center, where a strike by the staff was in progress. In a suitable juxtaposition of her politics and personal life, she and Joe started to get to know one another while walking that picket line. He was the first to call her "Tish," not "Letitia," and the new name stayed with her. "We took to each other immediately," she said. "I felt a very strong chemistry be-tween us. The first night we had dinner together and talked for hours. I arranged his speaking engagements while he was in town for three or four days. By the end of that time we were going to bed together and had established a bond. I knew this was *it*, this was the one I was not going to let get away."

Tish felt relieved and excited by the possibilities. She longed intensely for a new and more permanent relationship. Her deter-mination led to an unusual approach for her. She pursued him, rather ardently. They kept in touch by phone when he returned to his job as a nuts-and-bolts company sales representative in New York. They got together at the Cornhuskers Hotel in Iowa for a campaign meeting. "I suggested maybe we should get married, but I got a rebuff—not so fast. I was very anxious to settle down. He was ten years younger, so he wasn't quite as anxious as I was. But he was in love." Throughout their courtship, she continued to work with Youth for Wallace. The presidential campaign ended with less than a million votes for Wallace and a victory for Harry Truman. All during that time, she and Joe wrote letters and talked on the phone.

Her feelings for Joe crystallized. "My mind was made up. I then applied for the job of cultural director for the national Young Progressives. It wasn't the usual way of applying. I think there was some party assistance, at least in making contact, but anyway I was offered this job in New York. My reason was, and I expressed it frankly, to be where Joe was." This proved once again that Tish could count on her political network. Comrades in the party assisted in getting her the job, and once she arrived in New York she was surrounded by people who dedicated their lives to politics. Decades later, OWL benefited in a similar way from the community of feminists and their contacts in the women's movement.

Throughout her twenties and thirties, Tish experienced the chaos and boom of wartime Los Angeles as she gained in political sophistication. Other women, also California activists, like Jessica Mitford and Rose Chernin, recalled their days in the Communist party as crucial to their lifelong political development.[29]

As Tish saw it, "While Rose Chernin was involved in the heart and soul of the Communist organization as a functionary and an open Communist, I was of that more middle-class segment of the movement. We were trying to change ideas, involved in organizing, but holding on to roots of the American mainstream. Because I could 'pass,' could be part of the mainstream and yet move people along, I could be convincing to that group. That's where I've been most effective as an organizer throughout my life." She came to realize that "in the latter part of my life, my class background has been an advantage. I've been able to work with the establishment in rather creative ways."

Tish, *at center,* getting out the Young Progressives vote in East Los
Angeles for the Henry Wallace presidential campaign, 1948.
Photograph courtesy of Sy Kaplan.

Tish saw another fundamental difference: Chernin's views
didn't change over time. "She never lost her faith in the Soviet
Union, she never questioned the dogma. Most of us did, and in
that questioning we moved on. We either moved out of the movement entirely, or we found a new way to work."

Tish believed that Mitford's experience more closely mirrored
her own: both realized their full potential after leaving the Communist party. In *A Fine Old Conflict*, Mitford speaks of the party as
a Head Start movement in training, in the practical skills of organizing. Tish felt "She and I had the same reaction to language,
the turgid translation from the Russian sound of party documents. We used to laugh about it, but we believed this was
scientific socialism, and you had to have special language with
special meaning to Communists who really understood. In mass

work, I tried to avoid political cliches. I reserved those for Party meetings and educationals."[30]

Tish expressed regret that her own party loyalty led her to accept the Japanese internment policy during the war. She spoke quietly about her meeting in 1942 with Yuriko, the dancer who was about to be sent to an Arizona camp: "She was lovely, light, lithe, ethereal, really beautiful." Tish didn't quite know what to say, so she just urged Yuriko to keep up with dance. "What a time to be upbeat," Tish ruefully noted. After the war and two years of internment, Yuriko was able to rebuild her professional career, becoming a central performer for the Martha Graham group. Tish saw Yuriko only once after that, in an elevator in New York City in the 1950s. "She was most gracious but bitter about the loss of time." Tish was embarrassed and chagrined by her own compliance with the party's political stance. "But that was the patriotism of the times. We didn't see it as concentration camps then."[31]

In a more positive reflection about her later evolution as an organizer, Tish noted her ability to synthesize: "I have successfully taken pieces out of my own life, my strengths, the talents, the training and the various other things I've had, which came out of the party discipline and dance, and put it together into new shape in organizing." Nevertheless, there was a tremendous amount of turmoil and change in that earlier era and she wondered, "How did I manage to get through those years? I was so mixed up and frustrated, so unable to realize myself. Today I feel that I'm doing the best that I can. At that time I don't think I felt that way. I felt I was always not making it, not reaching my capacities."

Despite her status at war's end as a respected full-time organizer with leadership skills, Tish felt uneasy and unfulfilled. True, there was harmony between her work life and her ideals. But not even her new relationship gave her peace of mind. As a woman in her mid-thirties she felt uneasy and disharmonious.

Sweet Southern Magnolia

As I've grown older, I feel very little motivated by guilt.
It's as though the task is the motivating thing, and not the
sense of self.

I want an activist death like I want an activist life. I want
to be in control.

The ambivalence and lack of self-knowledge that flavored Tish's
earlier years were nowhere evident in 1985. She was focused, re-
lentless, driven by her will and vision. By February, the pendu-
lum had swung back toward active control of OWL. There was
no more talk of balance. She was content to relinquish the focus
on her physical and psychological self and devote her efforts exclusively to the organization. "Here it is five years after the death
sentence, and these have been the most productive and rewarding
years of my life. Actually, I'm at the height of my ability to cope
organizationally in spite of the cancer and that's the drama of it.
There is this tremendous drive to leave a legacy."

Her involvement with OWL was in full swing, stimulated by
a crisis at the national office. The Board learned at its November
meeting of a $67,000 deficit for 1984. There was also bitter inter-
nal staff dissension in Washington. The director resigned, and
Tish agreed to take her place in the interim as well as to loan
OWL money until new proposals were funded. Tish's inherited
money had always subsidized the organization, and in this transi-

tion period she shifted some stocks. "I see the money that I have as a means of making sure that what I want to get done is done. Not in basic support, but to fill in the holes. Theoretically, if all goes well and if my health maintains, we get some new grants, etc., I should be able to work out of that by the end of the year. By that time I plan to put my money in an endowment for OWL."

Tish admitted the pace was frenetic, but she felt vibrant and energized. "It's certainly been an all-out thing, requiring all the energy I can muster to keep things going and moving forward. It's like starting a new organization again. We've got to go out and raise funds, but this time we have a monthly payroll to meet. I'm going to New York, then in two weeks after that I'll be back in Washington to interview candidates for the director's position."

Tish was aware that she walked a fine and dangerous line: "I'm holding the fort, but I can't hold it too long. Physically and emotionally, it's too much. Too much to be the interim director, live on the West Coast and make daily decisions for Washington." But these demands fueled her political passions. "I feel I've been managing very well. I'm back in the heart of it again. With the last director, I had this feeling of competition, not wanting to get in her way, and still not being completely happy with things. Right now that's no obstacle. It's all very exciting and yet so nerve-racking."

Her physical vulnerability worried her, but not enough to slow her efforts. "I know I'm taking a risk, not only financially, but in shortening my time by going all-out now, and by stopping chemotherapy. I haven't yet told my oncologist that I'm stopping the chemo. He must have guessed it since I've not been back." Tish rationalized by arguing this was a short-term effort. "If I can get past this period, get the right executive director, and if I can help that person to raise funds and find my replacement as OWL board president. Well, then I can ease up a bit."

And yet she knew she hastened her own death. "I know damn well by the physical growth of the tumors all over my body and groin area that my health is affected. The death is growing inside as well. I could be stopped in my tracks any week now, in the sense of being able to function."

She attended Hemlock Society meetings in Los Angeles, focused on voluntary euthanasia and the nature of a "good death." Tish ruminated about methods, "How can I be sure? My current thought is to use the plastic bag over my head plus the sedatives. I ask myself if this is the best way. . . . Timing is extremely important." But the physical act of suicide was only one part of her dilemma: "I want to avoid risking legal problems for anyone. I started to think about people who would be able to help, who would be left with the least residual guilt." Grappling with these questions was difficult beyond description, and not only for Tish: "in my cancer support group, everybody is philosophically in agreement with staying in control and not wanting to go on to the bitter end. But there isn't one who's gone through with it."

She worried about pain control and loss of her mental faculties. She wanted to keep out of the hospital—that remained a primary goal. After she pondered a few more grisly technical possibilities and difficulties (pills? what if you throw them up? injections? what if it's too late to inject yourself?), she temporarily concluded, "I don't necessarily want to die by suicide, and I don't want to implicate anyone else. I just don't want to lay this on anybody." Tish had no negative feelings about talking or thinking about dying. "It doesn't depress me. I want an activist death like I want an activist life. I want to be in control. I want it to be something positive in terms of the people around me that I care about."

Plans for her own death, if not her daily physical comfort and well-being, permeated her thoughts. She talked about her needs: "I don't want to become a cog in the medical scene, to end up with prolonged dying, kept alive artificially or not allowed to find the best time and place. I see no reason why non-depressed terminal cancer patients can't decide to take their life at the time when it seems like everything meaningful has been cut off." She

expanded on these ideas in a videotaped interview, and about the
need for better communication in doctor/patient relationships and
the patient's right to participate in medical treatment strategy.
Tish, wearing a rose-colored sweatsuit, responded to a question
about depression: "After all, I'm a fighter, so lows don't last long."[1]

She took several concrete steps to remain in control: as a
member, she followed the Hemlock Society reports on the current
status of right-to-die legislation; she prepared her durable power
of attorney regarding health care; and she filed a living will with
her physician. She explained her views to her doctor, emphasizing
her strong desire to die at home without medical intervention.
Still uncertain as to her actual course of action, she said, "I don't
know if I'm going to be able to do this, but I want to have that
choice and be ready for it."

Her readiness to facilitate her death was new. She told the
interviewer she hadn't thought seriously about suicide prior to
her cancer recurrence. "I have found life very rewarding. There's
something about having cancer that's not all bad. . . . I was an
organizer before, and cancer has made me select priorities, feel
closer to people." Then she leaned forward, laughing and spread-
ing her arms. "And it's amazing how if you have a birthday party
and people think you're going to die, you can bring 'em all in.
You know, 'last time to see Tish'—and they're ready to come!"

In fact, Tish felt clear, whole, and increasingly sensitive to
others since her terminal illness—in ways that exceeded anything
she'd known in health. "It may seem strange because I have a lot
of discomfort, but these past six years have been the most self-
actualizing of my whole life. . . . I think I'm a better person. I
have more compassion, and though I feel tremendous urgency in
time, I think I can listen better." Tish found comfort in this
acuity. Little solace came from religion, since she had been a
nonreligious activist most of her life. But she did get a spiritual
lift "from the concept of trying to move society along in a positive way, and from the fact that I'm going to be leaving some-

thing of a legacy." As part of that legacy, she returned to contemplation of her post–World War II experiences.

In 1949 her political activism embodied the same philosophical goal: generate political and personal change by moving society in a positive way. The next step toward that vision was reported in *The People's World*: Letitia Innes was leaving for New York, to assume the job of cultural director for the Young Progressives. Tish was thirty-four.[2]

For the first time, however, her political direction was swayed by her search for a personal partner. She took a little apartment in Chelsea, and Joe moved in with her. They lived together for a period of about five or six months. "After that, he thought we ought to get married. So we did. We agreed, in light of Joe's family, that I should convert to Judaism. I did some studies with a rabbi, read some interesting historical books. Since I hadn't any particular religion, I [thought I] might just as well convert to Judaism as well as anything else. I certainly was pretty psychologically Jewish by this time." It was an expedient move to mollify Joe's family, who adored their only son and had reservations about his marriage to this sophisticated older woman. Nevertheless, it was also a consistent step for Tish, who had strongly identified with the experience of German Jews, and for several years been involved with Jewish friends and co-workers, including her first husband.

Tish and Joe had two happy years in New York, though she hated the noise and dirt of the city.[3] They were in love, and it was a period of affirmation. On weekends they visited Joe's sister Anita Gurion and her family, enjoying the cheerful noisiness of children in that household. At work, there still seemed to be a possibility of major social change; Tish's faith in a better future had been bolstered by the Prague Youth Festival. She was doing a good job for the party and was close to people on its national task force on youth movements. "It was a very rich period, a lively and changing one. Still, McCarthyism was coming in, and the Young Progressives was going through a terrible disintegration."

After the 1948 presidential election, the Progressive party began to crumble. The decision was made that the Young Progressives was no longer a viable organization and would soon be disbanded. Tish took over one of their last projects, a peace festival in the Midwest. About this time, Joe left his nuts-and-bolts sales job to work in an appliance factory organized by the United Electrical Workers union. But there he met a major struggle to oust suspected Communists from the union. In light of this, and with Tish's job over, they talked about where they should go from here, what they should do.

The change in public climate was dramatic. In 1949, the Smith Act trial of eleven members of the Communist party's National Board laid the legal precedent for arrest and prosecution of other radicals. Thousands lost their jobs or were threatened by the House Committee on Un-American Activities and the Internal Security Committee in the Senate. As Joseph Starobin, former party member and one-time foreign editor of *The Daily Worker,* noted, "Communists, and anyone accused of any association with causes or groups said to be Communist controlled, found themselves pariahs. The tolerated status they had enjoyed for two or three years after the war had suddenly and mercilessly been reversed. Near-hysteria gripped the nation."[4]

The 1950 Internal Security Act identified communism as inherently "a clear and present danger to the security of the United States." Mobilization for the Korean War was matched with anti-Communist fervor. Historian G. Perrett described the climate: "Government employees who subscribed to *The Nation* or the *New Republic,* owned records by Paul Robeson or read avant-garde literature, practiced yoga, or showed an interest in Eastern Europe, China, or the Soviet Union ran the risk of being secretly denounced and of then being forced to defend themselves against vague accusations made by faceless accusers."[5] Some of Tish's friends completely withdrew from politics and went to work in family businesses to avoid the witch-hunt. Many old friends, including employees of the Los Angeles housing projects, lost their jobs.

The FBI continued to track Tish's activities in New York. It noted her presence at the Young Progressives office, her picture in *The Daily Worker* at a Bedford-Stuyvesant youth forum protesting housing conditions for blacks, and recorded that she was a delegate to an American Women for Peace march in Washington, D.C., to protest the atomic bomb tests and the Korean War.[6]

Tish chose not to retreat into familial or domestic enclosure. Knowing the dangers involved, she made the decision to remain politically active amidst public persecution. Tish commented, "Those of us who were in the radical movement were very well aware that our names were on various lists. There was certainly the feeling that the party per se was going to be under direct attack. . . . I wasn't afraid of going to jail, but I certainly had the feeling that this was a time when everybody 'comes to the aid of.'" As later, she was willing to take risks to fulfill her commitments.

Rather than retreat, Tish and Joe chose a more positive track. They both had strong feelings of commitment to do something about racism and knew the party was trying to get people to go south to organize around this issue.[7] "I think it was my suggestion that we consider going south. It seemed like a very logical, sensible thing for committed people to do." The ominous general climate also affected their decision. Joe had been in a prison camp during the war, so he was completely dedicated to preventing the United States from going the way of Germany. They both felt fascism could easily happen in this country. They believed that, just as in Germany, recent purges in the unions, antiworker labor laws, and certainly antisubversive legislation could be the first steps toward totalitarianism. On a more personal level, Tish acknowledged her unabashed dislike of New York. Joe loved the city but responded to her wishes. They met with party leadership, who determined that Birmingham was a good place to go.

George Charney, writing about his own experience with the party's inner circles in the 1950s, described its stance this way: "The main endeavor within the party was now to slough off all weak or unreliable elements and reduce it to the hard core that could cope with the crisis. It was a period of testing, of verification, of weeding out, and of steeling the cadre."[8] The motto, adopted from Lenin, was "Better fewer, but better." Tish made the "cut."

One part of the party's process of internal change was the campaign against "white chauvinism." It began in 1949 with an article by Pettis Perry, the chairman of the party's Negro Commission. He urged the party to acknowledge the potential of the Negro liberation movement and "to take the offensive against chauvinist moods and themes within its own ranks and among its sympathizers." He and others were no longer willing to accept "unity" for the war effort as an excuse for minimizing the concerns of blacks.[9]

Tish recalled vividly the general tension of that anti–white chauvinist period. Many meetings were dominated by confrontations and accusations of racism. She remembers being accused and bursting into tears. She was absolutely devastated by the idea that she had behaved badly. "I don't know if I was charged with anything particular, but there was the whole sense of guilt for a lack of sensitivity to racism, and not seeing racism in ourselves. . . . Then I saw that it isn't that you have to understand it all, but you have to want to *do something* to change yourself. . . . This realization pulled me through that moment because until then I just felt completely worthless." Her recollection of those heavy-handed sessions remained acute decades later, yet she also felt that the resulting clarity was worth the struggle.

Hence, political introspection was commonplace and often ended in a clearer vision, but she was vulnerable emotionally. During a lunch conversation with a black party member, Tish was chain-smoking, her response to the pressure. Her comrade made a negative comment about smoking. At that point, Tish put the cigarette out and never smoked again. "It had to do with the fact that I was trying to prove something to a black comrade." She was also exhibiting her tremendous self-discipline and will power.

Joseph Starobin, Steve Nelson, and other leaders within the party felt that the antiracism goal was valid but the results damaging. The idea was a traditional American Communist one, "that part of the fight for civil rights involved self-purification and self-liberation from anti-Negro prejudice." A similar anti–white chauvinist concern had been raised in the 1930s in the party. This time, however, critics saw that "both whites and blacks began to take advantage of the enormous weapon which the charge of 'white chauvinism' gave them to settle scores, to climb organizational ladders, to fight for jobs and to express personality conflicts which, by Communist definition, were never supposed to predominate over political objectivity."[10] In short, race was used by some to advance personal goals.

The Communist party also began to organize an underground operation due to their expectation of repression and potential international war.[11] By 1950–51, party membership was below forty thousand, and the FBI estimated half of those were in New York City. David Shannon's *Decline of American Communism* put it this way: "Scores of important party leaders left their homes, assumed new names, and lived a clandestine existence. There were two reasons, . . . to obstruct FBI agents and to form the nucleus of a party for the future. . . . Those who went underground—or became 'unavailables' as they were commonly called within the party—were important leaders but [were] not from the very top leadership."[12]

Tish and Joe were part of this underground effort. They were "colonizers," party members who relocated and concealed their affiliation. They intended to become part of and influence the southern climate. Early in 1952 they told friends they were leaving, but not where they were going. This was a new kind of partnership for them, and there was an added dimension to their voyage: at thirty-seven, Tish was several months pregnant. She convinced the party that she could have a baby in Alabama just as well as in New York. But she began to hemorrhage on the train to Birmingham and miscarried at a Virginia hospital. "I must have been four or five months pregnant, and had taken DES to keep from losing it. At the hospital there were only student interns. Every medical student there seemed to have a hand in, literally. I lost the baby, but got through it and continued on." She offered little reflection on the emotional impact of the miscarriage. In retrospect, getting through and carrying on struck her as more important than the experience itself.

They soon resumed their trip to Birmingham, the "Pittsburgh" of the South—at the end of the Appalachians in wooded, hilly country rich in coal, iron ore, and limestone. The city had an active history of violence against blacks and union organizers when Tish and Joe arrived. In his autobiography, Hosea Hudson, who organized sharecroppers in the 1930s and steel workers in the 1940s, described the terror: "When Negroes were arrested they were not merely taken to jail, they were whipped and left for dead in the cornfields. It was in 1935, during the Sharecroppers Union struggles that we heard many reports that Negroes were kidnapped from the fields in broad daylight and taken away, never to be seen again."[13] Fear of racial integration was increasingly blended with hatred of "subversives."

Works Progress Administration writers described Birmingham as "at once a well-planned city and a hurriedly-built boom town. . . . Fog often lies thick in the trough of Jones valley, and when it blends with the smoke from many giant stacks it forms a heavy grayish-yellow haze, locally called smog."[14] One resident recalled, "When I was growing up, people didn't think about pollution. The air was so full of dirt that you couldn't go out without having your nose and throat stop up and your white gloves get dirty. It meant that Birmingham was prosperous."[15]

Southern racial politics were painfully learned by Anne Braden, an unlikely political pawn. Anne, who grew up in Birmingham, accepted segregation without question. She learned from her mother the differences between blacks and whites: "You never call colored people ladies. . . . You say colored woman and white lady—never a colored lady."[16] Braden and her husband Carl later lived in Louisville, Kentucky, a city they at first thought much less racist than Birmingham. But in 1954 the Bradens were charged with fostering racial unrest by attempting to support neighborhood integration: a house the couple sold to a black family was allegedly bombed by Communists. Under Kentucky antisedition laws, Carl was eventually sentenced to fifteen years in prison, a saga told by Anne in *The Wall Between.*

Tish and Joe were not prepared for these Southern realities. "Our going to Birmingham turned out to be a rude shock." They really had no idea of the extent of racism or isolation they would face. To satisfy their underground status they fabricated a background. They left out Joe's education, for example, but didn't change their names. Tish believed that with this scant cover they were easy to trace. In fact, it took the FBI some time to find them. They learned that the Sommerses had left New York in January 1952. Obviously aware of Tish's pregnancy, they checked California birth records to see if a child had been born. But it was late in 1953 before the FBI located Tish working for the city of Birmingham.

By then Tish and Joe had settled in. He had a job as a trainman for the Louisville and Nashville Railroad. She taught Sunday school at the Presbyterian church and had a job at a city recreation center. About the time Tish and Joe realized the FBI had been checking with some of the neighbors, asking them to take photographs, she was given notice to leave her city job one day before her probationary year was over. The FBI had also intervened at the Birmingham mayor's office in August 1953, noting that Tish came in contact with "hundreds of young boys and girls" in her work at Harrison Park. Tish left the job within the month. Their years in Birmingham were frustrating, given the harassment and local biases.

After her experience with the city, Tish never held a full-time job; she did only part-time or volunteer work. Though she had years of organizing and sustained enthusiasm, her new role as "traditional" wife, along with anxiety about the FBI, restricted her options. Like many women of the 1950s, Tish turned to volunteer work with the neighborhood church and the League of Women Voters, intending these activities as a base for future political impact. The league's main focus was on the accumulated poll tax. "It kept women as well as blacks from voting. If you didn't pay it, that poll tax added up at two dollars each year to a maximum of thirty-six dollars. Since a lot of people couldn't pay during the Depression, they ended up owing thirty-six dollars. It was a great League of Women Voters issue, which we fought and won."

In 1954 she organized a League of Women Voters branch in Fairfield, a fact noted by the FBI in November. The next month they interviewed someone in the league about her. The field office accepted Washington's assessment, via J. Edgar Hoover, that this was not a subversive organization. Tish did not know about the interview, but she did recall accidentally delivering a box of Communist books instead of other innocuous materials to someone in the league. "The woman telephoned me, saying sharply, 'Some of your things are over here.' 'Oh,' I said when I got there, *'those.'* I took them, talked about something else as I went out, and never tried to make an explanation because I couldn't think of one that would work." The woman never said anything more about it; however, Tish's fortunes seemed to wane in the league after that. "I was never asked to take on any key tasks."

Any political activism was undertaken with the utmost care. They hid a small mimeograph machine in the house's crawl space. Once a month they got it out to print their "Communist" publication: educational material on basic democratic principles or "brotherhood." They used the library and issues in the local paper for their content and distributed copies at night in lower-income neighborhoods. "Every time we went out with those papers, my gut was in my throat. I was scared to death."

Joe and Tish were cautious for two reasons: they were probably under FBI surveillance, and the climate in the South was hostile to any attempt at racial integration. Southern columnist Harry Ashmore wrote, "The bombings of black leaders' homes became so frequent the area where most of them lived was christened Dynamite Hill. The active presence of the Klan was attested by fifty cross-burnings and numerous threats against local synagogues. Night-riders castrated a black man and whipped a black preacher with chains."[17] Harvard Sitkoff, another historian of the period, commented: "White supremacists . . . claimed repeatedly that agitation against Jim Crow sowed dissension among the American people. . . . Segregationists missed no opportunity to link the black struggle with Communist ideology and subversion."[18] With the Supreme Court's school desegregation decision in *Brown v. Board of Education* (1954), tensions escalated. Senator James Eastland of Mississippi claimed the Supreme Court bowed to "pressure groups bent upon the destruction of the American system of government, and the mongrelization of the white race. . . . The Court has responded to a radical, pro-Communist political movement in this country."[19]

Even in this hostile climate, Tish and Joe made one brief connection with black sharecroppers. These older people had been party activists in the 1930s, when the Communists organized blacks in rural Alabama. Tish and Joe were dropped off at a crossroads by their contact. This couple lived like those captured in Dorothea Lange's Depression-era photos of southern poverty. "We gave them encouragement and maybe a little money, and let them know they weren't alone. That was a very moving experience."

In the spring of 1955, the papers were filled with news of labor disputes in many industries. Among them were strikes at the Southern Bell Telephone company and the L&N Railroad. Eventually thirteen southern states were affected by the fifty-eight-day railroad strike.[20] Reports of violence and bombings were carried in national newspapers and in *Life* magazine.[21] Joe was a well-liked leader in the local union by then, and some of his black co-workers at L&N had become social friends. Tish's personal memory of the strike was limited, though she did recall bringing together the wives of the segregated unions. Under her leadership, the racially integrated women's auxiliary served doughnuts to both black and white switchmen on the picket line—a first for the L&N line.

Joe and Tish were truly "underground"—out of touch for those five years. "Absolutely nobody, friends or relatives knew exactly where we were. There was a mail drop, and the one time my mother visited we developed an elaborate subterfuge about the kind of life we led." On the surface Tish seemed the dutiful and dependent wife, fitting in as best she could with white Southern culture. Looking back, she perceived the strain of that double life, looking conventional while trying to hold to her inner belief that she was as good as her husband. She felt that they were still partners in work and marriage, but her own role as an activist was increasingly confined by gender expectations.

"It was tough and frustrating. People were very cautious. In a sense it was a hell of a lot easier in the South for Joe than for me because he had a clear-cut arena to work in, man-to-man with the other fellows on his work site." Tish's choices were more limited, particularly as there was no real work site. And her work with the union auxiliary and church were hard in another way. The political level was very low among the women who had not voted because of the poll tax. "The conversation was all on babies and recipes and clothes and it was very hard to talk about anything else. The most I was able to get going, and that was early in our stay, was to have little meetings at my house to talk about the vote." Tish laughed as she remembered, "I talked about 'our three-part system of government.' I don't think it was very successful, but we did have a few meetings." After more than a decade of sophisticated political analysis and activism, Tish had to work hard to communicate at this level. Twenty years later, the effort had its rewards, as OWL members who had never been "political" found her easy to communicate with, not "above them."

It took a long time, but they gradually built a number of

contacts with like-minded people. Joe was very sociable and made friends at work. They also met people at the local Unitarian Society, or by responding to liberal letter-writers in the newspaper. That's how they met a couple from the small Jewish community in Montgomery, about a hundred miles away. They were visiting them when Rosa Parks started the bus boycott in 1955. During the yearlong struggle, they read reports about what was going on in the white community of Montgomery. "The women especially, were very dependent upon black servants to do their cleaning. They weren't about to give that up, so they organized car pools to get their servants to work. For some it was personal, but some supported the boycott out of conviction. There was a strong liberal current, particularly in the Jewish community. So there were a lot of white folks picking up blacks and taking them to their jobs."[22]

Virginia Durr, a white supporter of the boycott, gave another perspective on the bus strike: "I would see the black women walking to work every morning and walking back at night. It was like the black tides would come up out of the black section of town and go to work and then sweep back again. . . . There was phenomenal support for the boycott. Absolutely phenomenal. The unity of the black people was the most amazing thing I have ever seen in my life."[23]

During this dynamic period, Tish and Joe bought a small tract house at the end of Oak Street, thinking they were going to stay. It was cheaper than renting and gave them a lot more privacy. In this more-isolated location they were able to have their black friends visit. They arrived at night, surreptitiously. At one point, Tish found paid work doing opinion and product research; one assignment was a survey on attitudes toward race. She was fascinated to find that everybody thought their neighbors were more prejudiced than they were. A couple of active racists did get very suspicious about this door-to-door survey, and "they followed up and wrote to me, phoned, claimed this was a plot. And this was just a business venture for me. It was interesting how they were right without knowing it! There was some mild threatening. It never came to anything but was a little scary." Tish knew she couldn't accomplish a great deal, but she realized things were ripening in Birmingham as a result of the boycott.

With limited political outlet, Tish's focus shifted to the personal realm. Her biological clock was ticking loudly. "By this time I was very, very anxious to have a child." She went to a Birmingham doctor; she and Joe were tested, but there wasn't anything definitive. She recalled, "I went through some routines, like using baking soda, and we used temperature charts to find the day of ovulation. After about four years there, in my early forties, finally I did get pregnant and miscarried again."

This miscarriage coincided with her mother's visit. Tension was historical with them, and Joe and Tish were still maintaining a fictional "cover" for her family. Kate criticized the attempt to have a child, challenging their motives. She observed that Tish wanted a baby for Joe and Joe wanted a baby for her. While there was a degree of truth to that, it overlooked Tish's heartfelt desire to have a child. "For myself, it really was a strong urge. I can't explain it, but from the time I had that first miscarriage, I had a drive to have a kid. This seems to happen to many women who are getting near the end of the line as far as child-bearing is concerned. Whether it's biological or just socially induced, the fact was I had the drive." One explanation for Kate's reaction was that she didn't particularly want to have grandchildren and thought women were better off without children. Toward the end of her own life, Tish understood her mother's view that being a single mother outweighed the joys of child rearing, but she continued to resent what she saw as her mother's totally self-centered perspective.

A final factor in Tish's desire to have a child went virtually unanalyzed. The fact was that she had dramatically changed her way of life. She had lost her identity as a leader and organizer. Thus having a child seemed more and more important. She tried an adoption agency, but they made it clear that there were no

Jewish children available. They also made it clear that they didn't approve of "mixed" adoptions. Tish and Joe began to look for other, less formal sources. She was having her hair cut when she heard about a child whose mother had died. He was being pushed out of the home of a great-aunt who couldn't care for him. They went to investigate and met with the natural father, who was quite agreeable. The midwife who delivered the baby was the intermediary. "After we bought one of her quilts, she was able to help with birth certificate information. This was a real Appalachian-type scene in the hills, and some of our friends from the railroad were very helpful in communicating. Finally we got proper papers and agreement from the person caring for the child, and we took possession."

Making two trips in a week to see the boy, they felt it was important to act quickly. "He was a year old, and didn't have a diaper, let alone anything else." Tish recalls, "I didn't even know how to hold a kid!" Things seemed to be moving along quite nicely at first, and Tish was delighted with her neighborhood baby shower. She was moved by the unexpected warmth: "A couple of people who didn't know me at all came. It was a nice party, and Bill was such an adorable child. After he was cleaned up, he really looked good. He had all kinds of scale and sores on his head, but they cleaned up with proper care." A Birmingham lawyer helped them begin the adoption process, but there was a long, elaborate struggle.

This was not a blissful time in their lives as they had hoped. When they first had Bill, Joe received a notice to appear before Senator Eastland's committee investigating the role of Communists in labor unions. Tish was sobered by the memory. "We were scared to death! We thought the sheriff would come and take the child away. So we headed out, left that night. We had decided we couldn't risk keeping our child in Alabama." Later they went back, cleared out their belongings, and sold the house within a week. The night they drove away with their household goods, they were followed by the sheriff to the state line. The FBI report noted that on 15 October 1957 the Jefferson County Department of Pensions and Security recommended to the Judge of Probate Court that the adoption be disapproved given the "unwholesome atmosphere for the child."

The FBI file further reported that Joe, Tish, and Bill left the Birmingham airport at 12:45 A.M. on 26 June 1957 for New York. Joe quit the L&N Railroad on 1 July, and the FBI records their departure for Wisconsin as two days later. A front-page article about them appeared in the *Birmingham News* on 11 August. Its headline read, "Pinks Worked under Noses of Union, City." The text noted that "it was through the efforts of another union official that Sommers' past came to light." The FBI file shows that their interest in Joe was stimulated by the earlier strike at L&N, but the copies the agency released are too censored to be certain exactly what they were doing or concerned about. Tish had ceased to interest them; her file had already been shut down for a year.

The newspaper echoed the style and format of the FBI documents. It reported their fabricated background, false job references, and Joe's membership in suspect organizations. Very little is said about Tish, except that as "Letitia Innes" she was known as a worker for the Young Progressives.[24] The very next day, the *Birmingham News* reported that the fireman who bought Tish and Joe's house was worried by "numerous persons [who] have driven by. He thinks some of them may be seeking Sommers." He was anxious for the public to know "that his only connection with Sommers was the purchase of the home through attorneys here."[25]

Their life switched dramatically again. They stayed briefly with friends in New York and then moved to the Midwest. They chose Wisconsin because it was said to be a good state for adoptions, mixed marriages were more tolerated there, the age difference between Joe and Tish might not matter, and the political situation was more liberal. Their personal network in New York provided contacts with Milwaukee.

The summer of 1957 marked the beginning of Tish and Joe's

close friendship with Alita and Leon Letwin. They met in Milwaukee while Joe was searching for a way to earn a living. Alita recalled Joe's interest in Leon's recently deceased father's spice business. Leon's father "had gone from one grocery store to another selling these cellophane packages of spices. We knew his suppliers but didn't know to whom he had sold, so we organized a telephone campaign to call every single grocery in town to put together a list."[26] The business thus assembled, Joe quickly bought it.

Tish stayed with Bill in New York while Joe made these decisions. She worried what might be next. "Joe came back all elated. I was a little startled, because Joe wasn't one to do things rapidly. He was a very deliberate person who took things one step at a time." She was amazed when he told her his decision. "Later on, Joe said I'd always made the decisions and taken the lead. I certainly did in some cases, as in some ways I was 'more advanced,' being ten years older and having been in the party that much longer." Tish believed that over the course of their marriage it was a fifty-fifty decision-making partnership. In this instance, however, Joe led the way.

Now owners of the small spice business, they moved to Milwaukee. Tish recalled, "We packaged the spices while we watched television. The red chilis would get on your hands and in your eyes. Joe put the pungent herbs, peppers and dry mushrooms in the trunk and drove from store to store." He was a very intense person who built up the business, developed strong good will and did very well. But it was quite clear after a year that he was getting bored.

Their primary concern now was to be "respectable" citizens. According to state adoption requirements in the 1950s, a stable family needed a full-time housewife.[27] The process of approval took over a year from the time they moved. Finally they appeared before the judge, who had gotten reports on them from Alabama. This was still the McCarthy period, so the lawyer knew they would have to handle the political questions. "The strategy was that when the judge said, 'Are you now or have you ever been, . . .' the lawyer would interrupt and say that was not a constitution- ally permitted question, and then we should interrupt him by saying we're not members of the Communist party. All of which was correct because we had no ties at that time, but we wouldn't say anything about the past. And it worked. So we celebrated. It had been nearly two years we had been fighting for Billy."

With the adoption behind them, they began to talk about the future. Tish subsumed her energies into the supportive domestic role. Without doubt, the focus was on Joe: "I did most of the probing with him, asking 'What do you want to do, what are you interested in, what kinds of work would you like to do?' He recalled how much he had enjoyed languages as an undergraduate at Cornell." His high-school friend, Sol Saporta, had gone on to become a linguistics professor, so Joe decided to talk to him about the possibility of going into academic life, getting a Ph.D. and going into a university.

Bob Notestein, family friend and professor as well as chair of anthropology and sociology at the University of Wisconsin, also spent hours with Joe talking about graduate school and univer- sity life. The families often shared meals, and when Tish sepa- rated foods out of a casserole for Bill, she noted apologetically that he was more used to her plain cooking. Doris Notestein recalled, "She self-deprecatingly mentioned her levels of accom- plishment had not graduated beyond a wedding gift cookbook, *My First 21 Meals* (or the like)." Sometimes Tish and the Notestein's daughter executed dance steps in the living room, and Joe teasingly exaggerated a mock ballet glide for their amuse- ment. Not a dance fan himself, Joe teased about Tish's "long dancer's legs," insisting she needed the aisle seat at plays and concerts.[28]

The Sommerses were fully attuned and committed to family life. By the time the adoption process was completed, there was no question of going back into politics. The requirement that Tish be a full-time homemaker had its impact. "I think we be-

Tish in Wisconsin, ca. 1956. Photograph courtesy of Anita Gurion.

came very child-centered, particularly with all the attention on the adoption and the upsets that went with it. I got involved in all kinds of domestic activities. I remember fantastic Christmas decorations, including Santa Claus and life-sized elves on the roof."

Another motivation fueled Tish's political retreat: disappointment with what was happening to global communism. While she acknowledged that things had been falling apart within the movement for some time, she looked back and saw that the revelations about Stalin were the most important factor. There were also numerous discussions at the time about problems in the American party. In addition to the events in Hungary and the Stalin revelations, leaders initially jailed under the Smith Act came out of prison with different ideas and added to the dissent over the direction of the party in the United States. "The point is, it wasn't an easy thing to go back to activism when you knew everything was in terrible disarray."

As with many formerly active members, the party never initiated contact and neither did they. However, they were still hounded by the FBI, who tried unsuccessfully to interview Tish in 1958 and 1959.[29] She staunchly refused to let them in the house. Generally, the Sommerses felt they were in personal transition, that now was not their time to get involved in politics.

Tish tried to go on with her life, but her personal peace of mind was disturbed. "I was finding even in the early stage that I was having some difficulties in the parenting role. I was really anxious for child care relief, as the twenty-four-hour job didn't appeal to me. I got tense and uptight." Joe's plans were determined by the availability of Woodrow Wilson scholarships, designed to encourage people to go into university teaching. When he was awarded one at the University of Wisconsin, they found a small apartment and moved near the Madison campus. Tish decided she should also go back to school, also in Hispanic studies.

That memory made her chortle. "Joe was working very hard, taking a heavy load. He took more courses than he could manage,

Tish and her son, Bill, ca. 1959.
Photograph by Leon Letwin, courtesy of Anita Gurion.

so I began to help. I remember writing one of his papers. It was
such fun, I really enjoyed it, and he got an 'A.' Later, when I
returned to school, that same professor said I couldn't possibly
manage his very difficult course, that it took analytical and writing ability. I had to bite my tongue so I wouldn't tell him I'd
already done well on one of his assignments!" Tish could not be
publicly acknowledged for her auxiliary role as Joe's academic
helpmate, or for her own talents.

Still seeing themselves as partners, Tish chose Hispanic studies to help Joe with research on Spanish literature. She was enthusiastic about studying again and took anthropology, art history,
and literature classes. She loved everything except the language
classes, which had never been easy for her. About their relationship, Tish commented, "We had been helpmeets all this time and
it seemed only natural to continue. I was really naive in that
sense. I thought of people as teams, the old Communist way of

working. Joe was very much for it, he appreciated all the help he could get. But actually, ever since our time in the South, I had done the housework. He would help, there was no question, but it was 'helping' as opposed to doing. The basic responsibility was mine, as it was with child care." These changes, accepted in the South because of political necessity and then because of the adoption, became a way of life that continued when those justifications no longer existed.

During this period the Letwins and Sommerses expanded their friendship. The two couples had similar political ideas and experiences and had sons the same age. There are photographs of family outings, camping and swimming, including one of the "authentic teepee" Tish made for the boys, a wonderful replica of a Plains Indian dwelling. Their Thanksgiving turkey snapshot, with Alita and Tish bent over the stove, was the portrait of smiling domesticity. The women's friendship developed around mothering, the simple outdoor pleasures, and long, involved talks about politics and where they were headed. They all loved camping and planned vacations together. Once the Sommerses got to their site early and posted a sign to direct the Letwins. It said, "Camp Meshugana" or "crazy" in Yiddish.

It was on that camping trip that Tish first discovered a lump in her breast. She was forty-five years old. Her description was terse, the recollection still difficult: "I went to the doctor, who sent me immediately to a surgeon, who immediately said, 'Go to the hospital.' I was in the hospital the next day, and when I woke up there was no breast. It all went so fast from the point of seeing that first doctor. It was as big a shock as it is to everybody." She remembered weeping in the hospital room and the nurse consoling her. "I said, 'They'll take the baby away now.' I wonder why I thought that? It must have had to do with that year of probation. The idea was you had to be in good health." She was in shock. "Of course it was also the mutilation with no preparation for it. You sign before you go in that they'll do whatever they need to do. The radical mastectomy was done without any question, with no time between. There was no alternative treatment for breast cancer then." They took out lymph glands, half of which were malignant, so the cancer had already traveled to some extent. The doctors told Tish there was a 50 percent or greater chance of recurrence.

As soon as she got out of the hospital she needed to occupy herself, so she took a course in sculpture. She forced herself to use her hands to make sure her arm would not atrophy. Though she was very frightened, it helped that Joe was extremely supportive. "I remember the first time getting into bed without the breast. He was very sensitive about it and could not have made it easier for me. Really, after that I had no problems. I know there's so much written about loss of sensuality, but I didn't feel that." She joked, "Of course, he wasn't particularly a breast man. I mean he was adaptable, or at least he never expressed any reservations to me. We were not that open about our feelings. We were sensitive to each other, but there were always certain shut doors."

What followed was a period of change and fighting back that would inform her similar struggle twenty years later. She went into the sculpture class, continued to work toward her master's degree, and worked very hard to get well. Even before she got out of the hospital, she was doing ballet exercises and raising her arms despite the pain. When first home, she hung the laundry by hand because the stretching was supposed to help. "Looking back, I did right on the whole business of getting well. But, as happens with most cancer patients, there's always that terrific fear of return. Whenever I went for my six months' checkup, there was always something, some lump in my throat or elsewhere. Once the doctor gave me the all-clear sign, those lumps would disappear." Her fears returned in spite of keeping busy, in spite of denial, for a very long time.

Tish sounded matter-of-fact at seventy years of age when she told the rest of this story. She was engaged in a new struggle with cancer and sounded very distanced from that earlier fear. Thirty years had provided some buffering for her. Calmly she talked about her second mastectomy a year after the first, done because there were so many lumps. They called it prophylactic surgery. "The doctors said, who needs it, get rid of it so you don't have to worry about it. I agreed, and it wasn't particularly a painful recovery. Since my breasts were fairly heavy, having one was worse than none." She had a third operation within the next six months for removal of a small lump which was cancerous but encapsulated. So cancer was a recurrent theme in these years. "I was generally being as positive as possible." Looking back, she minimized any adjustment difficulties, Joe's reaction, and any affect on her sexual self-esteem.

Tish's parents died the next year, within a week of one another. The FBI carefully checked Murray's will in case he left money to Tish (he didn't) which might be used for subversive purposes. The FBI neglected to check her mother's will and so missed the $250,000 Kate left to Tish. Since Tish and Joe no longer had any connection with the Communist party, none of her inheritance went in its direction.

With the inheritance in 1960, Tish entered her "other" economic life. She was much more financially secure than during her childhood when she lived as a "poor relation" to her father's well-to-do family. She and Joe rose now to a higher economic bracket: the money became a factor in their decision-making. Initially it enabled them to travel comfortably. Joe was working as hard as he could to finish his degree and, in the process, applied for a fellowship in Mexico to support his dissertation research on the role of the literary figure as agent of social change. His focus was on Latin America, where writers of fiction had a much larger impact on society than in the United States. They went to Mexico for a year, and Joe moved in a circle of intellectual writers. Though they did not know it, the FBI followed their movements there.

But Tish's life in Mexico was not as stimulating as Joe's. Her days were filled with child rearing and isolation. She had trouble with the Spanish language and felt foolish in conversation. By this time Bill, in the American School in Mexico City, was also having to learn a new language and meet new friends. When he was home she had to be with him all the time.

She had to have another focus. When Bill went off to school, she had more free time and immediately went down to the Mexican archives. "I had learned to read old Spanish, and had an idea for a novel related to the seventeenth-century collection. It was intellectually exciting and gave me a purpose, a reason for being there, other than being wife and mother." Migration to the north had fascinated her when she worked on the master's degree, and she saw the potential for a novel set in the seventeenth-century expansion period around silver mining. At one point she and Joe followed as much of the northward trail as they could, taking pictures for reference. Tish decided to tell the story of the migration from the perspectives of several participants, including a Spanish priest, a well-to-do Mexican, and a poor Indian. She planned to give the class a religious view of each man's progress.

Soon she had another new activity, for which she was also full of enthusiasm. While they were in Mexico City, Joe got a job offer from the University of Washington. Joe's high-school friend Sol Saporta now headed the Linguistics Department, and having him in Seattle made the job even more attractive to Joe. Being back on the West Coast also appealed to Tish. She remembered "getting all these 'house and garden' type magazines, and making a book, 'The House,'" before they went. "I suddenly had this new project—had to have a new house. For one thing, we could now afford it. And it gave me a sense of permanence. My mother had always been frustrated by the fact that we moved around so much and she never had any one place." Joe had finished his Ph.D. and she her master's degree, and Joe was headed for a permanent academic position. "We were going to have a house, to build a new life for ourselves."

Tish approached her roles as wife and mother with the energy and creativity she had always given to politics. But the results were very mixed. As discussion led away from strict chronology toward reflection and analysis, the subject of mothering was raised. "I used to wonder why I couldn't be the kind of mother that others were. I don't think, whatever maternal strengths are, I had much talent in that direction. I found it difficult all the time," she admitted, "from the beginning. I tried, but I would say of the various facets in my life, mothering was the least successful."

Tish was aware of several logical reasons for her difficulty in mothering. One was being over forty at a time when older women weren't having or adopting children. "But there were a lot of factors, possibly my lesser talents in that area, the fact that I was older, the fact that the child was adopted, that the child was not a dream child. And also, I think, perhaps the fact that motherhood was much overrated." She was a forty-year-old who had been a youth organizer, who had worked in the South, a person who had been involved in ideological struggles, a person who had great confidence in herself, and a person with leadership abilities. "Here I was, faced with a full-time job of working with a kid who was anything but appreciative of my overzealous efforts at being a good mother."

She acknowledged in 1985 that Bill had suffered from his first, neglected year, and he was a very active child in a time before hyperactivity was recognized. Too, they moved from place to place six times before he was ten years old. Alita understood Tish's disappointment: "The thing you have been longing for comes to pass, and it's so unsatisfying. It must have been a tremendous blow to your self-esteem."

"It was." Tish concurred, sinking back, sighing. "I had just assumed I could do it. There was no question in my mind. I had all kinds of illusions." She digressed, momentarily, to the present. "We were sitting around the kitchen table at the OWL office a couple of days ago. Every woman there had one kid who was affected by the 1960s period, when Billy was a teenager. Either these kids dropped out or went down the wrong alleys, or whatever, but they were seriously damaged." Tish found solace in this commonality.

She expressed her sense of personal failure with Bill, a sentiment rarely expressed about other aspects of her life. "I haven't recovered completely. There are hangovers. I feel there's nothing I can do. And I surely contributed to that which I feel has made life for him not as full or rich or valuable as it would have been under other circumstances." In his late twenties, Bill still seemed without focus, unable to take charge of his life or manage his own role as parent of a small child. Tish looked for a bright side: "Of course, intellectually I can say, compared to his original circumstances, I saved him. I remember discussions about 'did he want to know his parents,' and his saying he had no desire to look into that. 'You've been my parents,' he said. I don't think he feels we messed him over, but that in some ways he failed us."

Her pain was palpable. She had not revealed her full angst and sadness to her son. "I don't know what I could say. It's hard to articulate because I don't want to convey to him that I think he's been a failure or that his life is less than it could be. That would reinforce the idea that what has happened to him is less than I wish it could have been." This was an unfinished piece of her life. She admitted she had not resolved it, except financially.

In a halting voice, Tish explained how unresolved her relationship with Bill was and how he viewed her as a flawless, "all-successful," public role model for others. Her tearful state reflected her pain and the distance between their two perceptions. This conversation left those in the room with her with a sense of sadness and poignant intimacy.

It was fall of 1985. The bar was smoky, the airport dingy and crowded. The best view of the Oakland airport comes from the plane flying low over the salt flats when the pampas grass is in bloom. As I waited for my flight to San Diego, most planes were two hours late. Tired and cranky travelers wandered around, and the bar overflowed. The delay gave me more time to chat with an OWL member, and we recalled how we each met Tish. We were enjoying one another's company, relaxed and weary. Our conversation turned to Tish's decades of activism.

The slender older woman turned her head and spoke softly so no one else in the bar would hear. There was a tentative note in her voice: "Was Tish a member of the Communist party?" Learning she was, she asked, "You won't put that in the book, will you?" She was worried about the possible impact on OWL members, fearing their reaction.

In the early taping sessions, Tish wasn't sure she wanted the fact of her Communist party membership acknowledged. After all, she had talked about her history in speeches for years without ever mentioning it. However, over time Tish came to feel that it was better to reveal this important aspect of her life. She thought the film *Seeing Reds* captured the excitement she'd felt, the feeling of being part of a large social movement—and her revelation might increase others' understanding. She became more interested in sorting out what difference being a Communist had made in her life.

But her anxiety about revealing a Communist past was real, and shared by several people close to her and by a few in OWL's membership. They didn't exactly want to suppress the truth, but they felt admitting past membership was dangerous. They collaborated in making their own lives invisible. When we interviewed significants in Tish's life, we felt such questions might be threatening and so did not ask them. Only a few were open about their party membership. One letter we received responded to a notice placed in the *Los Angeles Times*. The writer asked if Letitia Innes were "a young woman active in dance, and interested in 'progressive causes.'" That became the code response—"Well, we were all progressives in that time," or "That was a progressive kind of activity." One person, extremely cautious, refused to be taped; she never mentioned any radical or progressive connection, though we had been told it was there.

Most interviewees knew some people whose lives were drastically changed by the Red Scare of the 1950s and the ensuing investigations. One old friend of Tish's paused in telling a story, revealing his anxiety. "Well, maybe I shouldn't be telling you this. But what the hell, what are they going to do, take away my Social Security?" It was a joke, but not a funny one. Several we interviewed had lost their jobs in the 1950s, and their lingering anxiety was evident. Few took the stance that Tish eventually did, that it was necessary to talk about what being a Communist meant, important not to let it disappear as if thousands of people had never made that commitment. She said, "It's important to see those roots, and acknowledge that they were positive roots which made it possible for me to be an effective founder of an organization like OWL."

Join Hands: Racism and Sexism

It is when we tell our stories and find out what we have in common that we realize that many of our personal problems are really social problems. It is then that sisterhood becomes powerful.

It was as though a new phase was about to be born and I was aware of it.

Tish's success in developing OWL from 1980 to 1985 was reflected in varied ways. In spite of the territorial problems resulting from moving the office from Oakland to Washington, D.C., and Tish's discomfort with its rapid bureaucratic growth, OWL became a recognized force in legislative circles. Tish spoke frequently before Congress and local and national groups addressing the need for health care access, pension rights, and employment needs of older women.[1]

Through Alice Quinlan, OWL participated in the Coalition on Women and the Budget which brought together fifty-five organizations to watchdog the effects of the Reagan administration's policies on older women.[2] Tish also initiated a Citizens' Council on Earnings Sharing, co-chaired by Arthur Flemming (former head of the Civil Rights Commission) and designed to bring together experts in economics and aging. These experts included Lou Glasse from the New York State Agency on Aging, who later replaced Tish as OWL's president. The council monitored the Reagan administration's mandated study of earnings sharing for

Social Security credit by couples during marriage and critiqued the report when it finally appeared in 1985. OWL formed coalitions to fight for Social Security reforms, struggled to develop guaranteed access to health care for divorced women, pushed for legal changes to permit military pensions to be shared by ex-wives and spouses to be notified about survivor's benefits in pension programs. They also raised consciousness about care giving and death.

OWL chapters flourished, so that membership grew from that first three hundred to nearly twenty thousand. Membership remained primarily middle-class and white, though OWL did sponsor a conference on older black women and frequently emphasized minority women's special concerns in the *OWL Observer*. [3]

Though Tish was eager to stir all OWL members to action, she gradually realized that many women wanted social contacts and emotional support as well. Laurie Shields legitimized that need through the *OWL Observer*, which reported on chapter brunches and walking trips as well as legislative action. Personal letters attesting to the comfort and pride women found in their local meetings were also included to give support to those who came to OWL out of loneliness. Blending the personal with the political, OWL began to use Mother's Day as an annual reminder to legislators. Their first greeting card in this campaign said "Your mother didn't bring you up to let other mothers down." A later one pointed out that health care should be "a right, not a privilege."

OWL educational materials were made available through the newspaper, through special flyers, slide shows, and training sessions. The *Wingspan* handbooks laid out a series of workshops each chapter might hold, beginning with "What Kind of Older Woman Do I Want to Be?" and moving to those focused on pensions, Social Security, or housing.

Countering stereotypes, Tish often began her speeches by asking women to look in the mirror at the lines in their faces, which made them more beautiful than when they were sixteen. Dressed

Older Black Women Conference, May 1984, sponsored by the Berkeley Bay Area Alumnae Chapter of Delta Sigma Theta. *Left to right*, Dorothy Pitts, Ida Dunson, Josephine Robinson, Homerzell Swisher Harris, Barbara Belford, Frances Catlett-Crawford, Eugenia Hicks, Lillian Kelly, Judi Freeman, Phyllis Harris. Photograph courtesy of OWL.

in earth tones, her dancer's arms spread wide, her hair in a flattering "natural" perm, she provided an attractive, graceful image to her audience. She urged them to pay attention to their gains, to cherish experiences and places they'd been, to accept their own maturity and strength. These workshops always included political agendas, and many women who had never before been active found themselves speaking out and demonstrating at their state legislatures. OWL chapters operated in many states to press for greater awareness of older women's needs, and the network they formed provided a grass-roots base for OWL's national agenda.

Tish's work with OWL was the culmination, the final ripening of her talents as an organizer. Late in her life, decades after she first organized her fellow students in dance performances, her skills were at a peak. Success was grounded in her reemergence as an activist in the 1960s through the civil rights movement and then the women's movement. This transitional period was stimulated by her personal frustration with parenting and her domestic role as well as by the drastically changed political climate. As the decade of the 1960s began, her husband was a faculty member at the University of Washington. Tish was wife, mother—and now, faculty spouse.

At first her "dream house," in the north end of Seattle, overlooking Lake Washington, gave her a time-consuming and self-fulfilling focus. She devoted her time and energy, nurtured "forty-seven varieties of rhododendrons," and was a Cub Scout den mother. Tish spent a lot of time working with Bill on school problems. Still a highly active youngster, he wasn't doing well at reading. Years later they realized he had problems with letter reversals common to dyslexics, but that diagnosis was not available then. Tish painfully recalled: "I was doing everything I could to do things right and the harder I tried the worse the results seemed to be."

Her situation only worsened. She continued to work on the Mexican novel, but her eyes began to bother her, and she developed headaches. Before long, someone complained that as a faculty wife she shouldn't be allowed to use a library carrel. Thus slapped down, she set the book aside. Menopausal changes made her feel distracted and uncomfortable. Beset by depression, she viewed her faculty wives' gatherings as horror shows. There was nothing she could relate to, the women didn't talk about issues at all, and stimulating conversation among the men and women was nonexistent since the sexes were totally separated at social events. It was 1965, a time for change.

The turning point in this gloomy period was a visit with Alita. Tish knew the Letwins were having hard times and that Alita had been stricken with lupus. In need herself and longing for companionship, she offered Alita a plane ticket to Seattle. They talked fervently at the house and in restaurants, over several days and nights—about what they might do, what might make them feel a renewed sense of mission and fulfillment. Tish felt she had no identity of her own to give her a sense of value. Feeling some of that herself, Alita raised the idea of going back to social activism. "It was very momentous for both of us," Tish recalled. "Enough time had passed that we knew if we were waiting for a resurgence of a radical movement we might have a long wait; this was a time to make our own path."

Tish was rejuvenated by their intimate brainstorming. She wrote Alita: "We seem to communicate on the same wave length. The result is our get-togethers put wheels into motion that had slowed down. . . . Now I feel very much as I did the day I walked out of the hospital with one breast less and my first face-to-face encounter with death. Sky was never bluer, grass greener."[4]

The time had come to take action. Tish, with her earlier background in anti-racist work in Los Angeles and the South, was sensitive to the burgeoning civil rights movement. Her own acuity was echoed by the national media, which for the past few years had focused on racial conflicts in the South. Television brought the 1963 confrontations in Birmingham close to home. Lerone Bennett, Jr.'s *The Negro Mood* captured the social context: "Thou-

sands were arrested and humiliated amid scenes of incredible bru-
tality. Some demonstrators were attacked by police dogs; others
were bowled over by high water hoses. . . . Negroes rioted, burned
the stores of white businessmen, and fought."[5] Thousands dem-
onstrated as the civil rights movement grew, and many were arrested.

Seattle prided itself in being above such conflict, but when an
open-housing ordinance was defeated in 1964, Seattle Urban
League Director Edwin T. Pratt charged: "Now Seattle cannot
point its finger at Birmingham and call it bigoted. Seattle by a
vote of two to one said, 'no,' to open housing. . . . Those who have
strong feelings against non-whites have found a way to come
before the public and say so behind the closed curtain of a voting
booth."[6] That same year the local Congress of Racial Equality
(CORE) chapter (two hundred members, about half of whom were
white) aligned with the NAACP and the Baptist Ministerial Alliance to push local supermarkets to hire blacks, and Freedom
Patrols were established to monitor police activity in the predominantly black Central Area.[7]

Ripples from the civil rights and peace movements reached
the Northwest. A number of Seattle programs were being planned
or getting underway to take advantage of federal funds. Even the
PTA had become energized. One morning in a heated meeting, a
group of liberal parents successfully opposed the showing of a
"decency" film sponsored by the John Birch Society. Everything
was escalating. There was to be a Vietnam teach-in on campus,
and Joe moderated a panel on Santo Domingo's political unrest.
Tish chose the Seattle League of Women Voters' "equal opportunities" study as her way of getting into action. She reported to the
league on the progress of proposals for the "war on poverty."

She was particularly drawn to the growing activity in Seattle's
black community.[8] Located on hills east of downtown and south
of the University of Washington, the Central Area housed the
majority of Seattle's forty thousand blacks, including the poorest.
The area was marginally integrated, particularly in the Madrona

and Leschi neighborhoods. To the north, more white residents lived, and to the south more poverty and a higher percentage of all-black neighborhoods bordered the community.

Liberal whites who lived nearby the Central Area worked with blacks for open housing, school integration, and improved employment opportunities. One was Carol Richman, faculty wife and community organizer. She was especially concerned about schools and saw the upcoming poverty program funding as a great opportunity. Twenty years later, she explained: "We thought if we could just get the whole community organized, we could have a ten-thousand-person march anytime. . . . The idea was we were going to have this great uprising and bring about massive change."[9] It was indeed a time of optimism and hope.

Seattle moved toward President Lyndon Johnson's "Great Society" with dispatch. The Central Area Community Council and the Urban League were prime sponsors of a $350,000 grant proposal to the federal Office of Economic Opportunity. They planned ten after-school study centers, community block workers to organize citizen councils, and vocational guidance.[10] Funding arrived in August 1965, the month of the Watts riots in Los Angeles. The first three paid staff members of the Central Area Motivation Program (CAMP) began work before Labor Day in the old cinder-block building behind the East Side YWCA.[11] Among the first to volunteer was a very proper-looking white woman, Mrs. Joseph Sommers, who quietly suggested a program to recruit volunteers for the study centers to be held after-hours in local schools.

Tish was back in action! Not surprisingly, her program had lofty goals: "to bring together adults and youths in meaningful understanding, . . . to improve the overall interracial climate in Seattle and combat factors leading to poverty and prejudice through individual and organizational involvement of dedicated and creative volunteers in a two-way exchange within and without the Central Area."

CAMP, like other poverty programs across the country,

brought together civil rights activists from several segments of the black community. In the early months the mood was optimistic, and the energy level high. The staff moved to a three-story Victorian house when funding arrived for a multiservice center. Under the direction of Walter Hundley—a black social worker, minister, and CORE activist—new projects began to share the space. The mood was exuberant, and plans were made for day-care centers, a community-run credit union, youth programs, and general family services.

Nearly ten thousand people came through CAMP's door that year. The staff learned how to write the ever-multiplying government reports and laughed about, but got good at, "body counting." The services endeared the center to the community, as evidenced by the impressive community mobilization that took place when a boycott was called—for several days the Central Area schools were shut down. The demonstrations did not end de facto segregation in Seattle schools, nor did they lead to community control, but they did lay the groundwork for more serious negotiations and concessions from the school board. In 1969 the board agreed to a Central Area School Council, to which several former CAMP staff members were elected.

Staff members were also elated by another "victory." The after-school study centers in the Central Area's eleven schools were successful beyond anyone's expectations. Children trickled in to play games or work on homework with volunteers. Then friends came, word spread, and more staff were hired and trained. More and more students arrived until some three thousand dropped by each week. Volunteers provided most of the help; bringing them in was Tish's full-time, unpaid job.

Helping black children do better in schools was appealing to many whites who believed education would be a racial equalizer. Tish, realizing this, recruited six hundred whites through church and school groups from all over Seattle. Central Area groups also involved black parents and students from the area's high school. Tish elicited quite an array of donations, as her correspondence showed: "Thank you for the decorated egg cartons for our math games," "and for the musical instruments," "and for the fascinating science demonstration."[12]

Roberta Byrd Barr's Seattle-based TV program, "Face to Face," addressed a range of civil rights issues in the late 1960s. Tish spoke on the show about CAMP and opportunities for volunteer contributions. She also attended her first School for Community Action with five hundred others (primarily concerned white women), held at the activist Mt. Zion Baptist Church in the black community. These one-day sessions were designed to build awareness and support for racial harmony in the larger community. Tish also recruited many of these women to work in the Central Area.[13]

Tish was CAMP's full-time (unpaid) volunteer coordinator. Her life hardly paralleled that of a "lady bountiful" from the suburbs, condescending to do "good works." She gave the program the same dedication she had given to her earlier anti-racist work in East Los Angeles. The staff was impressed by her commitment; her word was as good as an action completed. She listened, responded to the study center teachers, and developed volunteer orientation programs. She was soon considered a pivotal staff member, included in weekly meetings, strategy sessions, and plans for expansion. This situation suited Tish well because initially the funding seemed limitless, and the CAMP director was open to her ideas. Soon, Tish sought economic support for the day-care center and a performing arts festival. The latter grew into a program. Then it blossomed into play writing, a film unit, an African boutique, and plans for an opera production. Eventually CAMP acquired an abandoned fire station for performances. Her days were full and stimulating. Menopausal depression lifted as she focused less on her domestic role.

Over time, Tish felt more drawn to the Central Area. She and Joe bought a wooded lot on its edge and built a lovely new glass-walled home overlooking Lake Washington. This decision had to do, Tish said, "with working in the black community and wanting to be a part of it. I felt isolated out in the north end; it was a psychological contradiction living in a white community and in my heart and soul being a black." Tish identified with blacks once again as she had earlier empathized with Jews, Mexican Americans, and black youths in the 1940s. Now her enthusiasm and sense of moral obligation motivated her to move into this community.

Tish never approached any project halfheartedly. She and Joe were both very busy and involved: he continued his literary research and supported Chicano students on campus; she worked on CAMP's multiple projects. By the second year a new focus on Afro-American heritage was added to the study centers, now politically renamed Action Education Centers. Consequently, Tish revised her approach to volunteer recruitment: "This was the first time I presented the new 'hard-line' volunteer approach (you came not to give but to learn—what you take back is more important than what you bring)."[14] Using her new strategy, she worked with a CAMP group on "Fences," a play about race relations, later used in training sessions for volunteers. She also developed proposals for noncredit courses in Afro-American heritage.

Black pride, black self-determination, and Black Power were gaining momentum—ideas that stirred both blacks and whites. The Southern Christian Leadership Conference (SCLC) had yielded to the Student Nonviolent Coordinating Committee (SNCC) in the South, with increased control by blacks and rejection of white leadership. Media reports quoted Malcolm X's black-centered politics, and the culture began to absorb a new language. Articles pointed out the new emphasis on black pride: "All across the country now one can find blacks wearing their hair 'Afro' style. . . . Friends are often admonished to 'think black.' People are often criticized for 'sounding too much like whitey.'"[15] Black historian Lerone Bennett, Jr., castigated liberals: "The reputation of white liberals in the Negro community is at an all-time low. . . . Because their aims are so narrow, white liberals are of limited value to Negro leadership. . . . [They are] paternalistic, patronizing, condescending, . . . [and they] cannot convert anyone in America until they convert themselves and their constituencies."[16]

These issues were not new to Tish, as they echoed her earlier confrontations over the role of whites in supporting anti-racist work. She understood the depth of distrust involved and was aware that she must work even more in the white community if she were to remain effectively legitimate in the eyes of her black co-workers.

These same issues confused and overwhelmed twelve-year-old Bill, whose youthful concerns took precedence over ideology. He was caught between two forces not of his own making: first, the growing anger among blacks about white oppression. Once they moved into their new house near the Central Area, Bill attended the local elementary school. At first he enjoyed it. "I felt really comfortable there because I was around kids who were a lot like me. I didn't feel like I fit in with the rest of the middle-class society. . . . [There] they all had problems similar to mine with math and reading."[17] Tish remembered the elementary school as partially integrated. Moving to junior high school, however, was difficult for Bill. He recalled: "They had little race wars where they'd set off fire extinguishers in your lockers. I think the thing that bothered me most was that Roscoe—a friend [from his elementary school]—completely turned against me. I could see his situation, he couldn't associate with a white boy at that time, but it bothered me." This occurred when Bill's parents were intensely focused on their political work and not aware of the depth of his confusion.

The second force that had an impact on his life was the growing drug culture of the 1960s. The "Age of Aquarius" let in more than long hair and sunshine. Bill had never had an easy time with school, but by junior high there were new pressures all the time. "It was scary really, living in that area. I was afraid to go anywhere, walk anywhere. I had nightmares, and we also had a break-in at the house. I didn't feel safe at all. . . . At that point I just decided I wasn't going to have anything to do with school, and I started getting into drugs, . . . smoking grass, a lot of acid, we called it LSD." He remembered coming home high many times and wondering if his parents realized it. Years later, Tish recalled, "I don't think we would accept the idea, we didn't believe it, not then." For Bill, his parents' inaccessibility due to their activism, the racial hostility toward whites in school, and the easy availability of drugs all intersected during his adolescence. These were empowering and exhilarating years for Tish, but for her son they were painful and, ultimately, debilitating ones.

Several whites continued to work with CAMP although they were no longer as welcome due to the growth of Black Power ideology. Federal funding became more unpredictable, so Tish wrote more requests to private foundations. She decided to spend at least half her time in the white community, working with church and human rights organizations on civil rights issues. Adjusting to the change in political climate, she became a proselytizer among whites against racism, moving away from CAMP without feeling betrayed or unappreciated. Not only did she have very positive working relationships in the black community, there were real allies for her in the fight against racism in the white community. Recognized as doing the job that a white should be doing, Tish had found her niche once again.

Racial explosions nationwide, particularly in summer 1967, caused the Seattle establishment to leap at quick remedies. Their strategy: keep young people off the streets. To this end, programs were hastily concocted, some recreational, others city-based employment. This "band-aid" approach was essentially ineffective, and Seattle, too, had a three-day riot by summer's end. The Rev. Dr. John Adams, pastor of the First AME Church in the Central Area and involved in CAMP from its beginning, responded in the Seattle press to the findings of the National Commission on Civil Disorders, "I think the commission report is naive in saying that riots can split America into two societies—one white and one black. America has always had two societies. What happened last summer did not create that condition. What went on the last several hundred years created that condition."[18] Tish shared his view.

Changes within the black community spurred Tish and others from CAMP to organize a "Soul Search" course at the University of Washington in the spring of 1969. Each session presented a speaker on black oppression, followed by open discussion. Symptomatic of the times, however, CAMP was seen by younger Black Power advocates as too "Uncle Tom," too establishment.

Most Central Area gatherings in this period were marked by conflict within the black community. Disagreements over strategy and opportunities, including who should speak and lead, were common. Conflict extended to the campus, where several young men who had worked with SNCC in the South formed a Black Student Union. Tish reported: "The first session [of Soul Search] started with a BANG! Two hundred students attended, including twenty-five members of the Black Student Union, who joined with great hostility to the whole idea. However, the confrontation that resulted, while shaking up many people, appears to have had generally positive results."[19]

The course ultimately led to some changes. The Black Student Union (BSU) became instrumental to the class and presented a memorial to Malcolm X, their own view of the black revolution, and a lively closing session on soul music. Representatives of the BSU continued to lead discussion groups and share in the planning for each week's session. The course received frequent, positive coverage in the campus paper and was approved for another term. Soul Search had made possible a new liaison between black students and the administration.

A variety of other political issues also occupied Tish and Joe in the late 1960s. Anti–Vietnam War demonstrations accelerated; in 1969 Tish and Joe joined the Letwins for a San Francisco march against the war sponsored by Women Strike for Peace. Joe continued working with Chicano students and organizers among the Yakima Valley farm workers. He also started Chicano literature classes for inmates at the nearby federal prison. They hosted a reception for members of the Watts Writers' Workshop, and when one poet, j. kurtis lyle, decided to stay in Seattle, Tish recruited him for the CAMP theater project.[20]

But Tish's primary role was increasingly as an anti-racist leader in the white community: she was involved with human-relations councils and the YWCA-sponsored School for Community Action. She helped them get started by providing materials and helping them develop program ideas. She continued to affirm that relatively intelligent, committed people could take a problem and brainstorm a solution.

One organizing effort culminated in Join Hands, a group modeled after a Los Angeles effort among concerned whites that Tish learned about from Alita. In one action, the Seattle group picketed a shopping center that did not hire blacks. They learned the pricing code for one store and passed out leaflets advising customers to buy only below-cost items. "It was like a reverse boycott," Tish laughed. "Everybody enjoyed that, loved getting a bargain, and knowing the secret code."

The laughter ceased when, in January 1969, Ed Pratt, a charismatic black leader who had worked toward racial harmony both behind the scenes and in public life, was murdered at the door of his north-end Seattle home. He had been central to the local poverty program's successes and was widely respected by both blacks and whites. Join Hands prepared a pledge of commitment to continue the struggle to secure black civil rights and circulated it at the downtown memorial march attended by nearly five thousand people. It read: "So that Martin Luther King, so that Edwin T. Pratt did not die in vain, let us Join Hands." It listed a ten-point pledge, including confronting one's own fear and prejudice and striving to eradicate them. It exhorted, "This is a commitment to action, not just words."[21]

His death seemed to mark a transition from the optimism of the Johnson administration's early War on Poverty to the bureaucratic Nixon years. Riots were fewer, and federal monies were

Padua Hills Theater, Los Angeles, 1968. *Left to right,* Joe Sommers,
Tish, Tomas Ybarra-Frausto, Pat Huckle, Alita Letwin. Photograph by
Leon Letwin, used with permission.

shrinking. Seattle was chosen to be one of the first "Model Cities," 150 demonstration projects that were supposed to foster the
meshing of local government and minority community action
projects. CAMP leadership was absorbed into the city-controlled
structure. The emphasis shifted very quickly to endless citizen
planning meetings instead of action. Tish felt there was too much
compromise, too much dilution of effort, and less room for free-
wheeling speculation or grass-roots projects. She gradually withdrew from the increased bureaucratic rigidity.

W. Ivan King, a staff member with the Seattle Urban League,
CAMP, and the Model Cities program, commented on the social

activists' transition from a "stay loose" approach to a "be efficient" mandate.[22] He recalled the initial flexibility of CAMP, the range of people involved, the hiring of indigenous, indigent residents, and the multiple programs in response to expressed needs: "special attention was given to mobilizing the (previously) most insulated, isolated and powerless group: blacks in poverty."[23] He commented positively on the use of volunteers and provision of meeting space for local groups.

King's criticisms included the brief period of federal support, changes in public reaction, diminished funding, and the effects of rapid growth and increased bureaucratization. There was limited coordination between new agencies and older ones, resulting in confusion on the part of those needing service. New or emerging activist leaders avoided government positions; they were replaced by social welfare careerists with "more credentials, but less charisma," as King saw it. According to him, decisions were made from the top down, with little feedback from the rank and file. This coincided with reduced or unpredictable funding as the public and government "romance with poverty" began to cool. His observations were echoed in the nationwide criticism of poverty programs.

CAMP provided hundreds of jobs in the short run, along with organizing experience for many. It also made careers for the most educated blacks able to assimilate into existing bureaucracies. As another activist-critic of the national programs noted, "Revolutionary fervor is transformed into bureaucratic meticulousness and regularity . . . [and] activists benefited much more as individuals than did the residents of the poverty areas collectively."[24]

Tish began to respond to the evolving women's movement during these turbulent days of 1969 as demands for day care and abortion reform bills were reported in the local press. She focused at first on the rights of women welfare recipients through the School for Community Action, as part of her anti-racist work. She also became a charter member of the Seattle chapter of the National Organization for Women (NOW). Retrospectively she recalled, "It was as though a new phase was about to be born and I was aware of it. I was beginning to move toward exploring women's issues."

The next year, 1970, Joe took a sabbatical at an academic think tank in Palo Alto. Tish left CAMP and Join Hands. The family rented the house and relocated early that fall. At the time, the move seemed a brief break from their political work. It turned out to be a momentous personal experience.

In Palo Alto, Tish continued to think about women's issues and the connection between racism and sexism. She wrote to a Join Hands friend: "Look back a few years. When people talked about the 'Negro Problem' it was in terms of housing—then some said schools—then others said it was a lack of jobs—and justice—and the matriarchal family, etc. . . . All kinds of remedies were tried (and failed) until at last we had to look at the whole pattern—systematic institutional racism." She went on to talk about organizing women: "plenty of problems—class, timidity, racism and general female bitchiness—but great potential. The more I study and the more I do, the more convinced I am that the status of women will be a dynamic issue—one that adds strength to others. And the questions of racism and sexism *can* be linked, in practice as well as theory." From the very beginning Tish viewed women's issues in a larger, sociopolitical context, not as isolated phenomena.

As her involvement grew, her letters to friends in Seattle sounded more agitated. "I've become involved with the women's movement. Ideas are generating lots of heat but with little outlet of energy. I'm a volcano ready to blow its top. I did that last night at a planning meeting for the August 26 Women's Strike Day." And in a prophetic moment, she mused, "It's too bad that the women's movement, like youth, is wasted on the young. I'm so sure I could run their movement better for them and let them know it." Tish had refrained from such confrontation within the black community but let her frustration out on this group of women; perhaps, because she was one of them, her urgency was greater. "I sure came down with a sledge hammer. Broke the first rule of organizing—listen, don't tell—and 'ran down' for them their errors from A to Z. Now I'm repentant."[25]

Temperamentally inclined to restrained, rational analysis, she was also impatient with the younger feminists' focus on personal anger. She found it a waste of time: "If the young dissatisfied women were putting their energies into organizing other women instead of complaining about their menfolk, their own gripes would have much more clout."

Gradually, Tish realized the women's movement could be a central force for change. "A few days ago it all came to me in a white flash. Revelation I think is the word for it. . . . Suddenly I *believed*. Women, that's the answer to it all. Women will give birth to the New Society (but probably not by natural childbirth)."

Tish envisioned a cross-racial and class-conscious movement built around common concerns—peace, child care, the end of poverty and racism. Her vision had a biting conclusion, indicative of the rage in that era: "we walk into the sunset with our admiring men from their impotent organizations asking if they can join us."

She was agitated, stirred by the energy she felt, and inspired by Kate Millett's *Sexual Politics* (1970). Yet when Vivian Caver, a black staff member from the Seattle Human Rights Commission, visited, her enthusiasm stalled. She wrote: "How easy it is to forget about the racism! When Vivian left I realized how far away it all seemed. Living in my white ghetto, involved with the woman issue with largely middle-class whites, becoming more and more aware of the parallels but not the differences of the two caste systems. I have moved backward on the race question—and I know darn well if that happens to me, it will happen faster to others." She believed that racism by omission was an implicit posture of many in Women's Liberation. She knew that some feminists treated minority women in the same way women claimed to be treated by men. Aware of this schism, she felt the urgency of "linkages—not in theory but on practical matters."

Yet she felt torn on the race/woman dilemma. It was so much easier to organize on the woman question, so much more personally gratifying. Publishers were crying for materials on the subject, and she realized she "could probably get a book published and maybe become a somebody." She was conflicted between principles and expedience or personal ambition.

Tish's ideas began to crystallize. Her personal letters during the summer of 1971 showed her development. "All the little pieces like a jigsaw puzzle seem to finally add up to that word, human." She saw all liberation movements as interrelated. "They're human—as opposed to what? 'Progress' (misapplied technology), inhumanity of man to man, racism, war, 'military industrial complex' nerve gas, sexism, oppression and all the 'againsts' you can name. . . . If we repudiate racism, if we now repudiate sexism, why not repudiate the *whole* mess." She went on to name homosexual and environmental issues as ones of parallel concern. "It is not then a question of changing *human nature*, but making our *nature human.*" She envisioned her book as a how-to-do it text for rectifying all of these unequal states.

Her reading in preparation for the book was voracious and expansive though headaches and eye problems slowed her at times. She devoured Mary Beard's *Women as a Force in History*, Elizabeth Cady Stanton's *Woman's Bible*, and Cellestine Ware on *Woman Power*. She also wrote to prominent Women's Liberationists and attended political meetings.

Tish's private life was very unsettled amid this new intellectual context. Joe was spending most of his time at the Palo Alto think tank and working with graduate students on a collection of Chicano literature.[26] Her son Bill's problems with high school accelerated as he drank and avoided classes. He was out of control; his problems and behavior went beyond his parents' ability to cope. After much heated discussion, he was sent to an Arizona boarding school for students with academic and behavioral problems. At first Tish and Joe believed the experience was good for him. It certainly relieved them.

Tish spent more time in community work, and Joe continued his research. She organized a "Finishing School for Action" through the YWCA, focused on how to beat the welfare system. One protest against government restrictions included letters strung on a long ribbon stretched in front of the capitol in Sacramento. She also met with a group interested in forming a women's political party but was frustrated by their apparent lack of political savvy. "As it turned out," she said, "the group didn't amount to anything much. We were a gourmet cooking potluck group. My feeling was that it was a little off the wall. Given my experience, there didn't seem to be a seriousness about it. The idea was exciting at first, but it was clear these people weren't ever going to organize." Tish was searching for the right forum to use her own political background and skills. Tanis Walters, a member of the group, respected Tish's directness when she decided to leave; she told them she was impatient with endless talk since little was followed through.[27]

Undiscouraged by this episode, she attended a women's consciousness-raising group and explored her own emotions more. Open expression of feelings was never an easy or particularly appealing process for Tish. There was a reserve about her, a distaste for angry display and self-revelation. In her marriage she and Joe had always talked easily of externals. Political ideas and actions flowed, but intimate communication was difficult for them both. Tish felt Joe's reserve had increased over the years, in spite of their earlier counseling sessions about Bill. More recently Joe had also been attending an encounter-type group, where letting it "all hang out" in direct confrontation was the mode. "In the process of doing that," Tish recalled, "Joe and I opened up to each other a little bit." In the course of one talk Joe admitted that, "while he appreciated me and he liked me very much and thought I was a very good person, he didn't *love* me." Tish was stunned and shaken to her core.

This revelation, and her feminist readings and discussions, made her question the value of her marriage and place it within some manageable social context. Perhaps feminist consciousness helped deflect the pain; at least feminist support made the pain survivable. Her letters from that time showed confusion, adjustment, and a tinge of resentment. By Thanksgiving, Tish was uncertain about her future but already planned to leave Joe. "Where do I go from here? I've moved (in my head) toward friendly, human, 'cooperative' separation, ready or not."[28]

Throughout their marriage she assumed they shared a reciprocal relationship. Tish believed their most lasting bond was their political work lives—along with raising Bill, which, although a difficult task, was something they shared. Several months later, Tish cautiously broached the difficult topic with Joe: "Do you think we should get a divorce? If our marriage no longer has the same meaning to you?" Joe was surprised that she even brought it up. And yet he responded, "But what would you *do?*" Tish was dumbfounded, then enraged. He *presumed* that she wouldn't be able to do without him: this insulted and wounded her. At that moment she began to be convinced she could and would live on her own. They didn't discuss it in any depth after that one cryptic exchange, but Tish continued to make plans. Little by little they came to an agreement that they should separate, an agreement for which Tish was ready.

The next few months were extremely difficult for them both. They slept apart, and each struggled with the idea of living alone. She planned to stay in California, while Joe would go back to Seattle. Assuming their son came home from boarding school, Tish stipulated her unwillingness to care for him any longer. She felt she'd done all she could as a mother. She insisted Joe expand his relationship with his son. Thus she envisioned a dramatic role change for herself while Joe imagined taking on the sole responsibility for Bill's care.

The severance of their twenty-two-year marriage was poignant and painful, despite their best-intentioned efforts. Each re-

mained occupied and self-contained while readying for the chosen day of separation. On the last afternoon, Tish asked Joe for
some help boxing things and transporting them to Berkeley. He
responded, "Can't you get somebody, hire somebody to do that. I
have to go." Minutes before, he had asked Tish be sure to do the
wash before she left. Now her reaction was volcanic: "Suddenly *I*
burst out! I remember having a real tantrum. I broke down, and it
all came out at one whoosh! That was the only time I ever, ever
screamed at him." She attacked him for being inconsiderate, accused him of being totally self-centered. Most of their relationship had been quite controlled and polite. Perhaps the clash was
inevitable given her raw sensitivities and the dramatic break after
twenty-two years together. The air cleared after her brief explosion. Joe apologized and helped her pack and move to her new
loft apartment across the bay.

When she looked back, Tish felt age was a factor in the divorce. She was fifty-eight, ten years older than Joe. They had been
completely monogamous, and she thought perhaps the late–1960s
cultural emphasis on sexual freedom fueled his restlessness. Her
own decision was bolstered by the unappealing prospect of "following" him again back to Seattle and the university. On a milder
note, she was relieved to be done with wifely attendance at the
track; horse racing captivated Joe and bored her. More than a
decade later, she credited the dissolution to Joe's loss of "love" for
her. Her sense of rejection "was a hell of an important factor" in
her own willingness to seek divorce.

Tish's recollection of Joe's not loving her anymore was the
most painful interview session for the entire book. She held her
arms wrapped tightly around her thin body, rocking in the chair.
Her words were not fluid but halting. Years later, she was still
full of hurt. That day her honesty and grief numbed us all.

She recalled that experience with residual pain but also
pointed out that, after the first awkward years of separation, she
and Joe reestablished a positive relationship. She stressed their
agreement that it was time to move on and emphasized how

many good years they'd had in the marriage. Their primary concern was for Bill, who remained unfocused and troubled. Several years later, when Joe accepted a faculty appointment at the University of California at San Diego, their son stayed in Seattle, working as a casual laborer. Bill saw Tish a couple of times a year, and she continued to worry about his future but gradually detached herself from his ongoing problems.

Several years later Joe developed lung cancer, and his strength dissipated fairly rapidly. When Tish visited him, she was touched by his courage in facing his incipient death. He continued to teach and invited students to his home even though he required an oxygen tank when he walked around his small apartment located near his beloved Del Mar racetrack. Tish saw Joe as a positive and courageous role model who approached his death with admirable dignity.

When Tish flew to San Diego in spring 1979 for the memorial service for Joe, she was suffering from what doctors had diagnosed as a bladder infection. It later turned out to be her own cancer. Although she was uncomfortable physically, and knew only a few who attended the service, she was proud of Bill's tribute to his father. She was also moved by the memories shared by Joe's friends and colleagues, who admired his gentleness and continuous encouragement of students, which he maintained until just before his death. Ironically, in this last realm—their own deaths—Tish and Joe were ultimately comrades, too.

It had never occurred to Tish that she couldn't make it on her own after her divorce. She'd lived alone at various times in her life. Even more important, she had economic security with her mother's money. Her initial loneliness in solo living was mitigated by research for her book on organizing, her "wave-makers manual." She was also active in the NOW and Women's Liberation group meetings. As the pain subsided from the divorce, she felt a sense of the freedom. She defined her own life and grew in creative and exciting ways.

Displaced Homemakers:
Don't Agonize

There is a changing mood among women, a decided
shift of gears, which presages a new spirit of activism.

There are all kinds of feminists, . . . radical feminists,
socialist feminists. . . . I haven't a proper label for
myself. . . . I have broader political perspective than
a feminist perspective alone.

The 1970s marked a major transition for Tish. She moved into a
life of her own, becoming by the end of the decade a figure of
some national prominence. The conversion from her suburban
housewife role to the counterculture mode was rapid. Where once
she wore rather plain shirt-dresses, she soon chose colorful earth-
toned pants suits and foot-shaped Berkenstock sandals. She also
altered her concept of self, embracing the challenges of aging.
Two trips she took during the decade epitomize her inner process.[1]

In 1974 she and her younger housemate, Tanis, took off for a
three-month trip through Europe. She was shocked by her own
reactions—the sixty-year-old Tish's responses were radically different than they had been at thirty when she enthusiastically took
part in the 1947 Youth Festival in Prague.

Her awareness of age and waning physical attractiveness was
one theme in her trip journal. "When you are young, you may

feel unequal to men, but there is a strong sense of superiority in relation to older women. I used to look at my mother, then look at my own image in the mirror, or at my hands. Whatever she had that I didn't have—I had youth. . . . When you're older, this same competition is present, but you're on the losing side. The depression, the feeling of inadequacy are constantly present under the surface."[2]

Tish was confused and exhausted by the day-to-day problems of foreign travel. She couldn't understand the language or find her way around without help, and being assisted by Tanis irritated her. Troubled by her own diminished powers, Tish pondered: "How can older women maintain the skills of coping? Surely not by being cared for, by having things made easy. Would cooperative effort work? Suppose a group of women (three-four-five-six) traveled. Could they rotate or share responsibilities so each felt she was contributing more or less equally?"

The disjunction in her European experiences thirty years apart was most evident in Rome, where she was particularly upset. In 1947, Tish had enjoyed a lovely romance with a young Englishman who gave her a private tour and bolstered her spirits. By 1974 she had become the invisible older woman. She wrote in her journal: "The men definitely do *not* make passes. Not that Roman men have changed. I see them eyeing young women—making the expected comments, but they certainly don't *bottse* me or Tanis. Is Tanis out of the running at thirty? I certainly am, alone or in her company."

"I think of the young feminists who feel the most insulted by the sex object image. How will they feel in ten years walking down a street in Rome and becoming a *nothing*—an object without value, obsolete, valueless? One doesn't gain personhood, one loses the limited value one had."

There were physical and psychological symptoms as well. "I'm feeling remarkably depressed, as though I'm coming apart. Perhaps at home I put such positive energy into my activism and my sense of being a role model. Without that, the painful aspects of aging emerge. My back and shoulders have been giving me trouble for a long time, but now the aches are much more in my consciousness. The headaches have been there, but before I could submerge them with work."

Her sense of fatigue and invisibility permeated her thoughts. "Here I feel adrift, floating on all my body aches, with no energy to fight back. And I feel cut off from people. Last time I was here I was riding such a high after the youth festival that everything I touched was magic. I could 'relate.' Now I'm a stranger, as alienated as a Sartre character."

Only a few days later, Tish titled her journal entry "The Rebound" and analyzed her recovery from this most recent depression. She may have been feeling an echo of her menopausal despair a decade earlier: "It's happened so often before, but it's always hard to be sure that a depression is not an organic thing. (I'm all wrong, going to pieces, 'getting too old,' can't cope). But this morning there was another click—or a series of them, like tiny quakes, that seemed to put me at rights again."

Seeing the Roman baths helped; she felt alive again, but not certain why. Perhaps it was the rejuvenation they represented. More important, she was creative and thinking, interacting with the culture. No longer passive or alienated, she recovered her sense of active self.

Tish was stimulated by reading Spanish history in preparation for their trip to Barcelona and recognized that one source of her malaise was intellectual frustration. There had been too much moving about in recent weeks and not enough mental work to suit her. She also realized that tourism, beyond brief moments, bored her. "I'm an intellectual animal, and over time must use my intellect or feel frustrated, lost, disintegrating. . . . Now that I know what the problem is, I'm certain I can find solutions. These preparations—more so than what clothes to bring—are priorities that will turn me outward and active, not in against myself or against Tanis and the situation."

Her irritation with Tanis melted when they worked together

to find Tish's lost pair of glasses. "I was in a panic, feeling that even a temporary period unable to read would be another clipping of my wings, another physical limitation. At the fancy cafe on Via Venete we found them. Tanis and I had just decided to spend separate afternoons when I realized my loss. She jumped into the breach without hesitation, without a trace of condescension." Tish was comforted by Tanis's steady presence. "I need her strength and abilities. Today, feeling myself again, I no longer feel a dependent, but a co-equal—sharing of what we have, each with strengths and weaknesses."

Four years later, in 1978, Tish's trip to China had an entirely different context. She was a member of and recorder for a group of specialists in the field of aging. The trip was organized by her longtime friend Maggie Kuhn, founder of the Gray Panthers, a gender-mixed age activist organization. By 1978, Tish was increasingly recognized for her work on displaced-homemaker legislation and was much more at ease with herself. She played a leadership role in the delegation as a strong supporter of Maggie and enjoyed the company of her peers, who shared a common concern for the societal problems of aging women.

Tish felt self-confident and deeply involved in her own work. She went to China to relax and find refurbishment. "I had a marvelous time. I had a chance to think about my ideas about revolution, which I hadn't done for a long time. I decided that as an older woman I might like living in China—but only *if* I could be part of the power structure." Later she had second thoughts and decided she didn't like the restricted roles available to older Chinese women, who were expected to retire and become caretakers for the community as well as their grandchildren. Mandatory child rearing and neighborhood supervision didn't strike her as liberating.

Ira Hirschfield, then working at the Andrus Gerontology Center in Los Angeles, spent many hours in China walking and sharing ideas with Tish. He saw another side of her when one day, some children performed for us. At the end, they turned to us, and said, 'Won't you please perform?' We all looked at one another. Out of the clear blue, this very serious woman who had done nothing but focus on issues heard a little music in the background. She asked them to pick it up. She turned around and exquisitely danced before everyone. It was graceful, it was uplifting. It was the visual, physical expression of what I came to learn later was her commitment to social issues.[3]

What comes through in her journals, particularly from the time in Rome, is a sense of Tish's own private journey. The European journal reveals her use of abstract analysis to relieve depression. She utilized it in much the same way she used activism to propel herself to a more positive frame of mind. And in China, she was self-confident, so she could relax and flow into her own dance, her own rhythm. Thus her travels were both eminently political and intimately personal.

A decade after her trip to Rome, hospitalized with the cancer, Tish had time for reflection. She talked about her younger self: "I don't think I thought much about old age when I was forty."[4] She was then seventy years old and looking back. When she was younger, her parents seemed negative role models, and in her earlier years she had not had strong attachments to other older people. When Tish spent two weeks in 1960 with her mother before the latter's death at seventy-two, the daughter determined she wasn't going to be old in the same way. Tish was still put off by her mother's total self-involvement and resolved not to follow that pattern herself. "I wanted to keep what I felt was the essence of youth, but really is the essence of being alive. Of being part of positive things going on in society, of living my life that way as long as physically able." Tish was fulfilled during her last decade, so she felt pleased with her own last set of life choices. With a laugh she acknowledged only a few regrets. "After all, I never did learn to hang-glide or scuba dive."

Tish shared her mixed feelings about diminished opportunities for intimate relationships. "Oh yes, I *was* aware that nobody ever made a pass at me." Another time she mentioned the attractiveness of some young men with whom she worked, noting wryly that they probably had no idea of her sexual fantasies. She missed warmth and physical contact but also experienced a sense of relief. She could redirect the energy and emotion needed to select, keep, or look for a mate. "In other words," she said, "the sex drive has certainly lessened, and I consider that more a plus than a minus even though there is some sense of loss."

The ease Tish experienced late in life came when she blossomed as a leader. Though there were still moments of shyness, she had become an expert at public appearances. She was also surrounded by admiring co-workers, brought together by common concerns and Tish's vision. Much of her success was grounded in opportunities generated by the women's movement as well as the culmination of all her earlier experiences. That most fruitful period began just after her divorce, in midsummer 1971.

Tish was on her own in the middle of the women's movement, which was exploding. Dozens of feminist organizations blossomed in Berkeley, the West Coast counterculture's progressive hub. Reformers, radicals, and revolutionaries were publishing and attracting media attention.[5] The general public became increasingly aware of women's demands for change as the multiple strands of the movement converged. In every major city there were telephone hotlines for dealing with rapes; there were women's health collectives, socialist feminist collectives, and more traditionally structured equal rights groups.[6]

Tish attended NOW's annual meeting in Los Angeles that hot September and was elected to the NOW National Board. Aileen Hernandez was ending her term as NOW's president, followed the next year by Wilma Scott Heide, first the NOW chair of the board and then NOW president until 1974. It was a time when NOW's membership seemed to mushroom hourly, when new ideas challenged traditional views, when so much happened so fast it was hard to decide what should happen next. To deal with the problems generated by such rapid growth, the NOW board held a retreat at Alverno, California, to talk about the future.

Out of those discussions came a Policy and Planning Committee, which included Tish. The women met at the Los Angeles home of board members Toni Carabillo and Judith Meulli. "It was a time when there was all the overlay from the Women's Liberation elements, so we talked about sliding scale dues, and non-hierarchical chapter structures," recalled Toni.[7] Tish, Aileen, and Wilma joined Toni and Judith in sharing recipes—for food and for revolution. They played with structure, imaginative strategies, and ways to use NOW to change the world. The group was refreshed and stimulated by working together, sustaining over the next several years the personal bonds forged that weekend. Unfortunately, their proposals were too daring for the rest of the NOW officials, who responded negatively at the next meeting of the full board.

Tish saw a greater blending of conventional and innovative strategies when she transferred from the "rights"-oriented Palo Alto NOW to the more eclectic Berkeley chapter. The members were concerned about legal equality but also cared about radical restructuring of work and family life. Former and New Left radicals as well as "cultural feminists" infused Berkeley NOW with a more revolutionary style. Nationally, NOW's image was white, professional, and middle-class—its black president, Aileen Hernandez, notwithstanding. In the Bay Area the members came from more mixed economic backgrounds, though most were also white. Their structural emphasis was on participatory democracy, antihierarchy, and the use of consciousness-raising as a prelude to action. Exalting in "leaderlessness," the Berkeley chapter was operated as a "troika," with three women leaders. Tish enjoyed the experiment, even though it wasn't very practical and was eventually abandoned.[8]

She moved at age fifty-seven from her busy, rather conventional, middle-class married life into changes in dress, lifestyle, language, and ideology. Her neat slacks and shirts and thin graying hair built up by a hairpiece seemed bland in the Berkeley culture, where jeans and work boots or flowing ethnic costumes were the norm, and young women used empty juice cans to straighten their long hair. Stimulated by the cultural turmoil, Tish revised the approach to her manuscript. She shifted to a less theoretical "wave makers manual" which could help women organize action projects. She worked at the writing in her small apartment daily and set evenings aside for expanding her social and political network.

On the more personal front, Tish joined a radical psychiatry group. Spurred by her emotional vulnerability after the breakup with Joe, she was drawn to this effort to combine social change with new levels of personal interaction. As a young woman Tish would have found this self-indulgent and unappealing. Now she was willing to stretch herself emotionally: she was lonely and eager to learn new ways of relating. After several potluck suppers followed by lengthy encounter sessions, she decided this group was not for her. Years later she remembered their tone as incredibly ageist, indifferent to her needs. It was also the case for most of her life that she was uncomfortable with intense emotional confrontations. She was willing to experiment, but not at this level.

Still in search of community and emotional bolstering, Tish attended the Berkeley Breakaway "Free Form Retreat" for women.[9] Breakaway hoped to take new directions in educating women through self-taught courses grounded in feminist analysis. About a dozen showed up at a local Girl Scout camp, including a few children and Tish's Siamese cat, Opie. In the warm afternoons, some of the women sunbathed nude, and a couple wandered off to "drop acid." The oldest one there, Tish was shocked, surprised, and generally amazed at the youth of the others, their electric enthusiasm, and their political inexperience. It was exciting, even unsettling. "It felt weird and was a shakeup for me. I wasn't on the same wave length; the others all seemed to be

Christine Shields, Laurie Shields, and Tish, ca. 1976.

so loose." Also, it felt like the earlier Women's party meetings, where big ideas did not lead to follow-through.

Still, this eclectic weekend was a turning point for Tish, shifting toward a radically different lifestyle. With two young Breakaway founders, Tish soon formed a new living arrangement.[10] Both the other women were feminist activists in their late twenties.

One was Ruth Friedlander, soon to change her name to Spring, who worked as a city planner and drove a school bus. The other was Tanis Walters, at that time doing anthropological research and living in San Francisco, who knew Tish from the earlier Women's party organizing meetings. As Tanis recollected, these earlier sessions ranged "from highly theoretical analyses of power/class/race in the country and how that impacted the women's movement—to an exchange of recipes." Tanis saw Tish at that point as "a woman who moved with abrupt quickness, who was inflamed with a drive for action and movement. There was a sense of impatience and urgency. There was also a total lack of comprehension of what the hell we were up to. She was clearly not part of the alternative culture as we were, and was taken aback by our style and our lack of clear focus."[11]

In their new collective household, they saw themselves as a loosely connected alternative to a family. They were all committed feminists who valued sharing ideas, space, and the upkeep of the house. They originally planned to include a fourth person but bought as three and shared only temporarily with anyone else over the next several years. They found a large, slightly run-down, turn-of-the century home near the Berkeley/Oakland border. Including the enclosed back porch, den, and unfinished upstairs, there were eleven living spaces. Each had her own bedroom plus another room as office or storage. They shared the large living, dining, kitchen, and bath areas, which were brightened by several gallons of new paint applied over several weekends.

At Tish's suggestion, they named it Prudence Crandall House after the nineteenth-century white teacher who persevered in running a school for black girls despite strong community opposition.[12] They added some of Tish's teak furniture for the common spaces and moved in. Tanis laughed to recall: "I think at first Tish thought we were committed to living in grand squalor, since she had seen that my old place had only one lawn chair. She was relieved to realize we were quite happy to have her lovely Mexican art and fine furniture."

Tish had lived collectively before, in the 1940s, but this was quite a different experience. For one thing, their egalitarian idea of rotating all chores was a short-lived one. Conflicts arose, especially around their different standards for cleanliness. Eventually, Tish took on the primary responsibility for cleaning, since disarray and dirt bothered her most. Spring chose food buying, and Tanis was the only one interested in the garden. There were disagreements over fixing broken appliances versus buying new ones, and other minutiae connected with daily living. Some were a matter of lifestyle, but others stemmed from differences in income. Although Tish had lived at an economically low maintenance level during her days in Germany and later in Los Angeles, she had by this time become used to material comforts, and had resources the others didn't.

Tish and Spring were temperamentally so at odds that they went through an awkward period of adjustment. Spring's form was very freestyle. She preferred as little scheduling as possible and avoided conventional mealtimes. Further, her tendency to confront was jarring to the always organized and never loud Tish. They eventually brought in a feminist mediator to help them reach accord. "I was surprised at how willing Tish was to try," said Tanis, "and how she gradually accepted the endless emotional discussions." Despite the tensions, it was an exciting living environment.

Tish felt the personal was now political—the credo of Women's Liberation had entered her own life. It required greater flexibility and a more expansive acceptance of others on her part. These cultural adjustments and new interactive skills later served her well.

The collective household was an inexpensive way to live, given the niceties they enjoyed. Spring recalled she paid $2,000 and Tish $6,800 as down payment on the $29,000 house. Retrospectively, they estimated it cost about $200 each per month for utilities, the house payment, food, and entertainment. This appealed to Tish, who had always been financially cautious. "Always, from the time I first inherited $5,000 in my twenties, I have felt the necessity of some kind of financial security blanket. I never spent Aunt Clara's $5,000, it was always there for emergencies. When my mother died and I inherited much more money, I didn't significantly change my lifestyle. The dream house in Seattle was about it. Other than that we were relatively frugal."

Through the early 1970s, there was a steady flow of friends and co-activists through the Oakland house, brought together by feminist politics and activism. The three women were in separate orbits. Involved in their various projects, they used the house as a base. Meals were in the counterculture style: mostly vegetarian, often consisting of uncommon legumes and exotic sauces. Since cooking chores rotated, a fairly conventional meal prepared by Tish or a rather muddy red-bean stew might be the fare. "We soon learned not to invite guests for dinner on stew night," quipped Tanis. Everything was recycled, including some of the food. "You'd never catch me eating that stuff," said an old friend from the national NOW board. For Tish's more conventional friends, the blandness or strangeness of meals was disconcerting, but there was always lively discussion and serious debate to compensate for the plain meal. Breakaway classes met sometimes in the living room, and the phone rang constantly for arranging meetings or setting up demonstrations. Tanis researched cross-cultural hunting and gathering societies to study sex roles and the division of labor. She also organized a class on sexism and racism and met with her feminist consciousness-raising group. She encouraged friend Judy Syfers to write out her anger about housework in "Why I Want a Wife," later widely reprinted in feminist texts.[13]

One of Tish's projects was a pamphlet, "Volunteer Beware!" (ca. 1971) for NOW's Task Force on Volunteerism.[14] Tish asked Genny Guracar, a woman from an earlier YWCA community-action workshop in Palo Alto, to do some drawings for the cover. They soon agreed that Genny, known today as bülbül, would do cartoons for Tish's book, providing a light touch to illustrate organizing techniques. Reflecting on their work together, Genny realized that, even when searching for her own direction, "Tish was somebody who had a much stronger sense of herself. . . . I felt her life had a central stream." They were critical of each others' drafts, spread the drawings on the Mexican rug in Tish's living room, argued about what should be included. When Genny felt tentative, Tish urged her to move forward. "Tish was a touchstone of sanity, though I did sense there were certain areas I shouldn't probe in her life." And when Genny wanted warm, unquestioning mothering from Tish, she was told that was an oppressive demand, especially to place upon an older woman. Disappointed, Genny nevertheless continued to work with Tish over the next decade, garnering intellectual nurturing and support.[15]

Tish's book, *The Not So Helpless Female* (1973), brought together her tenets for organizing. Later she reworked many sections for her speeches. She also used these ideas for her manual on coping with bureaucracy, *How to Tame the CETA Beast* (1979), and the *OWL Organizing Manual* (1983). Her first lesson was to "Start with Number One," a feminist principle to draw out political action from the personal experience, encouraging individual strength and action. She used examples of simple individual steps, like letters to sponsors and legislators, drawn from her earlier NOW handbooks, "Volunteer Beware!" and "Write On." Her overall tone was upbeat, full of optimism and positive strategies.

The book is a good guide for beginning organizers, with its tips on setting up groups, running meetings, and selecting issues. In it she first used the slogan "If You've Got a Lemon, Make Lemonade." She also recommended role playing for public presentations to enhance effectiveness and build self-confidence. Pointing out the dangers of political isolation and negativism, she offered ideas for building alliances, coalitions, and conferences. Throughout, she reminded the fledgling organizer that "the fun is in the going. . . . The truth is that life has more zest if we participate actively in it, despite risks, setbacks, wasted effort, and even deprivation." As she also wrote: "For a new lease on life, effective social involvement is far better than a psychiatrist, and much cheaper. 'Volunteer for something' fits the old concept of womanhood. 'Help turn the world around' is more appropriate today."[16] She later wrote more sophisticated policy statements, but essentially she kept this view drawn from her decades of organizing.

Fiery and energetic Ruth McElhinney, former social worker and local activist, helped Tish edit her book. McElhinney had been consulting on affirmative action programs and wanted to move into organizing. The more they talked, the better the idea of collaborating on a Women's Action Training Center (WATC) sounded. They could train women to organize and develop action projects. Tish believed Ruth was a good organizer, with the necessary "hustle" to build an organization. In an act of generosity and political acumen, Tish offered to share the income from her mother's estate. Each would receive five hundred dollars a month to live on. Ruth solicited additional funds from a local church and, with Tish's help, went off to activist training at the Sol Alinsky School in Chicago, which specialized in community self-determination and citizen participation projects.

They considered the value a NOW endorsement would have for WATC. Ruth's instinct was to stay independent, though she acknowledged that NOW's backing might help them get grants. She discussed her fear of getting caught between factions within national NOW. Tish responded reassuringly. For one thing, "most women, even on the national board of NOW, are not very political and are quite personal. They tend to vote together with people they like when they are not sure of an issue." Tish's hesitancy to affiliate with NOW was more profound. She disliked the self-selecting process for leadership, the difficulty of and resistance to any innovations in the hierarchical structure, and the alienating board meetings. Further, NOW's conferences—with their ritzy and expensive hotels, champagne parties, and mimicking of a businessmen's convention—were hard to take. To Ruth, Tish confided that, at these functions, "Emotionally at least, I feel like

I'm back in Birmingham working in the Presbyterian church." It turned out the NOW board was ambivalent about sponsoring *any* centers, and approved having WATC as a NOW project by only one vote. With their reservations and this slim vote of confidence, Ruth and Tish decided to move on their own.[17] Tish once again preferred the "freelance" posture, retaining independence and control.

They set up the Women's Action Training Center in 1973 in an old church and offered classes in organizing and identifying issues. Employment was an obvious issue. Tish also wanted to focus on older women. "Nobody was doing anything about it, and I was aware from my own experience that issues like health care and Social Security needed tackling. " Since she did the women's news program on public radio station KPFA, she announced her "Fine 59" birthday celebration. Her idea was to "come out of the closet" on age, so she invited the public to an outdoor party at her home. Ruth helped paint the large banner, "Don't Agonize, Organize!"[18] The day of Tish's September birthday celebration was warm and sunny. She wore a flowing orange-print caftan, and clusters of women chatted, ate carrot cake, and sang. Tanis took home movies of their spirited circle dance. As a result of the party, Tish formed the "We Should Live So Long" collective.

Milo Smith joined that collective a few weeks later. The next year they produced a television program about women and aging for a local television station.[19] Her experience illustrates how Tish attracted and encouraged others to become activists. As Milo told it, "When we got to the . . . [television] studio, I froze. I wasn't going to go in the door and everybody else was already inside. I've told everybody since then that it was Tish's foot in my back that got me in there. She said, 'Too late, you've committed yourself and you're going in.' . . . I'll be forever grateful to her because she saw potential in me and she didn't give me a chance to say, 'I don't know how,' or 'I can't do it.'"[20]

The opportunity was ripe to widen Tish's activist sphere. She had very strong personal feelings about aging and saw that most other feminists ignored the subject or focused on middle age, not beyond. Her picture appeared in a *New York Times* article on well-known feminists along with Tish's definition of a feminist as one concerned with both sex and age discrimination.[21] Tish also realized that issues affecting older women could serve as a means to organize. From 1971 to 1974, she moved from the general principles of her book to define her political territory.

To focus her energies on older women's issues even further, Tish gave up NOW's national Task Force on Volunteerism. Sparked by Maggie Kuhn, founder of the Gray Panthers, and Marjory Collins, an earlier NOW convention had approved a mandate for work on older women's issues. Then Maggie chose to devote herself to the Gray Panthers, and Marjory started the newsletter *Prime Time* to publish articles about older women. Neither of them felt they could chair the new NOW effort. Wilma Scott Heide, NOW's president, urged Tish to take on the Task Force on Older Women. She agreed, and the TFOW became the base for her national network.

Sometime in 1973 Maggie Kuhn, founder and prime mover of the Gray Panthers, gave a talk urging development of a Berkeley chapter. Tish weighed founding that chapter versus continuing to concentrate on older women at WATC and the NOW task force. She reluctantly passed by the Gray Panthers opportunity to continue working in her own directions. Besides, this was Maggie's show and Tish wanted political turf of her own.

With mutual admiration and support, her link with Maggie Kuhn held over the next decade. Maggie was a member of the advisory board for the Alameda Displaced Homemaker Center at Mills College, and when OWL was formed in 1980, Maggie was the keynote speaker. Tish always admired Maggie's public presence and use of media; Maggie's porcelain-doll-with-white-hair image was an effective counterpoint to her radical pronouncements and calls to action. Tish did support the Gray Panthers, though she never ran a chapter. She was on the steering commit-

Maggie Kuhn, founder of the Gray Panthers, 1985. Photograph by Julie Jensen, used with permission.

Women's Action Training Center greeting card, 1973, by bülbul
(Genny Guracar), used with permission.

tee for their board for two years and contributed "Moving Right
Along," a regular column on older women, to their newsletter
from 1976 to 1982. Tish used the column to speak out on the
same issues she addressed in OWL—Social Security, pensions,
and age discrimination in employment.

Yet while Tish felt close to Maggie, they had significant differences in priorities and ways of thinking. Though a feminist
herself, Maggie and the Gray Panthers chose a cross-generational,
male-female coalition and focused initially on anti–Vietnam War
issues. Tish agreed on the general issues, particularly the need for
peace, but her political focus evolved quite differently.

On a personal level, Tish found the Gray Panther organization difficult. Many members were "old lefties who had found a
new reason for being, a new excitement in life. And many of
them brought all their old baggage, lots of political rhetoric and
not much action." She was particularly irritated at all the energy
spent in battling over "correct" wording of convention resolutions, while concrete action proposals would go by the board. "I

thought it was all backwards. It was all men who were fighting. I don't recall there ever being a woman trying to argue about those resolutions." In Tish's opinion the men talked on and on, but the prime movers were overwhelmingly the women.

Tish credited the Gray Panthers with changing the field of gerontology from a passive to a more active one. "They raised the basic question of what is the role of older persons in society. How can they be more productive? It was Maggie who raised those things and the Gray Panthers showed how it could be done. More than any other group, they have brought up such questions as mandatory assignments to Medicare, and war and peace issues."

By 1974 Tish zeroed in on issues facing older women. She had already developed the Women's Action Training Center in Oakland, which dealt with some age-related concerns. As a multiservice center for women, WATC located jobs, acted on consumer issues, trained women to organize and become activists, and taught fund-raising. Women drawn to classes on organizing were recruited for political action projects, such as the public protest where "over one hundred WATC supporters flooded the Park District's usually private Board meeting to request the district to adopt an affirmative action policy and program."[22]

A Jobs for Older Women (JOW) hotline was started, with Milo Smith from the We Should Live So Long collective on the staff. Milo had worked as a riveter during World War II, and JOW decided to interview women in the Bay Area who had also been "workers on the home front." The response was so positive they went on to set up a "Rosie the Riveter Reunion." One hundred fifty attended, more than half of whom had worked in factories during the war.[23] A young Berkeley student, Cynthia Gorney, interviewed several of these "Rosies" and wrote an article about the JOW project, which drew in more volunteers, including attorney Barbara Dudley who later became a central figure in the displaced-homemaker movement. Shortly after the reunion, Cine Manifest of San Francisco proposed a film based on "Rosie's" lives.[24]

Tish's work with the NOW task force and WATC/JOW was receiving new attention. Even their holiday cards were politicized with slogans and Genny Guracar's cartoons: "We're Not Agonizing—We're Organizing," the Jobs for Older Women slogan; a TV set with "We Should Live So Long"; a picture of an owl saying, "Give a hoot, we'll file suit," and "Women on boards and commissions." Genny Guracar also proposed a WATC quilt project as a fund-raiser, featuring well-known feminist signatures to be embroidered by local artists. The era and its participants were boundlessly energetic and optimistic.

Tish's political and home lives metamorphosed in the three years after she and Joe divorced. She cherished the woman-centered, feminist environment where the housemates shared ideas and provided mutual support. Tish sustained her radio program and contacts with national NOW board members. Already known locally because of the Women's Action Training Center and Jobs for Older Women Project, she was more and more considered a feminist resource across the country. Her orange business card with the cartoon witch read, "Tish Sommers, Freelance Agitator." She was "freelance," but within a web of supportive feminists. She was an "agitator" as well, but less in a traditional revolutionary mode than in the arena of cultural and policy transformation.

Tish received increasing numbers of letters through the NOW task force. And when she spoke she felt the audience's strong emotional response as she talked about combatting the negative image of aging and the economics of sex and age discrimination. Tish saw this new population—those women who had bought the traditional sex roles of wife and mother and found themselves out of that job in mid-life as a result of divorce or widowhood—as an up-and-coming disenfranchised political group. Devalued as "only housewives" and without adequate job skills, they were often in despair and full of rage. How could she capture that energy as a political force?

"She was looking for a 'handle,'" recalls housemate Tanis, "and had been trying out terms and approaches, certainly with lawyer Barbara Dudley and probably writer Cynthia Gorney as well."[25] Tish raised it at home while they were making dinner. Talking in perpetual motion, she turned from stove to refrigerator to table, revising her thoughts while she set out place mats, stirred the chicken casserole, stopped in the doorway only long enough to emphasize her point. "How about 'displaced homemaker'?" she said, waving the wooden spoon. For Tanis it seemed a negative image, reminder of war refugees, displaced persons. "But she was absolutely right, it was a brilliant choice."

The series of events that followed culminated in a national movement. The experiences of millions of women "forcibly exiled" from their traditional homemaker's role were chronicled in co-worker and partner Laurie Shields' book *Displaced Homemakers* (1981).[26] In 1975 the bill Barbara Dudley drafted urging job training and counseling for displaced homemakers was submitted to the California legislature, and the first pilot center, housed at Mills College in Oakland, was authorized four months later. Using feminist networks across the country, speaking dates for women's studies programs, the combination of "old girl" connections in NOW and more traditional church and civic groups, Tish and Laurie struck a resonant chord with a variety of constituencies across the country. The press responded to the often painful personal stories of deprivation and discrimination; they also reported the proposed solutions. Centers blossomed across the country between 1975 and 1978 when displaced homemakers were finally covered by federal legislation. By the mid–1980s, despite severe curtailment of public funding, one thousand centers belonged to the Displaced Homemakers Network that Tish and Laurie founded. The phenomenal success of this project warrants analysis: it's a classic case study in grass-roots organizing.

Tish set about the process of making middle-aged and older women a visible and demanding voice. Laurie Shields, who came to play a central role in her political and personal life, met Tish early in the process. Recently widowed, Laurie was trying at age fifty-five to get back into the world of work. She wasn't having much luck, and at the suggestion of a friend, Nancy Snow, she attended a meeting of Jobs for Older Women. Laurie recalled her first impression of Tish, a woman she clearly found charismatic: "She was wearing tailored slacks and a colorful blouse, a combination that emphasized her slimness and made her seem taller than she actually was." Laurie couldn't believe such a vital woman was sixty years old. "There was an unmistakable vitality about her, generally presumed to be the mark of the young. Her eyes were brown, and thick glasses made them seem enormously large. Her voice was low-pitched but not deep; and together with precise diction, graceful gestures, and a smile that literally lighted her face, it all added up to an attractive, openly friendly woman."[27] Yet even then Laurie noted that there was a sense of reserve that suggested Tish's personal space had perimeters no one could violate.

Laurie, somewhat to her own surprise, was drawn to this discussion of proposed state and federal legislation and very quickly agreed to head the newly formed Alliance for Displaced Homemakers, founded in 1976. She was a neophyte, only most casually prepared for such an effort, but Tish convinced her, as she did so many others, to join the cause. And Laurie's background in advertising was an asset; she wrote punchy, succinct press releases and made hundreds of media contacts. Neither Tish nor the others who agreed to work for the bill had much experience working with legislatures. As they trooped around Washington, D.C., lobbying aides on Capitol Hill, they made up tactics as they went. As a lawyer, Barbara Dudley knew how to draft the bill but not how to push it through. She remembers "learning from that period that we could do anything we wanted to do. Congress and Sacramento and all the rest of it were not closed to us. If we got pushy, we could open a lot of doors, particularly with an organization behind us."[28]

Tish felt it too: "We were all learning. We were all a bit heady, a little dizzy with success." They lobbied fast and hard, holding open meetings, drafting newsletters, fact sheets, and press

Laurie and Tish at Displaced Homemaker campaign meeting, ca. 1976. Photograph by Sydney F. Rutzebeck.

releases. Laurie's days as a "footloose organizer" were frenetic as she drove all over the state, urging local groups to support the new legislation. The California bill passed quickly and funded one pilot center—establishing the model for a national effort. Tish used her contacts with women's organizations and the NOW task force to develop support and plan further strategy.

Laurie was on the road, first in California, then throughout the country. She developed her own style with the crowds. "I told them my story and Tish's, explained the legislation, and invited their comments."[29] These personal conversion narratives proved most effective: she talked *with* them, not *to* them. As Tish put it, "Laurie took to organizing like a duck to water. She did some remarkable grass-roots work."

Tish's speaking style by now included her pointed and engag-

ing "ten commandments." She reshaped them to fit each audience. One such instance was the December 1975 Public Forum
on Domestic Policy, chaired by Vice-President Nelson Rockefeller,
where her speaking time was very limited. Her commandments
to these elected officials were:

1. Thou shalt honor thy mothers and thy fathers—all of them.
2. Thou shalt not devise fine programs for thyselves alone.
3. Thou shalt not design painful social policy for everyone but
   thyselves.
4. Thou shalt not program for failure.
5. Thou shalt not balance the budget on our backs.
6. Thou shalt not ignore us.
7. Thou shalt reward us on earth as well as in heaven.
8. Thou shalt not judge our value by two standards.
9. Thou shalt not put us in double jeopardy.
10. Thou shalt not try to understand all women through thy wife.[30]

She delivered all of these softly, expanded points to cover the
situation of displaced homemakers, and always smiled while delivering a slight sting. The lawmakers laughed, and got the point.

Several other state bills were introduced using the model developed by Tish and Laurie. Tish credited their success to good
timing. Barbara Dudley watched Tish "pick the issue, an issue
that was very hot, and move forward on it, mobilizing a group of
people who had never been organized before." Tish instinctively
understood what would grab people, what they'd mobilize
around. Her leadership role crystallized what was already there.
She put words to it and let people take off with it. She gave
displaced homemakers a name and a political base.

In 1976 a media breakthrough added steam to the national
movement. Cynthia Gorney's "The Discarding of Mrs. Hill," dramatically characterizing the plight of divorced women, was published in the *Ladies Home Journal*.[31] At about the same time, Tish
and Laurie appeared on the "Phil Donahue Show." Laurie joked
with Donahue and mentioned her husband, Irish actor Arthur
Shields, and his film-star brother Barry Fitzgerald. She told of her

experience as a widow who was told she wasn't employable because she "hadn't worked" recently. Tish and Laurie dressed conservatively and emphasized their bonds with other women.

During that first national television appearance, they spoke convincingly of the need for job retraining, the need for creative new job alternatives, the need for recognition and respect for older women and of themselves as being in the same situation as many others. The audience became supporters and admirers of these two women who spoke simply and whose lives seemed so like their own. Tish revealed her personal situation. "When I found myself divorced," she said softly, commenting that many other ex-wives also lose health insurance protection, she engaged many listeners with her straightforward, personal and moving account, and the exposure brought thousands of letters from women in need.

Then and later, Tish implied that her personal situation was like that of other women who had made traditional marriage bargains and then been abandoned. She would sometimes add that in her own case it was an amicable decision, but at other times she allowed listeners to assume a negative history in order to make a political point. A 1982 *Los Angeles Times* article stated, "Sommers' own life is an example of the realities the elderly confront. She coined the phrase 'displaced homemaker' to describe the situation: Divorced at fifty-seven, she had been out of the job market and dependent on her husband, and she found herself ineligible for Social Security. Further, she had had cancer some twenty years earlier and so couldn't qualify for health insurance on her own. . . . She survived, though, partly because she had a small inheritance from her mother and partly because she also had a social conscience that had always led her into activism. She did as her slogan suggests: 'Don't Agonize: Organize.'"[32]

While accurate in outline, this version Tish presented skimmed over her years as a full-time activist and minimized her substantial financial inheritance. It was clearly an effective political simplification of her more complex background. It worked politically, on television, in the press, and with funders as well as followers.

Simplification was not possible when Tish faced problems with that first Displaced Homemaker Center when it opened in May 1976. Maggie Kuhn served on the honorary board, and Tish headed the Steering Committee, recruiting Milo Smith from WATC/JOW as the new center's director. Their vision was very difficult to implement. This first center sought to create jobs and draw on the skills of women long out of the labor market, many with low self-esteem and rusty job skills. Tish believed many "traditional" women's tasks should be paid jobs and hoped the center would take the lead in transforming the structure of work, beginning with home health care as well as nutrition-related and paralegal employment.

The second center was headed by Cindy Marano, former Peace Corps volunteer and graduate student. The Baltimore center's program drew many women with very low incomes, about half of them black, a group the Oakland center had trouble recruiting. Cindy commented retrospectively that their desire to keep women out of dead-end jobs was too often unsuccessful. "I think we were economically naive. While we experimented with job creation and counseling displaced homemakers for nontraditional jobs, the barriers were substantial. We had very high expectations for the women we were working with and overestimated their capacity to take on new employment struggles on top of those they already had."[33]

Tish acknowledged that there was little employment innovation at the Oakland center, "but a considerable number of women did make it into significant jobs. The struggle developed capacities in them and confidence, so the experience was positive." They did little job creation, but Tish felt that this did not signal its impossibility. She believed concentration on a small number of women, working with them intensively to serve as models for others, could create new jobs which would affect other women's self-perceptions and possibilities. The leaders disagreed among

themselves as to their effectiveness. Some believed their job place-
ments had succeeded; others felt they were "only" providing essential mutual support, an aspect of the movement that gave it a
special quality but which fell short of the larger economic goals.

Whatever its shortcomings in those early years, the idea developed rapidly. Institutionalization of support services for their
clients was the major accomplishment. "The Displaced Homemaker Network today is a very active, strong, bonded group of
people working on issues they believe in," as Cindy said. "They
took on the Department of Labor and retained funding in a way
that few parts of the women's movement have successfully done."

In 1976-78, however, Tish's experience was marred by increasing tension between herself, Milo Smith, and others at the
Oakland center. As Tish put it, "Milo thinks I'm a hard person,
she thinks I took over, I manipulated. I think she had very little
objectivity. She was very difficult to work with in a partnership,
given our ideological differences, like my feeling that people at
the center should all be paid the same amount." In 1979 Milo
Smith told some of her side of the story: "In the beginning Tish
and I were a team and really complemented each other. Tish is
gentle on the surface; there's a steely woman underneath. I'm a
pushover compared to her."[34]

A typical point of contention was collective decision-making.
As Milo put it, "We started out with all staff members getting
the same salary and we used the consensus system to make our
decisions. . . . It almost put us out of business. . . . I just didn't
know how to deal with it. I had the title of director but I wasn't
directing anything. . . . I don't like consensus for the actual day-
to-day operation." On Milo's recommendation to the board, a
plan for a more hierarchical structure was adopted over Tish's
objections.

Money was another difficult issue. As Milo recalled, "When
we came into the center, we all got subsistence wages. Everybody
got the same amount. With the revolution [the upheaval within
the center over this issue] I got a raise and they got a raise, but I

got more of a raise than they got. That created havoc with the old concept of equality."[35] This seemed justifiable to her, however, because she had greater responsibility. Tish definitely disagreed with the unequal pay scale.

Disagreements between Milo and Tish escalated. There was bitterness on Milo's part, and pain and frustration for Tish, who felt ideological integrity was being usurped by expedience and self-interest. Margaret Malberti, a displaced homemaker then doing clerical work at the center and later co-worker of Tish and Laurie in Oakland, wept in retelling her observation of the difficult split.[36] In her view, Tish was forced out by Milo's hostility. On the other hand, Milo felt she'd been abandoned to carry out implementation of Tish's idealized goals. In this setting, as with OWL's shift to the national office, Tish broke away or withdrew from conflict. As Ira Hirschfield commented wryly about Tish, "I never said she was a good day-to-day manager." Tish deemphasized the emotional intensity and simply reported that she chose to leave the center.

She remained chair of the NOW Task Force on Older Women (1973–78) and became co-coordinator, with Laurie, of the Alliance for Displaced Homemakers (1976–78). That double role eventually troubled NOW. There was resentment about whether NOW was properly credited for raising consciousness on displaced-homemaker issues. After one national board meeting, Tish wrote a clarifying letter to the board saying, "Leadership problems of two separate groups—NOW's TFOW and ADH—can be resolved. The Task Force on Older Women has been eliminated (in NOW's reorganization) and yesterday, the board approved the creation of an Older Women's Rights Committee."[37] Tish disassociated herself from the Alliance for Displaced Homemakers. Laurie Shields withdrew as a member of the Older Women's Rights Committee and continued to function as national coordinator of ADH. Tish was irritated, but the conflict was arrested for the moment.

Tish stayed with the NOW committee through the end of

1978, though it was increasingly difficult to get responses from the national office. Ellie Smeal, NOW's president, did not support an age-specific designation in the federal bill on displaced homemakers, a source of conflict with Tish. "Ellie Smeal is fundamentally wrong on seeing an age focus as discriminatory to younger women. That is no different than saying that a program targeted for women discriminates against men. Sex plus age equals a double bind and must receive special attention."[38] In any event, NOW gradually narrowed its focus and eventually dropped all task forces to push for ratification of the Equal Rights Amendment. Tish disagreed with this decision as well.

Tish realized her dependence on political partners who she hoped would compensate for her own weaknesses when she reflected on those uncomfortable situations with the Oakland center and NOW and OWL. She felt that, at times, she had compromised her values for the sake of liaison and that, at other times, her work with women who had agendas entirely different from hers had resulted in very brief relationships. She used her partnership with Ruth McElhinney at the Women's Action Training Center as an example: "It wasn't too long after we were together that I realized we were on different wavelengths, not so much politically, but in style, commitment and various other ways. We played that out and she moved on." Tish felt it had been the same with Milo Smith: "I wooed her out of a job in the local Department on Aging to take the Displaced Homemaker Center job. I should have known better. The error on my part was in taking what was at hand rather than searching someone out."

Although she was hurt by these splits, Tish tried to view them not as personal failures but as part of the political process. Her partnership with Laurie, informed by these earlier experiences, avoided several of these pitfalls—and unearthed others.

A Fine Pair of OWLs

Friends, housemates, colleagues, co-workers, co-authors, co-founders of movements and, finally, care giver and care recipient, more perhaps than any two women of their generation, Laurie and Tish have taught us how to live . . . and how to die . . . and how to do both as women and as friends.

—Jill Miller, *Owl Observer*, 1989

Laurie and Tish. Tish and Laurie. The two were as different as they were alike. Perfect foils for each other—cool yogurt beside spicy beans.

—Fran Leonard, *Owl Observer*, 1989

Tish and Laurie worked and shared a house together the last decade of Tish's life. During that time they went from mentor and protege to full working partners and, at the end, care giver and care recipient. The partnership is a story in itself, one of the more fascinating relationships in Tish's history.

One key to successful organizing is the ability to spot and develop talent in others. Tish Sommers always had an eye out for potential contributors—labor or money, or both. She kept lists of her contacts on every trip, noted follow-up possibilities after each conference or speech, and paid attention to the talents of others around her. She gave courteous but quick attention to those who did not fit in with her plans but was willing to devote a good deal of personal energy to bring along those who had potential. When there was a spark, Tish went out of her way to sustain contact.

That's what happened with Cynthia Gorney, Barbara Dudley, Cindy Marano, and Fran Leonard, with whom she developed intellectual and personal bonds as well as task-oriented interactions. Laurie Shields was also one of her successful recruits, and her most intense partner.

Laurie Shields had been a widow for five years when she met Tish on 7 May 1975 at a Jobs for Older Women meeting. At age fifty-five Laurie was unemployed and not happy about it. The daughter of a Chicago homemaker and a candy-store owner, Loretta Mary Bailey had a background in advertising. She was full-time homemaker and mother to Christine, Arthur Shields's daughter, and hadn't been employed for the fifteen years of her marriage, nor for the five years since her husband died. She joked that her prior organizing experience was with the mothers' volleyball team at Christine's parochial school, but she had also been exposed to the Catholic worker settlement-house milieu when she lived in New York in her twenties. When she met Tish she was discovering that she was "overqualified" for jobs she sought, meaning "too old" to get a job.

In her own classic fashion, Tish followed up that Jobs for Older Women meeting by inviting Laurie to join the new displaced-homemaker campaign. She had spotted Laurie's knack for slogans and sensed her potential energy. "Laurie more than anybody was not only responsible for the organizing but for the movement aspect, in other words the character, the color, and the vitality of it. We could not have done it without her. . . . My major contribution was finding and developing her as an organizer."[1] Tish led and Laurie took off to become a circuit rider for the new movement. Her first success was with the California campaign, but Laurie was soon booking flights one after another, moving across the country to generate state organizations to fight for legislation. Tish worked on the first displaced-homemaker center at Mills College, developed the national campaign strategy, and made the contacts. Laurie hit the road.

Early in 1976, she went to Baltimore to look over the

country's second displaced-homemaker center. Cindy Marano, its young director, recalled their first meeting at the train station. She had no idea what Laurie looked like and was a little nervous about meeting one of the founders of this growing movement.

> Laurie came toward us on the platform, this very small woman in tennis shoes, totally talkative from the moment we met. She began to involve us in a movement we didn't even know existed. Laurie talked a mile a minute, and hugged us both. When we got back to the center, in an old three-story row house, Laurie must have been up and down the stairs four or five times in the first minutes. She talked to everyone, was very personal immediately, reaching out. Everybody felt wanted and wanted to belong to what was happening.[2]

With Tish's general vision and encouragement, Laurie's talents as an organizer developed rapidly. She had a ward politician's way of working a crowd: she moved around the room, impressed people with her recall of names and details about their personal lives, and urged them to make connections. Her talks were sprinkled with jokes and anecdotes as she aroused and excited her listeners. Fond of literary allusions, she often used a Doris Lessing quotation: "Any human anywhere will blossom into a hundred unexpected talents and capacities simply by being given the opportunity to do so." Laurie was a perfect example.[3]

They were both ready for a transition in 1976 and, once the national campaign was under way, decided to look for a house to share. The volume of mail and phone calls was intruding on Tish's housemates, and Laurie was sleeping in the back of temporary office quarters. They knew they wanted to continue working together, but Laurie had some reservations about their sharing a home. "It was partly the old idea that two women couldn't share a kitchen," she said. Tish was drawn in part by Laurie's sense of humor. "Organizing is heavy work, and I must say I've tended to look at things very seriously. . . . Additionally, Laurie had that terrific energy, we sparked each other." As they checked out possible places, they would point out space for Laurie's Alliance for

Laurie and Tish, ca. 1983. Photograph by Elizabeth Crews, used with permission.

Displaced Homemakers and Tish's NOW Task Force on Older Women work. Reflecting on their decision, Tish commented, "Once we moved to the house together we were very much a partnership, we needed each other, we complemented each other; we had different skills."

At the Harrison Street house, they planned offices downstairs and private quarters upstairs, though in fact they carried work with them everywhere. Laurie's quilt was blue and white, and large photographs of Arthur in a priest's robe for a film and in *Playboy of the Western World* were on the wall behind the bed. Old programs from the Irish Abbey Theater hung across the room from Martin Luther King's portrait. Her parents' wedding picture was on one table, under which she stored her own First Communion picture and one of herself as a young woman, blonde hair curled and makeup carefully applied. Some of the artwork Tish's mother had bought in China hung throughout the house, and her jade flower arrangement sat on top of the red colonial Mexican chest at the head of the stairs. When Tish moved out of the tiny bedroom in the back to the large room across the front of the house, she left most of the white walls bare—except for a jade ornament, a picture of her rafting companions, and one of the children's prints exhibited in 1942.

As they settled into their new living arrangement, they discovered that Tish loved to cook and Laurie to clean, so the expected domestic conflicts never materialized. Their food preferences were very different—"You eat no fat and I eat no lean," Laurie joked. So they compromised. Laurie fried her own bacon and eggs, and Tish ate Japanese food at restaurants with other friends. Together they went on picnics in the hills behind Berkeley, to Tilden Park or Grizzly Peak or Lafayette Reservoir. Tish might walk while Laurie read. On the way home they'd stop for ice cream at Fenton's. Sometimes they watched TV together, but not often. Tish watched more than Laurie, who preferred reading novels.

They looked and were quite different, "the Mutt and Jeff of

the women's movement," Laurie joked, "or maybe I mean the odd couple." Slender Tish moved with elegant grace while Laurie was "short, stout and spontaneous" as one reporter described her.[4] Wreathed in smoke, Laurie often wore her OWL sweatshirt while editing the *OWL Observer*. She wore her blue pantsuit only on "state occasions," when she also wore bright red nail polish. While she was generally cordial, Laurie's temper could be fierce, blasting over the phone lines or through the house. Her levity could also break the tension and clear the air. Tish valued Laurie's raucous sense of humor as ballast for her own seriousness, even when she didn't appreciate Laurie's jokes. One she said her woman surgeon gave her was: "What did the elephant say to the naked man she met in the jungle?" (Pause for effect.) "How do you drink through that thing?" (A roar of laughter.) Laurie loved to poke fun, often with herself as target. Of course, she had her serious side too, and was scandalized by political folly, fraud, or injustice.

While neither woman was religious in a conventional sense, both lived with a strong moral code. After they saw the movie *Cocoon* together, Laurie wrote to a friend, "I thought it was great— pure fantasy but funny. Sort of an *E.T.* for grown-ups. . . . But afterward we were talking about it and found that each of us wondered what decision we would have made—go off . . . or stay behind. . . . Tish immediately said she'd go for the moon or wher- ever but I found myself thinking of the promised eternity with loved ones and my Catholic past couldn't quite hack living for- ever away from that possibility."[5]

From outside, it seemed that Tish was more connected to others, gave and got nourishment in a wider variety of situations, while for Laurie there were many "people" connections and tele- phone friends but few intimates. She jealously guarded her close- ness with Tish, pushing others away when she could. Often Tish chafed at the protectiveness, but she was also grateful for the support. And when she felt overwhelmed herself, Tish sometimes sought Laurie's advice. In her medical journal, Tish wrote, "This morning I requested a 'counseling session' with Laurie (cheaper, and she's more knowledgeable than a prof. counselor, and can help me attack the problem, rather than talking about attacking it). Very successful. We went thru all the 'to-do's' and cut them down to size. Think I can get 'caught up' over the weekend, so next week can get down to business."[6]

They devoted themselves to building the new organization amid tremendous public response. The OWL acronym began to take over the house, what with the Barred Owls (a group of lawyers who developed policy papers), the "flocks" of members, the allusions to "making OWL fly" or the next "parliament of OWLs." The house filled with sacks of mail, and owl memorabilia. Owl cards, paintings, and photographs were standard. There were also tiny porcelain and medium-size embroidered owls, owl aprons and shirts, owl figures that were wooden, crystal, plastic and metal, fat and thin, hairy and smooth—the bad and the beautiful. "If I ever see another!" groaned Tish in mock exasperation.

More important was the fact that they made a great team, continuing their strategy sessions after Laurie shooed staff and volunteers away at 4 P.M. Over dinner and early in the morning they worked out new plans. And Laurie was Tish's greatest fan. If Tish came home elated after an effective speech, she had someone to cheer and pour the wine. When she left the Mills Center after the bitter split with Milo Smith, she was comforted by Laurie's total loyalty.

Tish continued her other friendships, allowing time with her former housemates for a trip to Yosemite every December and white-water rafting in the summers. She tried to combine speaking dates with a pleasant weekend visiting old friends in Los Angeles or San Diego. Tish also stayed physically active, an interest Laurie definitely did not share. Laurie preferred driving to walking, and reading novels to any other form of exercise. She did go along on a couple of raft trips and fished while Tish hiked in the mountains. Their differences were epitomized on a trip to Fran Leonard's lakeside retreat: Tish rowed vigorously while Laurie trolled her fishing line.

When Tish spent time with others, Laurie stayed home, took

car trips, or went out to dinner with her daughter Christine. The two older women enjoyed being together for picnics and holidays but were careful to give one another privacy. Most of the time they agreed, or argued briefly, but Laurie loved to tease Tish about being too cheap about tipping and called her "Frugal Fannie" when she insisted on bargain prices. Tish bridled at being called cheap but acknowledged she had a hard time spending money. In one journal entry she wrote, "My financial report for the year came in, and, for whatever reason, the net worth continues to grow. That made me think—'what are you saving it for'—at least spend all the income. I played around with ways to spend money and could come up with little that I really wanted or would be comfortable spending $ for. I'm truly committed to a modest lifestyle. So Saturday, when I'd completed my work, I treated myself to a walk down Grand Ave. and Lakeside—with their many shops. I managed to buy some low cholesterol cheese and licorice tea, and that was about all. Last of the small spenders!"[7]

By the time the Alliance for Displaced Homemakers was phased out in 1978, and the Displaced Homemaker Network was left to Cindy Marano's direction, Tish and Laurie's partnership was firmly established. The service centers worked on meeting employment needs of older women, but Tish wanted a broader arena. It was time for a new campaign. They both continued to speak across the country, giving and getting information on the needs of older women. Laurie worked on her book about the displaced-homemaker movement, and Tish developed educational materials under their new Older Women's League Educational Fund. OWLEF, structured as a fund-raising mechanism, allowed them to sell materials and apply for grants to study a range of issues. The plan for a new national organization was slowed down by Tish's recurrence of cancer, but by 1980 the two women moved on to establish OWL. Tish subsidized both the house and OWL while Laurie happily served as paid executive director to Tish's president of the board. It was a matter of pride to Laurie that she was paying her own way.

Ideas flowed rapidly as they multiplied their contacts and

decided on OWL's agenda. Laurie maintained an extended telephone network, then traveled again, organizing chapters. She
might go to a city where they knew one or two women, get them
together in a home, and by the end of the evening have a new
OWL chapter formed. Back home, she devoured newspapers and
magazines, circled items for Tish's attention, and picked over the
day's events for possible use in the policy oriented *Gray Papers* or
the OWL newspaper. Laurie shaped the *OWL Observer*, writing
editorials about Medicare costs ("A Far from Sickly Business,"
May 1983), proposed Social Security cuts, and other OWL issues.
She put together the "OWL Tie-Line" column for chapter reports: "Flash! NEW chapters sprouting like spring flowers. . . ."
She also encouraged writers and cartoonists, highlighted government spending follies in "Ruffled Feathers," and provided profiles
on inspirational OWL activists. The tone combined informal
warmth with cogent policy analysis in columns by Alice Quinlan,
Fran Leonard, and Tish. Laurie's approach gave a personal face to
chapters and helped publicize Tish's ideas. Together the two of
them decided the organization's direction, consulting with board
members infrequently.

That changed dramatically in 1983 when OWL's office moved
to Washington, D.C., and Shirley Sandage became the executive
director. While Tish remained president, Laurie's role diminished.
She continued to be paid as editor of the *OWL Observer* but no
longer had a free rein in decision-making. She never forgot the
day Tish stood in the kitchen doorway and told her the team
approach was over; they would have to operate differently in deference to the new staff. That was not easy for Laurie.

Hers was a politics of personality. Laurie reached out to people
on a direct emotional level, and connected viscerally. When she
was enthusiastic, as she was for example about Cindy Marano,
that person could do no wrong. And when she was offended, for
whatever reason, she could be vituperative. She was fiercely loyal
and could be unforgiving when she felt a principle had been betrayed. At times Tish used that tendency in Laurie, allowing her
to confront and argue loudly, then stepping in to sooth feathers.

"Sometimes Laurie was the stalking horse for a new idea," said Fran Leonard, who as OWL's legal counsel was able to observe them closely. Tish once commented that she was "giving Laurie plenty of room, but would rein her in when it was necessary."[8] Laurie was blunt, sometimes rough in challenging opponents, and when she held a grudge she was tenacious. Many rankled at her style. Of their own interactions, Tish recalled, "There were rocky moments, but I learned early on that Laurie could get very angry very rapidly, but she would cool off just as fast and then we could discuss whatever it was." Those who loved Laurie and understood her soft, generous nature, tolerated her periodic outbursts even when they disliked them. Tish's cool rationality had greater appeal, though Laurie could also charm people with her direct warmth and approachability.

About their political partnership, Cindy Marano said: "Tish's role was to articulate substantive reasons they were right, and then to let Laurie do the unpleasant task of being a pain in the ass. People never dealt with Tish in the nasty way they would Laurie. They were intimidated by Tish because she was so clearly focused on ideas and wasn't going to get into the politics of getting it accomplished. . . . She would set out the vision and really wasn't willing to engage. Laurie offended many."[9] Later, Cindy wrote:

> Laurie was a complex woman, whose drives were most often personal and individual. As an organizer, she had the capacity to be personal with thirty or more displaced homemakers or older women in a group. She would remember their names, stories, and family concerns five years later when she returned to the same city. She saw the world quite personally, problems personally, movements as personal. As with most of us, this was both her greatest strength and her Achilles heel. In the displaced-homemaker movement, in OWL, and in her work on care givers, it was the personal lives of those affected which motivated her. It was the personal struggles in building an organization that haunted her. Since she understood life in such personal terms, she was sometimes defensive, quixotic, intensely loyal, unreasonably generous, or sharply

combative when organizational or political struggles clashed with her personal realities. She feared that history might not be kind to her because of this. . . .

Irishness itself was important to Laurie. She carried much of what we think of as Irish traits proudly—her volatility; her dramatic flair; her love of politics, potatoes, and justice; her melancholy; her great charm; her endurance.[10]

Tish was the visionary leader who drew admiration and attention. Laurie accepted her secondary role most of the time, though she was irritated when her contributions to either the displaced-homemaker movement or OWL were or seemed to be overlooked. She was the less visible partner, the dedicated and loyal helper. It was an uneven distribution of power and recognition. As Tish became increasingly dependent on Laurie for personal care giving, she thought more about this shadow effect. She knew her own personal success owed much to Laurie's efforts, and she saw the potential emotional and physical cost to Laurie from the burdens of care giving. As Tish wound up her own life, she tried to compensate for that, in part by more frequent public statements about Laurie's central contributions to OWL. She acknowledged both Laurie's contributions and the problem when she recommended Laurie for a Senior Scholar Award in 1985. Tish pointed out that their strengths differed and had synergistic effects—two being able to accomplish much more than one. "The negative side is that Laurie is often in my shadow. I am more likely to be singled out for honors and recognition."

"But objectively speaking," Tish went on, "look at the special contributions which would make Laurie a strong candidate for Senior Scholar in her own right. She is a sixty-five-year-old widow who for the past several years has worked tirelessly as a volunteer on behalf of older women." Tish credited Laurie with primary responsibility of displaced-homemaker legislation in nearly two dozen states. "She wrote the definitive book on the subject. . . . She was a co-founder of the Older Women's League and as long as it was based in Oakland, was its executive director. She is currently vice-president and editor of the *OWL Observer*. She is the type of 'people person' which is the glue for an advocacy organization. Without Laurie, many of those things for which I am credited would not have happened."[11]

Tish and Laurie saw their relationship as special; Laurie thought it unique. But Tish felt other older women could share a home as they did. She spoke of shared housing from time to time, noting that the Gray Panthers had been active in this area, but she was sad that so many older women seemed tied to their isolated lives.

Collective housing for aging feminists was an idea she played with but never implemented. She wrote about her plans: "Our 'Last Perch,' as we called it, would be a home for aging activists. . . . We'd decide who could join, what food would be served at the table and what drinks at the bar, who could study us and what we could expect in return. For a price, we'd test all kinds of model equipment for seniors. We'd have our own television program or printing press to get the word out, and we'd have a marvelous garden to surround our last years with flowers."[12]

Were Tish and Laurie lovers? Several wanted to know, but the answer to the question is both simple and not simple. "Laurie was so homophobic it was amazing," said one friend. She worried that people would think she and Tish were sexually involved. Laurie stated emphatically that they were not lovers, and there is no evidence to the contrary. She always made a point of stressing her good marriage with Arthur. Tish didn't seem to be bothered and was openly grateful for the companionship and care giving Laurie provided her. Years before, Tish had written to a friend: "I have always felt closer to women. Despite close relationships with men, there is always a seventh (and maybe a sixth) veil. But you and I had a type of intimacy that went deeper; or Alita; and a few others. Is that homosexuality? I don't think so—I think it is closer akin to soul—a shared 'oppression.'"[13]

An intense couple relationship without sex does not fit our heterosexist model. The question about Tish and Laurie suggests the limits of our model for relationships, particularly where it is assumed that the cornerstone is genital sex. What Lillian Faderman wrote of nineteenth-century female couples seems applicable to Tish and Laurie in their older years: "we do know that these women spent their lives primarily with other women, they gave to other women the bulk of their energy and attention, and they formed powerful emotional ties with other women."[14]

As Laurie began to know more women who identified themselves as lesbians, she relaxed some. She came to understand that their double beds and women lovers were no obstacle to their political work. While she was upset that anyone might misunderstand her feelings for Tish and the context of their life together, always emphasizing their separate bedrooms, she didn't want to invalidate what she saw at last as a life choice for several close friends.

That said, their partnership, particularly as Tish's health declined, was most intense. There was intimacy and mutual solicitude. They shared the process of care giving and dying both as a public issue and alone in the middle of the night. In 1985 Cindy Marano was with them on a weekend of rest by the ocean. Tish was exhausted, in agony but refusing heavy medications, trying to complete her final list of projects. Cindy woke in the middle of the night; Tish was sobbing with pain. As she considered going across the hall, she heard Laurie get up and go to Tish. The crying stopped as Laurie crooned and soothed her like a child.

Laurie described it this way: "One night after a very painful bout, she began to cry. I walked over to her bed, held her, and then she said, 'I'm tired of being brave.' Gently rocking her a bit, I softly whispered into her ear, 'You don't have to be.' Then I pulled back and grinned at her as I told her, 'You can be my courageous coward.' The contradiction in terms seemed to amuse her, and the tears stopped."[15]

Staying in Control to the End

I face my own last transition with the sure knowledge that you will all go on to complete the tasks we have set for ourselves. And that is why I feel such joy and love.

But people fear death most who have not lived fully. Even when all seems lost, we can squeeze the sweet juice out of adversity, finding new incentives for making each day count.

"I kind of thought at the end, well, she'll pull it out of the hat one more time," said Fran Leonard. Tish felt more than once that she had only six months to live. During summer 1982, one lung filled with fluid and any activity exhausted her. Anxious and alarmed, Laurie invited old friends and organizers from all over the country to a birthday gathering at Point Reyes on the coast above San Francisco. Tish then left for what she thought was her last rafting trip. By the time she got back, her lung had cleared; she believed it was healed by the serenity on the river. So instead of tearful goodbyes, they enjoyed a weekend of celebration, including walks on the beach and a raucous auction of the last few beers and food. For six years Tish planned to be around only another six months. Finally, many just couldn't believe the cancer would get her.

"There they went," said Margaret Malberti, "Tish in her maroon sweats and red backpack and Laurie in her blue pantsuit, using her cane to limp out to the car." They flew off to a combined public appearance and vacation in Alaska. Tish was frail enough by late spring 1985 that she cancelled her plans to attend the International Decade for Women Conference in Nairobi but felt she wanted to make this presentation to Alaskan professionals in the field of aging. She shared with them her familiar exhortations: use the system, it has used you; create a vision of the future; hope is never out of season; have short-term goals and long-term vision; and honor thy mothers and fathers—all of them. She and Laurie stopped by the roadside to photograph a moose in the field, but Tish wearied quickly and was glad to get back to Oakland. In spite of the new, experimental medical treatment, she was losing strength rapidly.

One last public appearance was before her: the public forum in Washington on living wills and other advance directives. By July her hair was so thin that she chose a straw hat with scarf to match her loose rose-colored pants and top. "She loved the fact that it was a seven-dollar bargain, too," chortled Laurie. Tish led OWL into dialogue about death and dying; now she urged public officials to deal seriously with the ethical and economic tensions, introducing her remarks with "life and death are intertwined, for we are all terminal cases." She explained the public policy dilemma as she saw it: "On the one hand, we don't want to prolong dying when a person is ready to go. On the other we don't want it speeded up for economic considerations without thinking of the desires of the dying person." Both, she felt, had to do with the "right of each person to determine what is most appropriate for himself or herself."[1]

By then she knew her time was short. She signed on with the Alta Bates hospice program,working with her nurse, Lily, to cope with the increasing pain. Work continued around and with her in the old house, but Tish spent more and more hours upstairs. She was organizing now for her own death, making final lists. She wrote about her increased dependency on Laurie: "The process . . . of handing [my] autonomy over to another person whom I trusted

Tish at OWL's Washington, D.C., forum on death and dying, July 1985. Photograph courtesy of OWL.

Tish and Senator Jacob Javitz at OWL forum, July 1985. Photograph courtesy of OWL.

and loved, opened up for me another kind of experience. It was very enriching."[2]

She faced her imminent death. "I found that . . . coming to terms with death could be joyful, as well as painful. . . . I have felt myself, joyously, a role model for death."[3] Friends were asked to come by. Tish gave them her assessment of their talents and pressed them to continue their support for OWL. She decided who should get which gifts: the Chinese crane silk painting to one, the Mexican carved chest to another, her grandmother's Tiffany strawberry bowl found and polished for someone else. She also generated as much funding for OWL as she could and worked to educate Vicky Jaycox, the new executive director, on goals and strategies for the future.

Each last visit included instructions, but also Tish's gratitude and love for old and dear friends. As she accepted her own decline, she seemed less shielded, more able to express warmth and caring. Barbara Dudley wrote to Tish after their farewell meeting: "I think about you so often and have something on my mind I want to tell you, but I'm not sure I know what it is. That I love you—yes; that I have learned more from you than from any other person I can think of; that you move my life forward when it's stuck; that I look at all those lemons and think 'lemonade'; that you are and always will be a Jiminy Cricket on my shoulder, giving me very sound advice and prodding me along. You know all that I'm sure."

Barbara continued, saying she would build Tish into her heart, "so that you will live there forever. I will take many more raft trips with you, whether you are there or not. And I'll have hundreds more conversations with you—about the state of the world, the country, love, life and motherhood. . . . I know I'm not your only daughter, your only love, but that seems just to make it better. You are a very special and very loved woman, you made us in your image because you saw us in yourself. I love you."[4]

These sentiments were echoed and shared as women arrived at Harrison Street, reported on their projects, expressed love, and said goodbye. They then came downstairs to weep and hold one another in the sunny yard.

Tish was nearly overwhelmed by pain now, but refusing to take anything stronger than Advil. She was honed down to wiry will and bloat, but could still check off tasks and say goodbyes. Since the hospice nurse was only on call, the burden fell more and more on an exhausted Laurie, who was consumed with caring and fear as she ran up and down the stairs and gave phone reports on Tish's condition to her network. They had done all this very public planning, and Tish's bravery stunned many. However, the practical weight of day-and-night care nearly overwhelmed her partner.

One friend wrote that Tish's flesh had gone to the essentials, her face like an ancient Indian princess, high cheekbones, slim nose.[5] She had very little hair now, and reed-like arms. Tumors made her look eight months pregnant, and the skin on her swollen legs was drum-tight. Her dinner was sliced avocado and poached pear, though she ate only a little. She was holding off, planning to start morphine in a couple of days. One more meeting, one more planning session. *The King and I* was on the TV, and she asked Laurie to delay preparations for bed until Yul Brynner and Deborah Kerr finished their dance. Oddly, Yuriko, her friend from forty years earlier, choreographed and danced in the Little Eva sequence. After the movie, when the sheets needed changing, Tish stood alongside the bed. She wept with pain, threw up what little she ate. She had thought about taking pills to end her own life. But that was out of the question since she couldn't swallow, certainly not the sixty pills one source suggested.

Laurie slept when she could, in her rocker or the big recliner in Tish's room. She moved restlessly around in the night. By 5:30 A.M. Tish was awake, hurting but determined to review sketches for a new series of ads. The group arrived, clustered around the bed, discussed the artist's approach. Phones rang, more women arrived, someone sat on the bench crying. It was crowded in the kitchen. Margaret kept on with phones and copying machine and paperwork. She didn't want to go upstairs; couldn't stand saying goodbye.

At noon Rhonda, another hospice nurse, responded to Laurie's call. Yes, she told Tish, her bladder seemed to be sealed off. Rhonda and Susan, friend and volunteer, joked with one another and with Tish. Rhonda tried to replace the bladder catheter but couldn't get it in. Tish writhed, tormented but silent. When Rhonda suggested the hospital, Tish was adamantly opposed. Rhonda gave her the first morphine and compazine shots. They agreed to call in the physician.

Tish was more comfortable by the time he arrived; she was able to swallow some water and a spoonful of ripe persimmon. She and the lanky, bearded doctor had become friends and colleagues on this "project," her disease. Not long now, he told her, with one kidney gone and the bladder too. Maybe tonight, maybe tomorrow. Thanks and it's been a good relationship, she told him. He left and Laurie stayed with Tish.

Downstairs someone brought in Chinese food. For several days food appeared and was eaten, automatically, in brief moments. Laurie talked on the phone, gave reports, soothed friends and herself. In the night she wept by the bed, talking to Tish, grieving.

The next day was the most pleasant. Tish's pain was controlled by the morphine, the bladder blockage ended, the swelling receded. There were flowers in the room, Vivaldi and Bach in the background. Individuals came in, sat by the bed, holding Tish's hands, surrounded by music. Tish was quiet but not unconscious, responding occasionally to the talk in the room. "How nice this is," she said once, "It feels like family." In the afternoon she asked for Margaret. Tanis and Bari were there too; others wandered downstairs. The whole day was full of the flow of women, the storytelling in the kitchen or outside in the yard, waiting. Nurturing and empathic, they absorbed the pain, soothed one another. It was not gloomy, though there were tears along with the fond memories. At lunch there were funny stories, including one local scandal about the burial society that mixed up all its ashes. Fran couldn't decide whether to have her ashes scattered in the mountains or at sea.

Tish seemed to be dying in an ideal way. That made her a difficult role model to emulate, as did her public bravery in the last months of her life. Dying at home met Tish's needs for control but placed a heavy burden on her care givers, particularly since there was almost no respite or nursing care. Ironically, she pushed off her death because she had a long list of projects related to death and dying; however, the emotional and physical care-giving costs were high for those who survived her.

Tish took the first morphine on Tuesday. By pre-dawn Friday she was not responding at all, but slept on. She was not really there, had gone in every way but this last one. It was the final wait. Somewhere in the next hour her breathing stopped, and it was over. She had what she wanted. She died at home surrounded by people she loved and who loved her.

Afterword

"A Decade of Vision toward a Century of Change"
OWL Observer, 1990

What happened since Tish's death to those who were close to her? Tish's son, Bill, returned to his life in Seattle with his son, Jeffrey. Laurie Shields died at home (with full-time nursing care) in March 1989, after a long struggle with her own cancer. She chose to be buried in the same plot as Tish, at Mountain View Cemetery in Oakland. Tanis, Bari, and Spring, Tish's former housemates, are still taking hikes and fixing up the Prudence Crandall house in Oakland. Margaret Malberti and her husband Jose retired to Merced, where she has taken up painting and recently had a watercolor exhibit in San Francisco. Fran Leonard is still legal counsel to OWL.

The new executive director selected by Tish in 1985 resigned, and Joan Kurianski currently runs the OWL office, while Lou Glasse is still president of the OWL board. Cindy Marano served her last year on the board in 1989, as did Dorothy Pitts, and Alice Quinlan left OWL for a new job in Indiana. Although there have been internal struggles about the best direction and organizational shape for OWL, thousands of members continue in the activism Tish envisioned. There are now several state OWLs to coordinate legislative advocacy, and the board of directors is taking a much more active role in shaping OWL's overall direction. As Lou Glasse put it, "OWL has the reputation in Washington,

Pat Huckle and Tish's son, Bill, at memorial service for Tish,
November 1985.

D.C., of being on the cutting edge of issues affecting older women
and of being able to deliver grass-roots support."

She also wrote, "OWL is celebrating its tenth birthday in
1990. Our success is reflected in the increasing attention being
paid to older women by researchers, policy makers and other national aging and women's organizations. But studies show that
unless current policies are changed, large numbers of older women
will be plagued by low income and poor health care well into the
twenty-first century. The work begun by Tish and Laurie must
continue."[1]

A final image of Tish, contributed by Jeanne Saletan, long-time OWL member:

At the 1984 OWL convention . . . it was the last plenary. We were conventioned out and many were leaving to catch busses and planes. A resolution on Medicare was under consideration and Tish had appointed a small committee to . . . revise a draft copy. As we awaited their return, Tish (whom I knew already to be quite ill again) put on this cassette tape [Helen Reddy's "I Am Woman"] and began to dance.

She was electric, radiating her energy, her wonderful joy, her delight in the body moving again with grace and spontaneity. How we loved her as we began to dance, too, rising from our tables and chairs and coming forward to be nearer her. We didn't want it to stop. It's as if we could keep her with us if we could keep dancing, yet knowing that this might be her last convention with us. I like to think of her that way, dancing with us.[2]

The Silver-Haired Sisterhood
Historical Perspectives
on Women and Aging

By Susan E. Cayleff

The significance of this biography as scholarship, as well as the significance of Tish Sommers's life as an activist, are best understood within a historical framework. Both make unique contributions. The text is the first biography of a female age activist. Sommers was the first to found a gender and age activist political action group in the twentieth century.

Before the inception of the Older Women's League in 1980, Sommers's own life resounded with the disturbing issues she would soon address politically: she had "fallen" in social status from a comfortably middle-class wife to single—and vulnerable—status; she had breast cancer in her mid-forties, divorced at age fifty-seven, and lost her health insurance (and Medicare eligibility) six months before her sixty-fifth birthday and cancer's return. She was painfully aware of the myriad vulnerabilities that accompany aging in a society that equates youth—and not old age—with economic productivity, sexual viability, reproductive status, and general worthiness.

Yet Sommers was clearly empowered by this stage in her life. Authors on aging refer to it as "autumnal ripening" or transcendence: being at ease with oneself, no longer fulfilling others' ex-

Susan E. Cayleff is associate professor in the Department of Women's Studies at San Diego State University.

pectations. This empowerment resonates in the main text even when shadowed or tinged by the grueling limits she faced as an older woman. This personal context informed Sommers's activism in the political arena.

Scholarship in the Field of Aging: Is the Older Woman Visible?

Cultural concern with aged Americans (currently defined as those of forty-plus years) is a relatively recent development.[1] Academic scholarship, governmental studies and programs, and feminist analyses are all, with notable exceptions, newcomers to discussion and involvement. Furthermore, the vast majority of the existing studies focus on middle-class and, to a lesser degree, working-class and upper-middle-class heterosexual, married women of Anglo descent; the early work emanates from the Eastern portion of the country. Thus, the prototypical woman *activist* who emerges in the late nineteenth and twentieth centuries is middle- and upper-middle class.

Older women were virtually invisible—at best they were grossly underrepresented—in scholarship preceding the late 1970s' explosion of statistics, studies, and projections prompted by the maturing of baby boomers (i.e., those born between 1946 and 1964). This invisibility occurred even in historical texts exclusively *about* women.[2] Even texts organized on a "life-cycle" basis omit older women; the later years (post-childbearing, circa age forty to forty-five) go unmentioned.[3] The texts' implicit message: post-menopausal women are not worthy of study since their female duties are complete. Another interpretation suggests that the age of some scholars precluded their asking these questions. Yet the best explanation for the omission is ageism, the undervaluing of the aged through negative stereotypes and discriminatory practices.

Early to contemporary feminist scholarship, ushered in by the Women's Liberation movement of the late 1960s onward, also contributed to the invisibility of older women,[4] as do recent books (1980s) whose focus is on women's sexuality.[5] In 1970, Robin Morgan's eclectic collection of essays, articles, and poems, *Sisterhood Is Powerful*, chronicled women's anger and frustration with male domination and oppression. While the essays represented great diversity, only one entry in the 648-page volume discussed older women. Ironically, the author of "It Hurts to Be Alive and Obsolete: The Aging Woman," wrote under the pseudonym Zoe Moss while decrying her invisibility. "What, fat, forty-three (note that forty-three is deemed old!), and I dare to think I'm still a person?" she wrote. "No, I am an invisible lump. I belong in a category labelled *a priori* without interest to anyone. I am not even expected to interest myself. A middle-aged woman is comic by definition."[6] In 1972 the question was reposed as: "Why Is Women's Lib Ignoring Old Women?" The answer? "Ageism is a national habit which has yet to be challenged by even the old themselves."[7]

The frustration evident in the 1970s essays resounds in MacDonald and Rich's *Look Me in the Eye: Old Women, Aging and Ageism* (circa 1983), which discusses the invisibility they feel from society at large, and from the female and feminist realm: "All my life in a man's world, I was a problem because I was a woman; now I'm a problem in a woman's world because I'm a sixty-five-year-old woman."[8]

Widows, Wives, and Care Givers

But older women have not been entirely invisible in scholarship. Before the 1960s, they appeared *in relation to* others. Thus the status of widows received discussion as a contradictory time of vulnerability and opportunity for propertied older women.[9] They were vulnerable because their fates were determined by spousal wills and children's benevolence. As one historian noted, "The legal records of the colonies contain many instances of poor widows who were 'warned out' and forced to wander from one town to another."[10] The Civil War letters of Bethiah Pyatt McKoun of Missouri reveal that she was reduced to begging her children for assistance after her husband's prolonged illness left her widowed and penniless.[11]

Other "pre–age consciousness" texts address the relatively high status enjoyed by older women as wives and respected community members. For some, the occasion existed to own, manage, and act autonomously for the first time in their lives.[12] Yet this is contradicted by revisionist scholars who chronicle indigence and frailty, enforced institutionalized living, status loss or change through ceased reproductivity, and diminished youthful attractiveness and social significance.[13]

Largely unknowingly, historians have charted a third dimension of older women's experience: care giver. Older women care for aging and infirm spouses and "mother" adult children, thus servicing the needs of two generations. They also have taken care of needy community members where social services did not or do not exist.[14]

Changes in the Status of Older Women:
From Pedestal to Poverty?

A common, often unspoken premise holds that a "golden age" of older womanhood existed alongside the high *sentimental* (vs. political/economic) status women enjoyed as wives and mothers in the middle and late nineteenth century. In fact, several of the factors detrimental to the material condition of older women accelerated dramatically in that period.

Six factors played a dominant role in affecting older women's material conditions in the last one hundred years. First, although differences occur amongst races, an increased life span for all women helped focus attention. Women now become widows later in life and spend more years as widows. This was less problematic—but evident—in 1890 when the wife was the surviving spouse in 56 percent of all marriages. This meant that "about one-third of women age fifty-five to sixty-four were widows."[15] Since at the turn of the century only one person in twenty-five lived to be sixty-five or older, this kept the actual number of years lived alone low.[16] Also, a larger family size meant more children were potential care givers. The number of women surviving their spouses burgeoned as the century continued: to 60 percent in 1930 and 70 percent in 1964.[17] Simultaneously, the number of people living to be eighty-five or older increased 165 percent between 1960 and 1985.[18] Thus the number of years a woman lived alone after her spouse's death increased from a maximum of five to ten years in 1890, to fifteen years in 1960, and eighteen years in 1970. The 1980s provide the biggest contrast: the average age of widowhood (among ethnically and economically diverse women in California, circa 1980) was fifty-six. Thus surviving "white" wives can live an average of twenty-four years after their spouses' death; nationally, in 1975, the average age at which women were widowed was sixty-eight.[19] This was accompanied by shrinking family size and fewer children as potential care givers.

Third, present chances of remarriage are quite slim. The 1950s marked the first time women of all ages outnumbered men of all ages in the United States.[20] For example, at present in the sixty-five to sixty-nine year old age bracket, women outnumber men 100:81; this increases to 100:40 at the age of eighty-five and above.[21]

Fourth, by the mid-twentieth century, more and more single heads of households emerged among widowed women. This was due in part to greater regional mobility between generations; a willing child care-taker was not necessarily nearby.[22] The increased life span of the surviving parent (taking in one's mother for five years is quite different from doing so for thirty years) presented new challenges to the American family, challenges they met alone. Governmental programs, which provided *some* economic relief to the elderly, made solo living possible though grim and meager. Contemporary statistics portray a startling situation: in 1984 the U.S. Census Bureau cited 68 percent of women aged fifty-five to sixty-four, 79 percent of those sixty-five to seventy-four, and 81 percent (3.1 million) of those seventy-five and older living alone.[23] Many of these women are in dire need.

By the 1980s and 1990s, these factors peaked. Severe economic and social difficulties (e.g., living arrangements, isolation) were common obstacles for greater numbers of older women. Labeled the "feminization of poverty," this means "females comprise nearly three quarters of the elderly poor, and their impoverished state is often linked with being unmarried."[24] Since the current average total death benefit to a California widow, for example, is only $12,000, it is readily apparent why as "early" as 1969 nearly 25 percent of white women ages fifty-five to sixty-four were living below the poverty level, 48 percent ages sixty-five and above; and among "Negro and other races" 58.3 percent and 77 percent respectively. The particular vulnerability of women of color and unmarried women is ever present.[25]

Today's 23 million women aged forty-five to sixty-four and the 17 million sixty-five and older are more likely than men to be: poor, without adequate Social Security and pension income (only 7 percent of women over sixty-five are in the work force), widowed, divorced and alone, employed in low-income jobs, and without adequate access to affordable health care.[26] And yet older women are care givers to other frail elderly individuals.[27]

Finally, projections into the next century yield the same problems in greater proportions. By the year 2000, one of every four adults will be over fifty; by 2030, one of six Americans will be over sixty-five, the majority of them women.[28] The care of the aged will likely continue to fall to elderly wives, daughters, and daughters-in-law; the period of physical disability and frailty will increase as longevity expands, and aloneness and economic want may continue unabated.

Yet, an ever-increasing *positive* trend is that "politically, the older woman is in a most advantageous position and it is likely to improve." Eleven million are potential voters, two-thirds are registered to vote, and those better off have the time and energy to lobby and campaign since 90 percent are retired from active employment.[29] Older Americans' potential political power is so great that in 1989 a *Los Angeles Times Magazine* cover story declared it the "Empire of the Old. It's Big. It's Rich. It Has Clout. And Its Members Will Dominate America into the Next Century."[30]

Old-Age Activism: In Search of
Gender-Conscious Historical Precedents

There are numerous historical instances of women who reached their peak political effectiveness while older. Among them are Jane Addams (1860–1935), Settlement House founder, social reformer, and peace worker; Susan B. Anthony (1820–1906), abolitionist, temperance and suffrage activist; and her co-worker and kindred spirit, Elizabeth Cady Stanton (1815–1902), who worked as a young woman against slavery and for temperance and later devoted herself to women's concerns. Another, Frances E. C. Willard (1839–98), worked during most of her adult life for the causes of the Women's Christian Temperance Union (WCTU), the most broadly based nineteenth-century national women's organization.[31] Interestingly, none of these women focused on older women's issues. This may have been due to personally comfortable circumstances, the ability of some intact intergenerational families to absorb their older females, fewer women living into old age, or old age as one item on an incomplete list of grievances. Yet the omission is striking. The WCTU and other women's clubs and their members, despite their comprehensive social critique, were silent on issues of aging. Willard's 705-page autobiographical *Glimpses of Fifty Years 1839-1889...* (1889) reveals no age-related political programs.[32] But it *is* quite likely that notable older women inspired others. For example, Harriet Paine, the early twentieth-century author of *Old People* (Boston, 1909), found many older women who inspired her. As her psychologist noted: "Mrs. Gilbert acted till over seventy; Mrs. Livermore, Julia Ward Howe, and others furnish examples which hearten her, etc. When the hair grows white it is possible, especially for women, to do many things impossible before."[33]

While these notable women were not "old-age activists," there were instances of women addressing concerns specific to older women. In the nineteenth century, a row of cottages called "Widow's Row" housed poor, old women in Mobile, Alabama;[34] a similar project began in New York City in 1814. The Association for the Relief of Respectable, Aged and Indigent Females (ARRAIF) assisted indigent women over age sixty, with the proviso that they be of respectable standing. In 1838, the society built an asylum for the aged. Before that date, recipients provided their own shelter and received help with rent costs. In its early years, this association did not provide medical services because it lacked a centralized facility. Thus those "women with extreme disabilities were usually removed to the public almshouse, where medical care and supervision was available." This changed with the erection of the asylum.[35]

Another association, the Society for the Relief of Poor Widows and Small Children, was formed by Mrs. Isabella Graham. Its constitution stipulated who would and would not receive help; the notion of the "worthy poor" reemerges. The charity helped "any poor widow of fair character" if she had two children under age ten, was a widow with one child under ten, cared for an aged parent, or had a child having any natural infirmity.[36]

In 1897, the Phyllis Wheatley Association of Detroit (an offshoot of the National Association of Colored Women [1896]), concerned with self and community improvement, established a home for "aged colored women," housing seven. The residents increased to twelve in 1901 when the committee purchased a permanent home and, by 1904–6, twenty-four residents resided at the home.[37]

Contemporaneously, twentieth-century women's religious orders also have provided for their older members. The Grey Nuns of Motherhouse in Yardley, Pennsylvania, serves its sisters of the Sacred Heart and houses their retirement facilities.[38]

One psychologist, G. Stanley Hall, pioneered in giving "sustained and serious attention to the subject of gerontology and discussing women as a separate entity in need of same-sex old-age activism. But his book *Senescence: The Last Half of Life,* published in 1922, 'fell dead from the press.'"[39] Better known for his work on adolescence, Hall discussed the stereotypes, problems, and possibilities for older women. He noted the importance of same-sex age groups in his description of the Sunset Club (circa 1920, diverse in locale). Comprised largely of women over sixty, "its purpose [was] not only to have old people help and be helped by others to useful occupations but to supply reading matter, chaperons, . . . help those in need [and] . . . those who need sympathy and companionship . . . [such as] the homeless, or they can simply form good cheer circles." This "silver-haired sisterhood," as he called it, brought usefulness into the lives of many. Hall suggested "the time is ripe for some kind of senescent league of national dimensions."[40]

Old-Age Politics:
Gender-Mixed Precedents

There are numerous examples of activism for the old *en masse* pre-1970. In the 1880s in California—a state that has often pioneered on this front—this type of attention focused solely on old-age pensions.[41] In 1927, California's Governor Young appointed Esther De Turberville, "an ace researcher in the State Department of Social Welfare," to investigate the plight of the aged. She depicted the problems forcefully but offered no radical solutions.[42] Another effort, more social than political, was the Borrowed Time Club of Oak Park, Illinois, that admitted those only seventy and older. Established in 1900, it reorganized in 1911, and in 1920 had 294 male names (only) on its roster.[43]

Upton Sinclair's California-based EPIC (End Poverty in California) Program of the 1930s sought to relieve the Depression's devastating effects. EPIC hoped to make the state's million-plus people on relief self-supporting by farming idle land or working in idle factories. Sinclair's gubernatorial campaign platform also contained an old-age pension plan.[44]

The Townsend Movement (1933–51), also based in California, had seven thousand clubs, with a membership of 1.5 million throughout the United States.[45] Townsend's plan spoke to "a dilemma confronted by most elderly people, a sense of purposelessness in a nation almost desperately directed toward the symbols of youth."[46] Membership in the early years "reported a predominantly middle-class participation: small businessmen and farmers, retired and otherwise, skilled independent workers and housewives."[47] Townsend proposed retiring all of those sixty and older on pensions of $150 per month. Forced to spend all of the money, they would bolster the fractured economy—thus keeping younger workers employed.[48]

The movement peaked in 1936 when "even conservative Maine elected Townsendites to Congress,"[49] but club membership declined by 98 percent between 1936 and 1951, due to: the enactment of Social Security law (1935); the lack of endorsement from a major political party; club members' frustration with the plans not being enacted; the Depression's abatement and the start of an economic upswing; and the leadership's inability to prepare and defend the bills.[50]

None of the national Townsend leadership was female, although women played a critical role on the state level, as the following example demonstrates. "After listening to a speech at the San Diego Women's Civic Center, the president . . . took one of the pamphlets home and read it. She then passed it on to a fellow club member and civic leader, Mrs. Sidney Scott, who organized the first San Diego unit espousing Townsend's plan."[51]

The Ham and Eggs Movement (1938–50) emerged as the next influential organization for old-age activism. It, too, sought to end poverty in old age.[52] It planned to raise and distribute funds weekly to every Californian fifty and older.[53] Membership grew at the rate of 600 per day in 1938–39, peaking at 362,000 in 1939. At that time the group's income was estimated at $55,000 monthly.[54] The *National Ham and Eggs* newsletter had a circulation of sixty to a hundred thousand. (Tish Sommers's first husband was an editor for this paper.) By 1942, the movement had been defeated in two elections; its popularity waned, and it ceased to function. Women are not mentioned in pertinent historical accounts of either the Townsend or Ham and Eggs Movements at the national level. It's likely they were active at the grass-roots levels, as noted above.

These movements died because of their impracticality, and because of the federal government's implementation, in 1935, of the Social Security Act, which adopted sixty-five as the age for eligibility for benefits; in 1973 the retirement age was dropped to sixty.[55]

Nationally, old-age activism, like feminism, had a diminished public visibility in the 1940s and 1950s. But in California, the state government took a particularly active role in response to the public's demands. In 1951 the governor called a Conference on the Problems of the Aging. Topics for the conference included: community organization, education, employment, housing, income, mental and physical health, and social welfare services. Women's issues were not specifically addressed.[56]

Citizen groups that focused on aging also organized and gained strength at mid-century: all were gender mixed. The National Association of Retired Federal Employees, a nonprofit organization, began in 1920. In 1946 Ethel Perry Andrus, California's first woman high-school principal, organized and presided over the National Retired Teachers Association (NRTA). The NRTA helped provide nationwide health insurance to retired teachers and lent assistance in starting second careers and doing voluntary community work. In 1958 Andrus founded the American Association of Retired Persons (AARP). It aspired "to promote independence, dignity and purpose for older persons."[57] By 1974, AARP/NRTA claimed over seven million members in over 2,500 local units. More than three thousand members joined *daily* in 1972. The dual group publishes two magazines, *Modern Maturity* and *NRTA Journal*. Andrus also built a nursing home, an apartment complex for convalescents, and a retirement home, "Grey Gables."[58]

The National Council of Senior Citizens was organized by conferees at the 1961 White House Conference on Aging. The council sought to represent "the views of older persons on major issues confronting the nation," but did not consider women's issues until 1981.[59]

Another activist contingency, the Gray Panthers, was founded by Margaret E. Kuhn in 1970. She, too, experienced mandatory retirement, which inspired her and five others to form an intergenerational movement "working for peace and human liberation and the elimination of discrimination on the basis of age." The group presently possesses more than a hundred local networks and an effective national organization. Kuhn co-founded the National Organization for Women's Task Force on Older Women in 1971 and has long supported feminist issues.[60] Still, few of these groups, despite extensive female leadership, addressed older *women's* issues as a separate and unique set of concerns.

Government involvement reemerges with the 1971 White House Conference on Aging: Toward a National Policy on Aging. Conference sessions were aimed at a culturally diverse audience; topics included: education, employment and retirement, physical and mental health, housing, income, transportation, programs and services, and planning and training. No special section on women was offered, although women were discussed as homemakers as well as home health aides and care givers; Mrs. Theodore Wedel, associate director of the Center for a Voluntary Society, suggested using women's volunteer labor to fill the need for those two services.[61] Sommers, then chairing NOW's Task Force on Volunteerism, took a position contrary to Wedel's because the latter's plan would reinforce women's unpaid care-giver role and sex-role stereotypes; it would impair the *care taker's* economic security as she would not be accruing retirement monies. Despite these governmental and citizen efforts, the attention, dialogue, and actions needed on older women's problems were virtually ignored.

Women's "Autumnal Ripening":
Modern Political Organization
by and for Older Women

To the frustration of contemporary gender-conscious scholars and activists, "many . . . continue to operate as if the elderly were a homogeneous sexless group, as if we know nothing of the sexual composition of the elderly population, or as if we know it to be predominantly male."[62] The androcentrism endures. Early feminist tracts and activists, as already discussed, were slow to include older women in their analysis of women's oppression. The movement for "Creating the New Woman" in the 1970s did not include those over forty.[63] Yet feminist literature of the decade did provide enlightening characters, especially Lessing's *The Summer before the Dark* (1974) and Arnold's *Sister Gin* (1975).[64] Also, the magazine *Country Women* (which had published eleven issues as of 1974) was collectively written, containing poems, letters, articles, essays, photos, drawings, and book reviews all pertaining to older women.[65] And, at mid-decade, academia began addressing older women's issues, although gender "blind spots" were far more common.[66]

Sommers was among the vanguard in linking gender, politics, and aging. Chair of NOW's Task Force on Older Women from 1971 to 1978, she also led the Displaced Homemaker Movement, from 1975 to 1979. The latter originally focused on divorce and widowhood for older women, then broadened to more general issues. In 1975 Sommers wrote: "As a feminist, I see the problem of aging in America as a woman's issue. The poverty, loneliness and neglect of older women is the payoff for performing women's traditional role. But as we grow stronger and move together we can change that and build a bridge between mothers and daughters."[67]

The Older Women's League, the first woman-centered political action group of its kind, was national in scope, clearly feminist, and boldly self-asserting. Founded in Oakland, California, in the fall of 1980 by Sommers and her partner and co-worker

Laurie Shields, it identified and addressed concerns of mid-life and older women. These included: retirement income inequities, divorce reform, problems of long-term care financing, and employment discrimination. In 1983, OWL moved its headquarters to Washington, D.C.[68]

OWL's first *Gray Paper* (1979) was a position and fact sheet outlining the agenda of the related organization that preceded the group's founding by one year. Sommers's and Shield's "The Coming Decade: American Women and Human Resource Policies and Programs," in that first issue, was presented before the U.S. Senate Committee on Human Resources "to review conditions and trends affecting American women in the coming decade." OWLEF (Older Women's League and Education Fund) and then OWL testified with the older woman's viewpoint. They identified the educational, health, employment, labor, and care-giving conditions facing older women at the close of the decade. They suggested policy, program, budget, and information measures.[69]

Sommers's message was clear: "Males and females do not approach the starting line of aging on an equal footing. Nor do they run the same course."[70] Beyond analysis, OWL's primary focus was education on issues—leading to action. This was epitomized in Sommers's slogan: "Don't agonize, organize." This woman-centered analysis appealed to many mid-life and older women, who, according to Sommers, "confront distinct gender related experiences in virtually all vital areas of life."[71]

Other early 1980s publications also spoke to older women. Laurie Shields's *Displaced Homemakers: Organizing for a New Life* (1981) reached many women who were new to politics.[72] For them, age activism made the personal political. A newsletter, *Broomstick: A Bimonthly Publication by, for, and about Women over Forty,* which began publication in 1980, seeks personal accounts by mid-life women. It functions as a voice and informational support system for older women.[73] Other newsletters, along with various publications, found an eager and receptive audience: *Prime Time* and *Hot Flash* best known among them.[74]

OWL was founded at the 1980 White House mini-conference on women and aging, which Tish Sommers and the Western
Gerontological Society organized. Out of this regional conference
came recommendations for the 1981 National White House Conference on Aging, at which Sommers was a keynote speaker and
delegate; through Sommers's efforts, older women were included
on the agenda. Included for the first time were forums with such
titles as "Concerns of Older Women" and "Growing Number,
Special Needs."[75] Relevant topics included economic, medical,
discrimination, services, and quality-of-life issues.

OWL and Sommers published regularly throughout the mid-
1980s and presented testimony before state and federal legislators.
Women Take Care (1987), a collection of stories Sommers coau-
thored with Shields, discusses women care givers as well as ana-
lyzing the social, economic, and emotional aspects of women's
care giving.

The prototypical OWL member was identified in 1985 when
the *OWL Observer*, the organization's newsletter, surveyed the
membership, revealing a range of women—many of them alone,
well educated, and economically vulnerable. The commonality of
age transcended regional, economic, educational, work, and rela-
tional status. Preliminary results showed 98 percent to be female,
a full 77 percent over fifty, and 58 percent living alone. Of these,
18 percent were widowed, 29 percent divorced, and 11 percent
single. Income for one-third of the membership ranged from
$5,600 to $15,000; the college and post-graduate degree holders
earned more. More than half were still employed, while a quarter
were retired. Membership was regionally diverse, drawing heav-
ily from the Pacific and mid-Atlantic regions. Questions were not
asked about ethnicity (one chronicler did observe a "sprinkling"
of minority women in the audience) or same-sex relationships,
though a lesbian caucus at the 1986 convention drew about a
dozen participants.[76]

Since the founding of OWL, writing and organizing on the
issue of aging has proliferated. *The Encyclopedia of Associations*

(1989), which chronicles national organizations in the United States, lists fifty-two age-oriented groups. Of these, four identify subcommittees on older women (*including* those using the "home-makers" category). Many others, while they have "care giver" committees, do not identify this as a gender issue.[77]

The "post–Tish Sommers" literature about, by, and for older women, referred to in one text as "autumnal ripening,"[78] spans a distinct yet diverse set of experiences. Thematic divisions are: older women as *speakers* defining and chronicling their aging; *descriptions* of the experience of aging (including changing attractiveness and vanity, caretaking of others, impoverishment, loneliness, frailty); and decreasing economic and age *status* of older women in different cultures. The last of these was termed the "double whammy" by Sommers, who saw women and the aged as two cultural "out groups." *Stereotypes* of older women as stagnant, uninteresting, asexual, invisible, waiting for children and others —and for death; *sexuality*; and *physiological/medical* aspects are also prevalent topics. The last chronicles myriad health problems, a changing relationship with one's body, cosmetic surgeries, medical advice, unwanted life-prolonging medical interventions, depression, frailty, and relationships with physicians.[79]

A final theme echoes Sommers's sense of empowerment as an older woman. Women authors describe personally unprecedented creativity and transcendence of cultural expectations in a genre loosely categorized as *"in praise and celebration"* of older womanhood. This theme resounds throughout nineteenth- and twentieth-century American women's literature. Demonstrably, Sarah Orne Jewett and Mary Wilkins Freeman, two late nineteenth-century authors, wrote about the world of women and the heroism of older women.[80] In 1911, Mary Heaton Vorse, an insurgent involved in feminism, socialism, and unionism, wrote in her *Autobiography of an Elderly Woman* that among the "Compensations of Age" that older women have earned is the right to do, say, and think as they please.[81] This was echoed in 1978 by a researcher in a community of aged Jewish women: "The old women . . . com-

municated a quiet conviction and satisfaction with themselves. . . . This is not scant comfort at looking back at one's life-
work."[82] Similarly a poet, writing in 1986, also reached self-
acceptance: "i find my reflection and begin to recognize me/ . . . i
am surprised i like my image, i look my age/i come home to my
time, my place, i am my age."[83] Finally, this acceptance and
comfort with oneself is evident in Lillian Morrison's "Body," in
the rebelliously titled collection, *When I Am an Old Woman I Shall
Wear Purple* (1987). "I have lived with it for years. . . . Though it
is aging now, I cannot abandon it nor do I want to. . . . It's really
pleasant to be with, familiar, faithful, complaining a little, continually going about its business, loving to lie down."[84]

Tish Sommers brought a dichotomous legacy to her activism
on older women: on one hand, historical disenfranchisement and
invisibility; on the other, empowerment "of a woman/turned and
tuned to her ripening, whose life is [as] dear as a signed first
edition."[85]

Notes

Unless otherwise noted, all quotations of Tish Sommers are drawn from over a hundred hours of interviews conducted by the author, 1982–85. All of these interview tapes and transcriptions are in the Tish Sommers Collection in the Special Collections Department at San Diego State University's Love Library. Materials in the collection are identified herein as "TSC." Unless otherwise noted, epigraphs for each chapter are from Tish Sommers.

Preface

1. Sherna Gluck, "What's So Special about Women," *Frontiers* 2 (1977): 3–14. See also: Daniel Aaron, *Studies in Biography* (Cambridge, MA: Harvard Univ. Press, 1978), Susan Armitage, "The Next Step," *Frontiers* 7 (1983): 3–8; Gluck, "Women's Oral History, The Second Decade," *Frontiers* 7, (1983): 1 and 2; Rita Mae Kelly and Mary Boutilier, *The Making of Political Women* (Chicago: Nelson-Hall, 1978); Ken Plummer, *Documents of Life* (London: Allen and Unwin, 1983); and Lawrence C. Watson and Maria-Barbara Watson-Frank, *Interpreting Life Histories* (New Brunswick, NJ: Rutgers Univ. Press, 1985).
2. Carolyn G. Heilbrun, *Writing a Woman's Life* (New York: W. W. Norton and Co., 1988), 129.
3. My thanks for the insights in Bell Gale Chevigny's essay, "Daughters Writing: Toward a Theory of Women's Biography," in *Between Women*, ed. Carol Ascher, Louise DeSalvo, and Sara Ruddick (Boston: Beacon Press, 1984); and Elizabeth Karnarck Minnich, "Women: The Act of Feminist Biographies," *Feminist Studies* 2 (Summer 1985): 287–305.
4. Heilbrun, *Writing a Woman's Life*, 128.

Chapter 1

1. Tish Sommers and Laurie Shields, *Women Take Care* (Gainesville, FL: Triad Publishing, 1987).
2. Their pioneering work is noted in a Senate hearing on S1107, Tish Sommers and Laurie Shields Displaced Homemakers Training and Economic Self-Sufficiency Assistance Act of 1989, U.S. Senate Committee on Labor and Human Resources, 1 June 1989.
3. Sommers, draft for "Perspectives on Aging," *OWL Observer,* 1985, in TSC.
4. Her endowment to OWL eventually totaled more than $750,000, built from funds inherited from her mother in 1960. Tish was not eligible for Social Security as she had only twenty-three of the twenty-five required earning quarters.
5. Sommers, draft for *OWL Observer,* 1985, TSC.
6. The banner design committee also included Susan Edenborough, who met Tish at the hospital radiation center and later worked as one of Tish's hospice volunteers, and Terri Clark who often drew cartoons for the *OWL Observer.*
7. According to Jill Emery, director of the Federal Women's Bureau, twenty-six states have displaced-homemaker legislation. The Women's Bureau has funded the Displaced Homemaker Network, Inc., since 1983, serving about one thousand programs nationwide: U.S. Senate, S1107, 1 June 1989, pp. 6 and 17. Also see Jill Miller, "Displaced Homemakers in the Employment and Training System," in *Job Training for Women,* ed. Sharon Horton and Ronnie J. Sternberg (Philadelphia: Temple Univ. Press, 1989), 143–65.
8. Tish taped this discussion with her cancer support group in Dec. 1983, TSC.
9. Sommers to KM, 2 Mar. 1985, TSC.
10. Leo Politi later illustrated several well-known children's books, among them *Pedro, The Angel of Olvera Street* (New York: C. Scribner's Sons, 1946), for which he received the Caldecott Medal in 1947.

Chapter 2

1. Lynn Smith, "Older Women's Advocate Dies at 71," *Los Angeles Times,* 19 Oct. 1985, 7.
2. Interviews with Leona Ludwig, Paula Krotser, Dorothy Pitts, Cindy Marano, Ira Hirschfield and Laurie Shields—all in TSC—were used as

background for this chapter; Tish taped an interview with her brother, Murray Innes, Jr., in Mar. 1984, also in TSC.

3. Author's telephone interview with Ira Hirschfield, 28 July 1988.

4. Wilma Scott Heide, "NOW, for the Feminist Menopause That Refreshes," in *The World of the Older Woman*, ed. Dr. Gari Lescnoff-Caravaglia (New York: Human Sciences Press, 1984), 167.

5. U. S. Public Law No. 95-524, Comprehensive Employment and Training Act, 27 Oct. 1978.

6. Tish's cancer journal, 17 Oct. 1979, TSC.

7. Now known as the American Society on Aging.

8. Comment to author by Jean Stern, founding president, San Diego OWL Chapter, 1988.

9. For example, Mildred Hamilton, "The Resolve of Older Women," *San Francisco Chronicle*, 7 Oct. 1980, 16, and Judy Klemesrud, "New Focus on Concerns of Older Woman," *New York Times*, 13 Oct. 1980, 16.

10. Tish Sommers, "Growing Numbers, Growing Force," report from White House Mini-Conference on Older Women. OWLEF and Western Gerontological Society, 1981, TSC.

11. Sylvia Porter, "New Older Women's League Helps That Invisible Group," *New York Times*, 13 Oct. 1980, 13.

12. Laurie Shields letter to Virginia Matthews, 28 Feb. 1982, TSC.

13. Murray Innes, Sr., letter to son Bill Innes, 19 Dec. 1939, TSC.

14. Murray Innes obituary, *San Diego Union*, 10 Aug. 1960, sec. B, 1.

15. "Bachelor Joys Revive," *San Francisco Chronicle*, 23 Apr. 1926, 22.

16. Murray Innes, Sr., letter to J. J. Lerman, attorney, 6 June 1933, TSC.

17. Kate Innes letter to Murray, 10 Apr. 1929, TSC.

18. Kate Innes letter to Murray, Jan. 1932, TSC.

19. Laurie first and most often used this teasing label.

20. Leona Ludwig and Paula Krotser interviews with the author, 1985, TSC.

21. "Boy Drowns in Riptide," *San Francisco Chronicle*, 26 Sept. 1931, 1.

22. Sommers, cancer journal, 2 May 1979, TSC.

23. Ibid.

24. Sommers, Salmon River journal, 1984, TSC.

25. Tish's draft for a speech to be given at CSU Chico during Women's History Week, Mar. 1985, TSC.

26. Rafting companions included Cindy Marano, Karen Kelley, Joyce Keating, and Barbara Dudley.

Chapter 3

1. Interviews used for this chapter include those with Cindy Marano, Laurie Shields, Fran Leonard, Margaret Malberti, Barbara Dudley, Alice Quinlan, and Tanis Walters, 1985–89, TSC.
2. The Alameda County Displaced Homemaker Center, the first such center in the nation, was opened on the Mills College campus in 1976.
3. Tape of Fran Leonard interview with Tanis Walters, Sept. 1988, TSC.
4. Quoted by Horst Koegler, "In the Shadow of the Swastika," *Dance Perspectives*, Spring 1974, p. 48.
5. Walter Sorrell, *Hanya Holm: The Biography of an Artist* (Middletown, CT: Wesleyan Univ. Press, 1969), 46.
6. For general background, see Raul Hilberg, *The Destruction of the European Jews* (New York: Harper and Row, 1961); Richard J. Evans, *The Feminist Movement in Germany* (London: Sage Publications, 1976); Yehuda Bauer, *A History of the Holocaust* (New York: Franklin Watts, 1982).
7. Lucy S. Davidowicz, *The War against the Jews* (New York: Bantam, 1976), 257.
8. See Ernst Scheyer, "The Shapes of Space: The Art of Mary Wigman and Oskar Schlemmer," *Dance Perspectives,* 1970, p. 57, and Koegler, "In the Shadow of the Swastika."
9. Mary Wigman, *The Mary Wigman Book,* ed. Walter Sorrell (Middletown CT: Wesleyan Univ. Press, 1973), 63.
10. Tish's letters to her mother, 1933–35, TSC. On Nazi attitudes toward smoking and lipstick, see Jill Stephenson, *The Nazi Organization of Women* (Totowa, NJ: Barnes and Noble, 1981), 191 n. 20: "For good health, the javelin or the pole-vault are of more value than the lipstick."
11. Scheyer, "The Shapes of Space," 11.
12. Florrie Gordon Thunen interview with the author, 1985.
13. Evans, *The Feminist Movement in Germany;* Stephenson, *The Nazi Organization of Women,* 133.
14. Koegler, "In the Shadow of the Swastika," 31.
15. Michael Young, *The Elmhirsts of Dartington* (London: Routledge and Kegan Paul, 1982), 225.
16. H. W. Koch, *The Hitler Youth* (London: Macdonald and Jane's, 1975), 167.
17. Mary Wigman, *The Language of Dance* (Middletown, CT: Wesleyan Univ. Press, 1966), 13.
18. Bauer, *A History of the Holocaust,* 101.
19. Wigman noted, in a letter to Kate Innes, that Tish would probably be a better teacher than a solo star performer, 6 June 1934, TSC.

20. Walter Sorrell, *Dance in Its Time* (New York: Anchor Press/Doubleday, 1981), 385.
21. C. P. Snow, "J. D. Bernal, A Personal Portrait," in *Society and Science*, ed. Maurice Goldsmith and Allan Mackay (New York: Simon and Schuster, 1964), 23. John Strachey, author of *The Coming Struggle for Power* (New York: H. Wolff, 1933), was later a member of the British Labour Cabinet. He was the son of St. Loe Strachey, editor of *The Spectator* and cousin of biographer Lytton Strachey.
22. Young, *The Elmhirsts of Dartington*, 4.
23. Ibid., 37–38.
24. William C. Seitz, *Mark Tobey* (New York: Doubleday and Co., 1962), 10.
25. Florrie Gordon Thunen interview with author, 1985.
26. Merle Armitage, *Modern Dance*, comp. Virginia Stewart (New York: A. E. Weyhe, 1935), 12.
27. Bauer, *A History of the Holocaust*, 101.
28. On emigration of young people from Nazi Germany, see Davidowicz, *The War against the Jews*, 257.
29. Tish did not know what later happened to Mr. Jacoby. Florrie Gordon Thunen believed he eventually escaped from Germany, but was not sure how or when.
30. Bauer, *A History of the Holocaust*, 104.
31. Emanuel Eisenberg, "Danse Macabre," *New Theatre*, 1936, p. 23.
32. Scheyer, "The Shapes of Space," 11.
33. Walter Sorrell, ed., *The Mary Wigman Book*, 162.

Chapter 4

1. Young & Rubicam, San Francisco office, staffed by Skye Halberg.
2. Sommers, "Coming of Age," OWL Annual Report, 1984, 8, TSC.
3. Susan Bales, "Spirit of the Place: A Tribute to 3800 Harrison St.," *OWL Observer*, Mar.–Apr. 1987, pp. 2–3, TSC.
4. Tape of Fran Leonard interview with Tanis Walters, 1988, TSC.
5. OWL's annual dues were raised to ten dollars in 1986.
6. Comment to the author by Cindy Marano, 1989.
7. Dance program for this event, and Tish's critical comments on performances, in TSC.
8. Letitia Innes, UCLA transcript, 1937–39, TSC.
9. Martha Deane, "Dance Education at UCLA," UCLA Oral History Program transcript in UCLA Library Special Collections, 1969.

10. Archibald MacLeish, *Land of the Free* (New York: Da Capo, 1977), used photographs taken during the Depression, commissioned by the Federal Resettlement Administration.

11. Zan Dubin, "Horton Tribute: Credibility Out West," *Los Angeles Times*, 10 Nov. 1985, Calendar, 46: "[Lester Horton] served as the primary mentor and teacher for a number of dancers (including his leading dancer Bella Lewitsky, [and] Alvin Ailey . . . who were later to become important in the field)." During Tish's time with the company, Rudi Gernreich was also a dancer, not yet a famous fashion designer.

12. Larry Warren, *Lester Horton, Modern Dance Pioneer* (New York: Dekker, 1977), 58–60. For the general political attitude among dancers of the period, see "Dancers Aid Democracy," *Dance Herald* 1, no. 6, Apr. 1938, Editorial, 2.

13. Nell Silva, "Horton Dance Group Relates Life to Art, *The People's World*, 28 Apr. 1938, 5.

14. Alita Letwin telephone interview with Bella Lewitsky, 4 May 1985. Alita's notes are in TSC.

15. "Hollywood Bowl Dancers Revolt, Demand Living Wage; Musicians and Famous Names Pledge Help," *The People's World*, 13 May 1938, 5.

16. California State Senate, Joint Fact-Finding Committee (Tenney committee), *Un-American Activities in California* (Sacramento, 1943), 43.

17. Tish Sommers (Letitia Innes Burke Sommers) FBI file no. 100-345618, copy in TSC.

18. "She joined the Communist Party in 1937 under the name of Mary Graham," FBI file no. 100-345618, copy in TSC.

19. Larry Ceplair and Steven Englund, *The Inquisition in Hollywood* (Garden City, NJ: Anchor Press/Doubleday, 1980), 183.

20. Alfred Miller, "Camacho Holds Big 3-1 Lead," *The People's World*, 11 July 1940, 1. "The dead in Mexico City today numbered 48 while the wounded are variously estimated at between 200 and 400."

21. Tish is listed in the brochure for the Elizabeth Holloway School of Theatre, Fairmount Hotel, San Francisco, CA, 1941, TSC. Tish filed for divorce in 1942, and it was final in 1943.

22. Mrs. Sigmund Stern's letter to Letitia Innes, May 1941, TSC.

23. Alfred Frankenstein, "'Park' Ballet: The Emphasis Is on the Modern Side." *San Francisco Chronicle*, 25 Aug. 1941, 9, TSC.

24. This was at the height of Dunham's success. She had recently completed the film *Stormy Weather* with other black stars, including Lena Horne, Bill "Bojangles" Robinson, and Cab Calloway, and she worked with Ethel Waters in *Cabin in the Sky*. See John Pittman, "Dunham Dance Group

Returns for Another San Francisco Triumph," *The People's World,* 2 Jan. 1942, 5.

25. "Plan for Nurseries Is Promoted in L.A.,"*The People's World,*" 16 Mar. 1942, 5.

26. "Children's Fair for Refugee Youth," *California Arts and Architecture,* Apr. 1942, p. 12, TSC.

27. Persis was working through the Unitarian Service Committee.

Chapter 5

1. Sommers, cancer journal, July 1979, TSC.
2. Ibid.
3. This section is drawn from a tape of Tish's discussion with her cancer support group, Dec. 1983, TSC.
4. Her chosen successor was Lou Glasse, whom she had met at a conference on aging issues.
5. *Wingspan,* 1984, a series of workbooks designed for local OWL chapters, focused on such issues as housing.
6. Known today as the American Society on Aging.
7. Mauricio Mazon, *The Zoot Suit Riots* (Austin: Univ. of Texas Press, 1984).
8. Bernice Griffith, *American Me* (1948; rpt., New York: Houghton, 1978), 63.
9. Mazon, *The Zoot Suit Riots,* 26. See also, Ismael Dieppa, "The Zoot Suit Riots Revisited," Ph.D. thesis, Univ. of Southern Calif., 1973.
10. Rodolfo F. Acuna, *A Community under Siege* (Los Angeles: Chicano Studies Research Center, UCLA, 1984), and Remi A. Nadeau, *Los Angeles: From Mission to Modern City* (New York: Longmans, Green, 1960), provide general descriptions of the community at this time.
11. Tape of Frank Wilkinson interview with Tish Sommers, Alita Letwin, and the author, 1984, TSC.
12. Griffith, *American Me,* 91.
13. International Institute brochure, TSC.
14. Acuna, *A Community under Siege;* John Caughey and Laree Caughey, *Los Angeles: Biography of a City* (Berkeley: Univ. of California Press, 1976), describe this shift.
15. The funds came from the Los Angeles War Chest, otherwise known as the Community Chest. See Roy Sorenson, *Recreation for Everybody* (Los Angeles: Welfare Council of Metropolitan Los Angeles, 1946).
16. Bari remembered that Beatrice Griffith, author of *American Me,* was the pianist for some of the PADG's rehearsals.

17. Tish was reminded of this episode by reading Danny Santiago, *Famous All Over Town* (New York: New American Library, 1983), a novel set in East Los Angeles in the 1960s.

18. Several of these appearances are mentioned in local newspapers, the *Belvedere Citizen* and *Eastside Sun*, 1943–47, on microfilm at the East Los Angeles County Library.

19. International Institute files for the 1940s, in TSC.

20. International Institute Executive Secretary Elsie D. Newton letter to Mrs. Edith Terry Bremer, American Federation of International Institutes, 21 Nov. 1945, TSC.

21. Aliso Village Victory Council letter to Los Angeles War Chest, 6 Aug. 1945, TSC.

22. Tish's report to the Los Angeles Youth Authority, 1947, TSC.

23. Interview with the author, June 1985.

24. For this posture on the "unfulfilled" woman, see for example, Marynia Farnham and F. Lundberg, *Modern Woman: The Lost Sex* (New York: Harper and Brothers, 1947). See also Karen Anderson, *Wartime Women* (Westport, CT: Greenwood Press, 1981), and D'Ann Campbell, "Wives, Workers and Womanhood," Ph.D. thesis, Univ. of North Carolina at Chapel Hill, 1979, and Susan Hartmann, *The Home Front and Beyond* (Boston: Twayne Publishers, 1982).

25. Walter Storm, "The World Youth Festival in Prague," *The People's World*, 13 Sept. 1947, 5.

26. FBI file no. 100-23650, Oct. 1946, TSC. Tish requested her files in 1984.

27. Tape of Annette Hazen interview with the author, June 1985, TSC.

28. "While Wallace Was in L.A.," *The People's World*, 4 Oct. 1948, 3, and Sidney Burke, "Labor Rally Goes Wild on His Arrival," *The People's World*, 17 May 1948, 1.

29. Tish met Jessica Mitford in Oakland through her high-school friend Paula Krotser. According to Laurie Shields, the encounter was not a raving success, as Mitford apparently criticized Tish's displaced-homemaker campaign as too middle-class in emphasis.

30. Paul Joseph, staff member at the Soto-Michigan Jewish Community Center in the 1940s, commented that Tish certainly knew the "party line" and chastised him for giving time to the bosses by coming to work early. Tape of interview with the author, Apr. 1984, TSC.

31. On Yuriko's later career see Barbara N. Cohen-Stratyner, *Biographical Dictionary of Dance* (New York: Schermer Books, 1982), 962.

Chapter 6

1. Videotaped interview with Dr. Stephen Blum, UCLA, Feb. 1985, TSC.
2. Ted Kalman, "Accent on Youth," *The People's World*, 4 Jan. 1949, 8.
3. General background for this chapter was contributed by Anita Gurion and Leon Wofsy in informal conversation with the author and Alita Letwin, 1985 and 1987. Notes on these conversations are in the author's possession.
4. Joseph Starobin, *American Communism in Crisis: 1943–1957* (Cambridge, MA: Harvard Univ. Press, 1972), 197.
5. Geoffrey Perrett, *A Dream of Greatness* (New York: Coward, McCann and Geoghegan, 1979), 131. As Ceplair and Englund noted in *The Inquisition in Hollywood*, 410, "James V. Bennett, director of the Federal Bureau of Prisons, announced in September, 1952, that $775,000 had already been expended for the 'activation and rehabilitation' of six relocation camps, which were capable of holding well over sixty thousand Communists."
6. FBI file no. 238,774, TSC.
7. For example, see Sam Hall, "South in Struggle," *The Daily Worker*, Harlem Edition, 13 Mar. 1949, 1, and David K. Dunaway, *How Can I Keep From Singing* (New York: McGraw-Hill, 1981).
8. George Charney, *A Long Journey* (Chicago: Quadrangle Press, 1968), 207.
9. Joseph Starobin, *American Communism in Crisis*, 199.
10. Ibid., 200.
11. Ceplair and Englund, *The Inquisition in Hollywood*, 382.
12. David A. Shannon, *The Decline of American Communism* (New York: Harcourt, Brace and Co., 1959), 230. The party underground is also discussed in David Caute, *The Great Fear* (New York: Simon and Schuster, 1978), 212–14, and Irving Howe and Lewis Coser, *The American Communist Party* (Boston: Beacon Press, 1957), 478.
13. Nell Painter, *The Narrative of Hosea Hudson* (Cambridge, MA: Harvard Univ. Press, 1979), 102.
14. *Alabama: A Guide to the Deep South*, comp. Writers' Program of Works Progress Administration in Alabama (New York: Richard R. Smith, 1941), 165.
15. Virginia Durr, *Outside the Magic Circle* (Tuscaloosa: Univ. of Alabama Press, 1985), 25.
16. Anne Braden, *The Wall Between* (New York: Monthly Review Press, 1958), 25.
17. Harry Ashmore, *Hearts and Minds* (New York: McGraw-Hill Book Co., 1982), 349.

18. Harvard Sitkoff, *The Struggle for Black Equality* (New York: Hill & Wang, 1981), 170. See also Jack M. Bloom, *Class, Race and the Civil Rights Movement* (Bloomington: Indiana Univ. Press, 1987).
19. Ashmore, *Hearts and Minds,* 225.
20. The strike was front-page news in the *Louisville Courier-Journal* the last two weeks of Apr. 1955. Their Sunday, 17 Apr. 1955, front-page headline reported, "Some 25,000 nonoperating L&N employees in 13 states went on strike 35 days ago."
21. "Burned Bridge on Struck Railroad," *Life,* 9 May 1955, 34.
22. See David J. Garrow, *The Montgomery Bus Boycott and the Women Who Started It (The Memoir of Jo Ann Gibson Robinson)* (Knoxville: Univ. of Tennessee Press, 1987).
23. Durr, *Outside the Magic Circle,* 282.
24. Edwin Strickland, "Pinks Worked under Noses of Union, City." *Birmingham News.* 11 Aug. 1957, 1.
25. "Story in News about Red Puts Fireman on Spot." *Birmingham News,* 12 Aug 1957, local news page.
26. Conversations between author and Alita Letwin, 1986.
27. According to the Wisconsin State Attorney's Office in Nov. 1989, this requirement was not written into the state law but might easily have been interpreted this way by local adoption agency officials.
28. Doris Notestein's letter to author, 1986, TSC.
29. Her FBI file was not closed until 1964.

Chapter 7

1. Taped interviews used for this chapter include those with OWL staff members Alice Quinlan and Vicky Jaycox as well as with Anita Gurian, Bill Sommers, Alita Letwin, Walter Hundley (former director of CAMP), W. Ivan King, Roberta Byrd Barr, and Vivian Caver, all in TSC.
2. Alice Quinlan, OWL director of public policy, "Inequality of Sacrifice: The Impact of Reaganomics on Women" (OWL reports, 1983–84).
3. OWL's 1985 membership survey reported that 4 percent of the four thousand respondents were members of ethnic minorities, 8 percent were full-time homemakers, 62 percent held college degrees, 90 percent owned their own homes, and 42 percent were married and living with spouses. A third reported incomes of less than fifteen thousand dollars.
4. Letter from Tish to Alita Letwin, ca. 1965, TSC.
5. Lerone Bennett, Jr., *The Negro Mood* (New York: Ballantine Books, 1965), 25–26.

6. Seattle Urban League Annual Report, 1964, TSC.

7. August Meier and Elliott Rudwick, *CORE: A Study in the Civil Rights Movement* (New York: Oxford Univ. Press, 1973).

8. The 1960s nomenclature for those now known as African Americans is used here. Terms included "Negro," "black," and "Afro-American."

9. Kevin Roderick, "Case History of a 20-Year War on Poverty," *Los Angeles Times*, 31 July 1985, 8.

10. Seattle–King County Economic Opportunity Board (SKCEOB), "Interim Report on the Central Area Motivation Program (CAMP)," 1966, TSC.

11. Lonnie Williams, Dorothy Whittington, and Pat Huckle were the first paid staff members. This was where I first met Tish.

12. Tish's CAMP volunteer coordinator reports, 1965–69, TSC.

13. "1966 School for Community Action," *Northgate Journal*, 28 Sept. 1966, 7, TSC.

14. Sommers, CAMP volunteer coordinator report, 3 Oct. 1967, TSC.

15. Julius Lester, *Look Out Whitey! Black Power's Gon' Get Your Mama!* (New York: Grove Press, 1968), 92–93.

16. Bennett, *The Negro Mood*, 125–27.

17. Tape of Bill Sommers's interview with Tish, July 1984, TSC.

18. Don Hannula, "Negro Leaders Hope People 'Get Message,'" *Seattle Times*, 1 Mar. 1968, 21.

19. CAMP volunteer coordinator report, 1969, TSC.

20. j. kurtis lyle's poetry is included in *Watts Poets: A Book of New Poetry and Essays,* ed. Quincy Troupe (Los Angeles: House of Respect, 1968).

21. "Join Hands" flyer, 1969, TSC.

22. Tape of W. Ivan King interview with the author, June 1985, TSC.

23. W. Ivan King, "Maximizing Feasible Citizen Participation," draft report, ca. 1968–69, TSC.

24. J. David Greenstone and Paul E. Peterson, *Race and Authority in Urban Politics* (New York: Russell Sage Foundation, 1973), 308.

25. Tish's letters to author, July and Aug. 1970, TSC.

26. Joseph Sommers and Tomas Ybarra-Frausto, *Modern Chicano Writers* (Englewood Cliffs, NJ: Prentice-Hall, 1979).

27. Tanis Walters, conversation with author, 1988.

28. Tish, without Joe, visited me over Thanksgiving, 1970, and told me she was thinking of divorce but hadn't yet said anything to Joe.

Chapter 8

1. Tish's journal and an interview with Tanis Walters were the sources for the following discussion of her 1974 European trip; on the trip to China, Tish was the group's recorder and kept a private journal. All of these sources are in TSC. Ira Hirschfield was kind enough to comment on the trip as well.
2. Tish's trip journal, 1974, TSC.
3. *OWL Observer*, Tish Sommers Memorial Edition, vol. 4, no. 8 (Nov.–Dec. 1985): 8.
4. Tape of Tish's interview with Betsy Blakeslee, 1984, TSC.
5. See Barbara Deckard, *The Women's Movement* (New York: Harper and Row, 1983), and Jo Freeman, *The Politics of Women's Liberation* (New York: David McKay Co., 1975), along with Celestine Ware, *Woman Power* (New York: Tower Publications, 1970), and Pam Allen, *Free Space* (Washington, NJ: Times Change, 1970), as general background.
6. Deena Peterson, *A Practical Guide to the Women's Movement* (New York: Women's Action Alliance, 1975), 8, gives an idea of the range of issues and activities.
7. Tapes of interviews with NOW members Toni Carabillo and Judith Meulli in 1985 and 1988, TSC.
8. Freeman, *The Politics of Women's Liberation*, 93.
9. *Berkeley Tribe*, 16 July 1971, 2, TSC.
10. Tape of Tish's interview with Tanis Walters, Spring Friedlander, and Bari Rolfe at Yosemite, 1984, TSC.
11. Tanis Walters, comments to author, Jan. 1989.
12. Prudence Crandall (1803–90) conducted a boarding school for black girls in Connecticut, *Notable American Women 1607–1950,* 3d ed. (Cambridge, MA: Belknap Press), 1974–75.
13. Judy Syfers, "Why I Want a Wife," in *Radical Feminism,* ed. Anne Koedt, et al. (New York: Quadrangle/New York Times Book Co., 1976), 60–62.
14. "Volunteer Beware!" NOW pamphlet, co-authored with NOW member Kerstin Joslyn, TSC.
15. Genny Guracar interview with author, 1986, TSC.
16. Tish Sommers, *The Not So Helpless Female* (New York: David O. McKay, 1973), 231.
17. Tish Sommers's letter to Ruth McElhinney, 15 Oct. 1972, TSC.
18. This was a slogan earlier used by union organizer Joe Hill and frequently quoted by black feminist Flo Kennedy in the 1970s.
19. "We Should Live So Long: A Program on Women and Aging," KQED TV script, 1974, TSC. Members of the collective included Milo Smith,

Lucile Dunham, Ruth Sheer, Tish Sommers, Jean Weinberg, Kay Nollenberger, Isabel Van Frank, Ethel Mengel, and Pat O'Brian.

20. Milo Smith, "It's a Poor Hen That Can't Scratch," in *Out of the Frying Pan*, ed. Karol Hope and Nancy Young (New York: Anchor Books, 1979), 122.

21. "A Feminist? Definition Varies with the Woman," *New York Times*, 8 Nov. 1975.

22. WATC files, 1974, TSC.

23. "Return of Rosie the Riveter," *San Francisco Chronicle*, 23 Sept. 1974, 1. See also "Senior Power," *Newsweek*, 16 Sept. 1974, 53–54. Both in TSC.

24. Tish's letter to Cine Manifest, Connie Field, and Susan Lyne, 22 Nov. 1974, TSC.

25. Tanis Walters, comments to author, 1989.

26. Laurie Shields, *Displaced Homemakers* (New York: McGraw-Hill Book Co., 1981).

27. Ibid., 42.

28. Tape of Tish's interview with Cindy Marano and Barbara Dudley, 1983, TSC.

29. Chronicled in Shields, *Displaced Homemakers*, but also discussed by Laurie with the author, 1985–89.

30. Laurie Shields, draft in Tish's files, TSC; used in several speeches, and in Shields, *Displaced Homemaker*.

31. Cynthia Gorney, "The Discarding of Ms. Hill," *Ladies Home Journal*, 21 Feb. 1976, 58+.

32. Kay Mills, "Aging Women Don't Agonize, Organize," *Los Angeles Times*, 21 Nov. 1982, sec. 4, 3.

33. Tape of Tish's discussion with Barbara Dudley and Cindy Marano, 1984, TSC, and Cindy's comments to author, 1989.

34. Smith, "It's a Poor Hen That Can't Scratch," 132.

35. Ibid.

36. Tape of author's interview with Margaret Malberti, 1986, TSC.

37. Tish to NOW board members, 4 Dec. 1977, TSC.

38. Tish to Arlie Scott, 1 May 1978, TSC.

Chapter 9

1. Tape of author's interview with Laurie and Tish about their partnership, June 1985, TSC. From time to time each also discussed elements of their relationship with the author.

2. Tape of Cindy Marano interview, June 1986, TSC.

3. Sommers, "Growing Numbers, Growing Force," 1, TSC.
4. Kay Mills, "Aging Women Don't Agonize, Organize." *Los Angeles Times,* 21 Nov. 1982, sec. 4, 3.
5. Laurie Shields to Ann Zimmerman, 2 July 1985, TSC.
6. Tish's cancer journal, 1 Nov. 1979, TSC.
7. Ibid., 21 Jan. 1980.
8. Tape of Fran Leonard interview with Tanis Walters, 1989, TSC.
9. Tape of author's interview with Cindy Marano, June 1986. This chapter is also informed by taped interviews with Vicky Jaycox and Alice Quinlan of the national OWL office, June 1986. All in TSC.
10. *OWL Observer,* Memorial Issue for Laurie Shields, Mar.–Apr. 1989, p. 5.
11. Tish Sommers letter to Carroll Estes, 24 May 1985, TSC.
12. Tish Sommers, draft article for *Perspectives on Aging*, July–Aug. 1985 TSC.
13. Tish to author, 20 July 1970, TSC.
14. Lillian Faderman, *Surpassing the Love of Men: Romantic Friendship and Love between Women* (New York: Morrow, 1981), 190.
15. Sommers and Shields, *Women Take Care,* 194.

Chapter 10

1. OWL, "Taking Charge of the End of Your Life," 1985, 9 and 12.
2. Sommers and Shields, *Women Take Care*, 197.
3. Ibid.
4. *OWL Observer*, Tish Sommers Memorial Issue, vol. 4, no. 8 (Nov.–Dec. 1985), 3.
5. Terri Clark, cartoonist for the *OWL Observer*.

Afterword

1. Lou Glasse to author, 9 Mar. 1990.
2. Jeanne Saletan to author, 27 July 1988, TSC.

Epilogue

Jennifer Watson of Poway, California provided invaluable research assistance in the preparation of this essay.

1. Eleanor F. Dolan and Dorothy M. Gropp, comp., *The Mature Woman in America: A Selected Annotated Bibliography 1979–1982* (National Council

on Aging, 1984), vii, shows 59 items published in this field in 1979, 79 in 1980, 92 in 1981, and 145 in 1982.

2. Natalie Shainess, "A Psychiatrist's View: Images on Woman—Past and Present, Overt and Obscured," in *Sisterhood is Powerful: An Anthology of Writings from the Women's Liberation Movement,* ed. Robin Morgan (New York: Vintage Books, 1970):257–274. Jo Alexander and Debi Berrow, et al., eds., *Women and Aging: an anthology by women* (Corvallis, OR: Calyx Books, 1986).

3. Gerda Lerner, ed., *Black Women in White America: A Documentary History* (New York: Vintage Books, 1973); and Judith Walzer-Leavitt, ed., *Women and Health in America: Historical Readings* (Wisconsin: Univ. of Wisconsin Press, 1984).

4. Representative texts include: Aileen S. Kraditor, *Up from the Pedestal: Selected Writings in the History of American Feminism* (Chicago: Quadrangle Books, 1968); Betty Friedan, *The Feminine Mystique* (New York: Dell Publishing, 1983); William H. Chafe, *The American Woman: Her Changing Social, Economic, and Political Roles, 1920–1970* (New York: Oxford Univ. Press, 1974); Nancy F. Cott, *Root of Bitterness: Documents of the Social History of American Women* (New York: E. P. Dutton, 1972); Adrienne Rich, *Of Woman Born: Motherhood as Experience and Institution* (New York: W. W. Norton, 1976); Lillian Faderman, *Surpassing the Love of Men: Romantic Friendship and Love between Women from the Renaissance to the Present* (New York: William Morrow Co., 1981); Mary P. Ryan, *Womanhood in America: From Colonial Times to the Present* (New York: New Viewpoints, 1975); Vivian Gornick and Barbara K. Moran, eds., *Woman in Sexist Society: Studies in Power and Powerlessness* (New York: Signet, 1971), a 704-page text with only one essay focused on older women, Pauline Bart, "Depression in Middle Aged Women," 163–86; Nancy Woloch, *Women and the American Experience* (New York: Alfred A. Knopf, 1984); and Zoe Moss' "It Hurts To Be Alive and Obsolete: The Aging Woman," in Morgan's *Sisterhood Is Powerful,* 188–194.

5. Carole S. Vance, ed., *Pleasure and Danger: Exploring Female Sexuality* (Boston: Routledge & Kegan Paul, 1984); Ann Snitow, et al., eds., *Powers of Desire: The Politics of Sexuality* (New York: Monthly Review Press, 1983).

6. Moss, "It Hurts to Be Alive," in *Sisterhood Is Powerful,* ed. Morgan, 188.

7. Myrna I. Lewis and Robert N. Butler, "Why Is Women's Lib Ignoring Old Women?" *International Journal of Aging and Human Development* 3 (1972): 223–31, quoted in Marie Marschall Fuller and Cora Ann Martin, eds., *Older Woman: Lavender Rose or Gray Panther* (Springfield, IL: Charles C. Thomas, 1980), 212.

8. Barbara MacDonald with Cynthia Rich, *Look Me in the Eye: Old Women,*

Aging and Ageism (San Francisco: Spinsters, ca. 1983), 30. These essays were written between 1978 and 1983.

9. See David Hackett Fischer, *Growing Old in America* (New York: Oxford Univ. Press, 1977); Terri L. Premo, "Women Growing Old in the New Republic: Personal Responses to Old Age, 1785–1983," Ph.D. thesis, Univ. of Cincinnati, 1983; Peter N. Stearns, "Old Women: Some Historical Observations," *Journal of Family History* 5, no. 1 (Spring 1980): 44–57; James W. Goodrich, ed., "The Civil War Letters of Bethiah Pyatt McKown, Part 1," *Missouri Historical Review* 67, no. 2 (Jan. 1973): 227–52; *Chimes of Change and Hours: Views of Older Women in Twentieth-Century America*, ed. Audrey Borenstein (Cranbury, NJ: Associated Univ. Presses, 1983). Also: Lois Green Carr and Lorena S. Walsh, "The Planter's Wife: The Experience of White Women in Seventeenth-Century Maryland"; Robert V. Wells, "Quaker Marriage Patterns in a Colonial Perspective"; Nancy Cott, "Eighteenth-Century Family and Social Life Revealed in Massachusetts Divorce Records"; Laurence A. Glasco, "The Life Cycles and Household Structure of American Ethnic Groups: Irish, Germans and Native-born Whites in Buffalo, New York, 1855"; and Judith E. Smith, "Our Own Kind: Family and Community Networks in Providence"; all in *A Heritage of Her Own: Toward a New Social History of American Women,* ed. Nancy Cott and Elizabeth H. Pleck (New York: Simon and Schuster, 1979).

10. Kate O'Neill, recorder, "Economic and Legal Status," as reprinted in *Chimes of Change and Hours,* ed. Borenstein, as cited in Fischer, *Growing Old in America,* 62–63.

11. Goodrich, ed., "The Civil War Letters."

12. Carr and Walsh, "The Planter's Wife"; Fischer, "The Exaltation of Age in Early America," in *Growing Old,* 63.

13. Michael Zimmerman, "Old-Age Poverty in Preindustrial New York City," in *Growing Old in America,* ed. Beth B. Hess (New Brunswick, Transaction Books, 1976):81–104; Helen Evers, "The frail elderly woman; emergent questions in aging and women's health," in *Women, Health and Healing: Toward a new perspective,* ed. Ellen Lewin and Virginia Olesen (New York: Tavistock Publications, 1985). Also: Robert N. Butler, "How to Grow Old and Poor in an Affluent Society," and "Houses of Death are a Lively Business," in his *"Why Survive": Being Old in America* (New York: Harper & Row, 1975); Howard P. Chudacoff, "The Life Course of Women: Age and Age Consciousness, 1865–1915," *Journal of Family History* 5 no. 3 (Fall 1980): 274–92, esp. 290; Elizabeth W. Markson, ed., *Older Women: Issues and Prospects* (Lexington, MA: Lexington Books, 1983); Stearns, "Old Women"; G. Stanley Hall, *Senescence: The Last Half of Life* (New York: D.

Appleton and Co., 1922); Leon Bouvier, Elinore Atlee, and Frank McVeigh, "The Elderly in America," Population Bulletin 30, no. 3 (Washington, D.C.: Population Reference Bureau, Inc., 1975): 3–4 in *Chimes of Change,* ed. Borenstein and Dolan and Gropp, *The Mature Woman.*

14. Hilary Graham, "Providers, negotiators, and mediators: women as the hidden carers," in *Women, Health and Healing*; ed. Lewin and Olesen; Dolan and Gropp, "Divorce," in *The Mature Woman;* Vanda Colman with assistance from Tish Sommers and Fran Leonard, *Gray Paper* no. 7 *Issues for Action,* (Washington, D.C.: Older Women's League) (Jan. 1982); OWL, "Women Take Care: A Workshop on Family Caregivers," *Wingspan:* Series Workbooks for Owl Chapters 6, Washington, D.C., May 1984; Florence Rush, "Woman in the Middle," in *Radical Feminism,* ed. Anne Koedt, Ellen Levine, and Anita Rapone (New York: Quadrangle/New York Times Book Co., 1973): 44; Alice J. Gonzales, "Aging: An Issue for Older Women, California's Efforts to Help Seniors Remain Independent," *California Women,* 2, California: California Commission on the Status of Women (1986): 1–2, 6; Marian Louise Moore, "Nursing an aging mother," in *The Female Experience: An American Documentary,* ed. Gerda Lerner (Indianapolis: Bobbs-Merrill Co., 1971), 172–78; Cott, "Eighteenth-Century Divorce Records," 109; Goodrich, "The Civil War Letters"; and Premo, "The Ties That Bind" chap. in "Woman Growing Old in the New Republic," 95–136.

15. Edward Wakin, "Living as a Widow: Only the Name's the Same," in *Older Woman,* eds. Fuller and Martin, 152; Geraldine P. Mineau, "Utah Widowhood: A Demographic Profile," in *On Their Own: Widows and Widowhood in the American Southwest 1848–1939,* ed. Arlene Scadron (Urbana: Univ. of Illinois Press, 1988), 141. The statistics cited apply to the entire United States although the study focuses on Utah.

16. Gonzales, "Aging: An Issue for Older Women," 1.

17. Mineau, "Utah Widowhood," 141.

18. Gonzales, "Aging: An Issue for Older Women," 1.

19. Wakin, "Living As A Widow," 152; Gonzales, "Aging: An Issue for Older Women," 2; and Joyce D. Goodfriend, "The Struggle for Survival: Widows in Denver, 1880–1912," in *On Their Own,* ed. Scadron, 172.

20. Robert Lindsey, "Gerontology Comes of Age," in Borenstein, *Chimes of Change and Hours,* orig. appeared in *New York Times* (Jan. 8, 1978): Education, p. 11; orig cited in: U.S. Dept. of Special Studies P23, No. 58 (Washington, D.C.: U.S. Govt. Printing Office, 1976), p. 3.

21. Gonzales, "Aging: An Issue for Older Women," 2; for a discussion of elderly widows' status throughout American history, see Robert W. Smuts, *Women and Work in America* (New York: Schocken Books, 1971), 52.

22. Greg Arling, "The Elderly Widow and Her Family, Neighbors, and Friends"; Elizabeth S. Johnson and Barbara J. Bursk, "Relationships Between the Elderly and Their Adult Children"; and Maureen Lally, et al., "Older Women in Single Room Occupant (SRO) Hotels: A Seattle Profile"; all in *Older Woman,* ed. Fuller and Martin.

23. Census Bureau, p. 20, No. 399 as cited in OWL, *Report on the Status of Midlife and Older Women in America* (Washington, D.C., 1986), 4.

24. Rita Freedman, *Beauty Bound: Why We Pursue the Myth in the Mirror* (Lexington, MA: D. C. Heath and Co., 1986), 206; Blanche Williams, "A Profile of the Elderly Woman," in *Older Woman,* ed. Fuller and Martin, 5–8, quotes the U.S. Census's far lower figures.

25. Gonzales, "Aging: An Issue for Older Women," 2; Yung-Ping Chen, "Income Background," and Technical Committee on Income, Roger G. Murray, Chairman, "Issues," both in *1971 White House Conference on Aging,* (Washington, DC, 1971), 66; Kathleen Kautzer, "Growing Number, Growing Force: Older Women Organize," in *For Crying Out Loud: Women and Poverty in the United States,* ed. Rochelle Lefkowitz and Ann Withorn (New York: Pilgrim Press, 1986), 150.

26. U.S. Dept. of Labor, *Employment and Earnings,* Dec. 1985; Fran Leonard, "Issues for Action: Older Women and Pensions—Catch 22," OWLEF *Gray Paper,* no. 4 (1980); OWL, *Report on the Status of Midlife and Older Women;* Gonzales, "Aging: An Issue for Older Women," 2; Jane Berry, "Do Special Folks Need Special Strokes? Counseling Older Women: A Perspective," in *Older Woman,* ed. Fuller and Martin, 45.

27. OWL, *Report on the Status of Midlife and Older Women,* 1. The *Report from the White House Conference on Aging,* no. 12, Aug. 1981, is ethnically and regionally diverse. It discusses aging among Asians, Hispanics, African Americans, and American Indians.

28. McDonald and Rich, *Look Me in the Eye,* 73, 48. Bernice L. Neugarten, "The Aged in the Year 2025," in *Older Woman,* ed. Fuller and Martin, 332–343, presents illogically "upbeat" projections. Also see Tish Sommers and Laurie Shields, "The Coming Decade: American Women and Human Resources Policies and Programs," OWLEF *Gray Paper,* no. 1 (1979).

29. Lewis and Butler, "Why Is Women's Lib Ignoring Old Women?" 221.

30. *Los Angeles Times Magazine,* no. 7, 12 Feb. 1989, cover, 8–13, 37–38.

31. Edward T. James, Janet Wilson James, and Paul S. Boyer, eds., *Notable American Women 1607–1950: A Biographical Dictionary* (Cambridge, MA: Belknap Press, 1974) , I: 16–21, 51–57, and 3: 342–47, 613–19. Also see Chafe, *The American Woman,* and Woloch, *Women and the American Experience,* 299.

32. Frances E. Willard, *Glimpses of Fifty Years 1839–1889: The Autobiography of an American Woman* (Chicago: Woman's Temperance Publication Association, H. J. Smith and Co., 1889).

33. Hall, *Senescence,* 103.

34. Nancy Breeze with the Crones Nest Committee, "Crones Nest: the Vision," in *Women as Elders: The Feminist Politics of Aging,* ed. Marilyn J. Bell (New York: Harrington Park Press, 1986), 7–11.

35. Hess, ed., *Growing Old in America,* 92.

36. Lerner, ed., *The Female Experience,* 194.

37. Ibid., 197.

38. Rita L. Margraff, "Aging: Religious Sisters Facing the Future," in Bell, ed., *Women as Elders,* x.

39. Historian David Hackett Fischer, quoted in *Chimes of Change and Hours,* ed. Borenstein, 24.

40. Hall, *Senescence,* 193–94.

41. Jackson K. Putnam, *Old-Age Politicos in California: From Richardson to Reagan* (Stanford, CA: Stanford Univ. Press, 1970), 17.

42. Ibid., 20–21.

43. Hall, *Senescence,* 154–94.

44. Putnam, *Old-Age Politicos,* 34–35; Butler, *Why Survive,* 335.

45. Abraham Holtzman, *The Townsend Movement: A Political Study* (New York: Bookman Associates, 1963), 47.

46. Paul David Lucas, *The Townsend Movement in San Diego County, 1934–1939* (San Diego, CA: San Diego State Univ., 1967), 8. Orig. cited in *San Diego Sun* (January 31, 1935), 13.

47. Holtzman, quoted in Richard L. Neuberger and Kelley Loe, *An Army of the Aged* (Caldwell, 1936), chap. 1. See also: Duncan Aikman, "Townsendism: Old Time Religion," *New York Times,* 8 Mar. 1936, 5, 25; Lewis Nordyke, "Report to the Editor: Old Age in Our Town," *Saturday Evening Post,* 216, 20 Nov. 1943, 6; Harry T. Moore, "Just Folks in Utopia," *The New Republic,* 85, 13 Nov. 1935, 9–10. All of the movement's leadership mentioned in the above sources were male.

48. Putnam, *Old Age Politicos,* 49–71; Butler, *Why Survive,* 335.

49. Butler, *Why Survive,* 335.

50. Holtzman, *The Townsend Movement,* 201, 203, 206.

51. Lucas, *The Townsend Movement in San Diego County,* 1–2.

52. Butler, *Why Survive,* 335.

53. Putnam, *Old Age Politicos,* 94–95.

54. Putnam, *Old-Age Politicos,* 89–115. Orig: *National Ham and Eggs* 8 April, 13 May, 27 May, 1939.

55. Beth J. Soldo, "America's Elderly in the 1980s," *Population Bulletin* 35, no.

4 (Washington, D.C.: Population Reference Bureau, 1975): 3–4, cited in *Chimes of Change and Hours,* ed. Borenstein, 8.

56. Edward E. Silveria, *Background Material for the Governor's Conference on the Problems of the Aging* (Sacramento, CA, 1951), inside front cover, 1, 49.

57. Butler, *Why Survive,* 335; David DeVoss, "Empire of the Old," *Los Angeles Times,* 5 no. 7, 12 Feb. 1989, 12.

58. Butler, *Why Survive,* 336; DeVoss, "Empire of the Old," 12.

59. Butler, *Why Survive,* 337.

60. "Margaret E. Kuhn, National Convener: Biography," pamphlet distributed by Gray Panthers, Philadelphia, p. 2; Maggie Kuhn, "Grass-Roots Gray Power," in *Older Woman,* eds. Fuller and Martin, 223–227. Orig: *Prime Time* 2 nos. 4–6, 1974.

61. White House Conference on Aging, *Toward a National Policy on Aging: Findings and Recommendations, . . . Final Report* (Washington, DC, 1971), 2: 119–20.

62. Janet Robuck, "Grandma as Revolutionary: Elderly Women and Some Modern Patterns of Social Change," *International Journal of Aging and Human Development* 17, no. 4 (1983): 251.

63. A notable exception is Lerner, ed., *The Female Experience,* especially the chapters, "Creating the New Woman," and "U.S. National Women's Agenda—1975."

64. Doris Lessing, *The Summer before the Dark* (New York: Bantam Books, 1974) ; June Arnold, *Sister Gin* (Plainfield, VT: Daughters, 1975).

65. Carmen, Diane, Harriet, et al, *Country Women* 11 (1974) included such titles as: "Ageism in Paradise," "Seventy Plus Has Many Plusses," and "Growing Older, Gracefully."

66. Sources including women are: Barbara Payne and Frank Whittington, "Older Women: An Examination of Popular Stereotypes and Research Evidence," in *Older Woman,* ed. Fuller and Martin, 9–30. Orig: *Social Problems 23,* 1976, 488–504, and Sarah H. Matthews, *The Social World of Old Women* (Beverly Hills: Sage Publications, 1979). Matthews discusses white elderly lesbians. Sources minimizing older women are: Butler, *Why Survive*; Arlie Russel Hockschild, *The Unexpected Community: Portrait of an Old Age Subculture* (Berkeley: Univ. of California Press, 1978); and *Aging International: Informational Bulletin of the International Federation on Aging,* ed. Charlotte Nusberg (Winter 1979–Spring 1982).

67. Quoted in Tish Sommers, "A Feminist? Definition Varies with the Woman," *New York Times* 8 Nov. 1975.

68. Fran Leonard, "Tribute to Sommers: Advocate for Older Women," *California Women* (Sacramento: California Commission on the Status of Women, II, 1986), 4.

69. Tish Sommers and Laurie Shields, "The Coming Decade: American Women and Human Resources Policies and Programs," *Gray Paper* no.1 (1979). Also see: Leonard, "Tribute to Sommers"; and Colman et al., *Gray Paper no. 7.*

70. Quoted in Freedman, *Beauty Bound,* 101–2.

71. OWL, *Report on the Status of Midlife and Older Women,* 1; Rush, "Woman in the Middle," 42–49.

72. Laurie Shields, *Displaced Homemakers: Organizing for a New Life* (New York: McGraw Hill, 1981).

73. Polly Taylor and Mickey Spencer, eds., *Broomstick: A Bimonthly Publication by, for and about Women over Forty* (San Francisco, 1980–ongoing).

74. Bell, ed., *Women as Elders,* ix.

75. White House Conference on Aging, *Toward a National Policy on Aging: Findings and Recommendations, . . . Final Report* (1971).

76. "Survey Results," *OWL Observer* 4, no. 2 (Mar. 1985): 1, 8; these were the preliminary findings. See also Kathleen Kautzer, "Moving Against the Stream: An Organizational Study of the O.W.L.," Ph.D. thesis, Brandeis Univ., 1988.

77. Several of these groups were founded before 1980. Karin E. Koek, Susan B. Martin, and Annette Novallo, eds., *Encyclopedia of Associations: National Organizations of the U.S.,* 23d ed. (Detroit: Gale Research, 1989), vol. 1, pt. 2, sec. 7–18 .

78. *Chimes of Change and Hours,* ed. Borenstein, 436.

79. In addition to items already listed, see: Tillie Olsen, *Mother to Daughter, Daughter to Mother: A Daybook and Reader* (New York: Feminist Press, 1984); Robert N. Butler and Herbert P. Gleason, eds., *Productive Aging: Enhancing Vitality in Later Life* (New York: Springer Publishing Co., 1985); William M. Kephart, *Extraordinary Groups: The Sociology of Unconventional Life-Styles* (New York: St. Martin's Press, 1982); Barbara Myerhoff, *Number Our Days* (New York: E. P. Dutton, 1978); and Tom L. Beauchamp and LeRoy Walters, eds., *Contemporary Issues in Bioethics,* 2d ed. (Belmont, CA: Wadsworth Publishing Co., 1982).

80. Barbara H. Solomon, ed., *Short Fiction of Sarah Orne Jewett and Mary Wilkins Freeman: Including the Country of the Pointed Firs* (New York: New American Library, 1979).

81. Mary Heaton Vorse, *Autobiography of an Elderly Woman* (Boston: Houghton Mifflin Co., 1911).

82. Myerhoff, *Number Our Days,* 268.

83. Sharon Mooney, "Is Every Kitchen Sink under a Window?" in Alexander and Berrow, *Women and Aging,* 108. This anthology reflects black, Hispanic, white, and lesbian experiences.

84. Lillian Morrison, "Body," in *When I Am an Old Woman,* ed. Sandra K. Martz (Manhattan Beach, CA: Papier-Mache Press, 1987).
85. Terri L. Jewell, "Investment of Worth," in *When I Am an Old Woman,* ed. Martz.

Bibliography

All of Tish's personal files, including letters, and OWL files are available in the Tish Sommers Special Collection at San Diego State University's Love Library along with the interview tapes and transcripts for this project.

Books and Articles in Books

Aaron, Daniel. *Studies in Biography*. Cambridge, MA: Harvard Univ. Press, 1978.

Acuna, Rodolfo F. *A Community under Siege: A Chronicle of Chicanos East of the Los Angeles River*. Los Angeles: Chicano Studies Research Center, UCLA, 1984.

Alabama: A Guide to the Deep South. Compiled by Writers' Program, Works Progress Administration in Alabama. New York: Richard R. Smith, 1941.

Allen, Pam. *Free Space: A Perspective on the Small Group in Women's Liberation*. Washington, NJ: Times Change, 1970.

Anderson, Karen. *Wartime Women: Sex Roles, Family Relations and the Status of Women During WW II*. Westport, CT: Greenwood Press, 1981.

Armitage, Merle. *Modern Dance*. Compiled by Virginia Stewart. New York: A. E. Weyhe, 1935.

Ascher, Carol, Louise DeSalvo, and Sara Ruddick, eds. *Between Women: Biographers, Novelists, Critics, Teachers and Artists Write about Their Work on Women*. Boston: Beacon Press, 1984.

Ashmore, Harry. *Hearts and Minds: The Anatomy of Racism from Roosevelt to Reagan*. New York: McGraw-Hill Book Co., 1982.

Barrett, Edward L., Jr. *The Tenney Committee: Legislative Investigation of Subversive Activities in California*. New York: Cornell Univ. Press, 1951.

Bauer, Yehuda. *A History of the Holocaust*. New York: Franklin Watts, 1982.

Beard, Mary. *Woman as a Force in History*. 1946. Reprint. New York: Hippocrene Books, 1985.

Bennett, Lerone, Jr. *The Negro Mood*. New York: Ballantine Books, 1965.

Berkin, Carol R. and Clara Lovett. *Women, War and Revolution*. New York: Holmes and Meier, 1980.

Bloom, Jack M. *Class, Race and the Civil Rights Movement*. Bloomington: Indiana Univ. Press, 1987.

Braden, Anne. *The Wall Between*. New York: Monthly Review Press, 1958.

Briegel, Kaye. "History of Political Organizations." Master's thesis. Univ. of Southern California, 1967.

Buhle, Mari Jo. *Women and the American Left: A Guide to Sources*. Boston: G. K. Hall and Co., 1983.

Bunch, Charlotte. *Passionate Politics: Feminist Theory in Action*. New York: St. Martin's Press, 1987.

California State Senate. Joint Fact-Finding Committee (Tenney committee). *Un-American Activities in California*. Sacramento, 1943.

Campbell, D'Ann. "Wives, Workers and Womanhood: Americans During World War II." Ph.D. thesis. Univ. of North Carolina at Chapel Hill, 1979.

Caughey, John, and Laree Caughey. *Los Angeles: Biography of a City*. Berkeley: Univ. of Calif. Press, 1976.

Caute, David. *The Great Fear: The Anti-Communist Purge under Truman and Eisenhower*. New York: Simon and Schuster, 1978.

Ceplair, Larry, and Steven Englund. *The Inquisition in Hollywood: Politics in the Film Community, 1930–1960*. Garden City, NJ: Anchor Press/Doubleday, 1980.

Charney, George. *A Long Journey*. Chicago: Quadrangle Press. 1968.

Chernin, Kim. *In My Mother's House*. New York: Harper and Row, 1984.

Clark, Kenneth B. and Jeannette Hopkins. *A Relevant War on Poverty*. New York: Harper and Row, 1968.

Cohen-Stratyner, Barbara N. *Biographical Dictionary of Dance*. New York: Schermer Books, 1982.

Cook, Blanche Wiesen. *Women and Support Networks*. Brooklyn, New York: Out and Out Books, 1979.

"Crandall, Prudence." *Notable American Women 1607–1950*. 3d ed. Cambridge, MA: Belknap Press, 1974–75.

Davidowicz, Lucy S. *The War against the Jews: 1933–1945*. New York: Bantam, 1976.

Deane, Martha. "Dance Education at UCLA." UCLA Oral History Program transcript. UCLA Library Special Collections, 1969.

Deckard, Barbara. *The Women's Movement: Political, Socioeconomic and Psychological Issues*. New York: Harper and Row, 1983.

De Kruif, Paul. *Microbe Hunters*. New York: Harcourt, Brace Jovanovich, 1926.

Dieppa, Ismael. "The Zoot Suit Riots Revisited: The Role of Private Philanthropy." Ph.D. thesis. Univ. of Southern California, 1973.

Dunaway, David K. *How Can I Keep From Singing: Pete Seeger*. New York: McGraw-Hill, 1981.

Durr, Virginia. *Outside the Magic Circle*. Tuscaloosa: Univ. of Alabama Press, 1985.

Endore, Guy. *The Sleepy Lagoon Mystery*. Los Angeles, 1944. Reprint. San Francisco: R and E Research Associates, 1972.

Evans, Richard J. *The Feminist Movement in Germany: 1894–1933*. London: Sage Publications, 1976.

Faderman, Lillian. *Surpassing the Love of Men: Romantic Friendship and Love between Women from the Renaissance to the Present*. New York: Morrow, 1981.

Farnham, Marynia, and F. Lundberg. *Modern Woman: The Lost Sex*. New York: Harper and Brothers, 1947.

Freeman, Jo. *The Politics of Women's Liberation*. New York: David McKay Co., 1975.

Garrow, David J. *The Montgomery Bus Boycott and the Women Who Started It (The Memoir of Jo Ann Gibson Robinson)*. Knoxville: Univ. of Tennessee Press, 1987.

Gold, Doris B. "Women and Voluntarism." In *Women in Sexist Society*, ed. Vivian Gornick and Barbara Moran. New York: Signet, 1971.

Greenstone, J. David, and Paul E. Peterson. *Race and Authority in Urban Politics: Community Participation and the War on Poverty*. New York: Russell Sage Foundation, 1973.

Griffith, Bernice. *American Me*. 1948. Reprint. New York: Houghton-Mifflin, 1978.

Hall, Fernau. *World Dance*. New York: A. A. Wyn, 1954.

Hartmann, Susan. *The Home Front and Beyond: American Women in the 1940s*. Boston: Twayne Publishers, 1982.

Heide, Wilma Scott. "NOW, for the Feminist Menopause That Refreshes! Or: Creative Leadership of Older Women." In *The World of the Older Woman: Conflicts and Resolutions*, ed. Dr. Gari Lescnoff-Caravaglia. New York: Human Sciences Press, 1984.

Heilbrun, Carolyn G. *Writing a Woman's Life*. New York: W. W. Norton and Co., 1988.

Hilberg, Raul. *The Destruction of the European Jews*. New York: Harper and Row, 1961.

Holm, Hanya. "The Mary Wigman I Know." In *The Dance Has Many Faces*, ed. W. Sorrell. New York: World Publishing Co., 1961.

Horner, Edward. "A Recreation Director of a Mexican-American Community." Master's thesis. Univ. of California, Los Angeles, 1945.

Howe, Irving, and Lewis Coser. *The American Communist Party: A Critical History, 1919–1957*. Boston: Beacon Press, 1957.

Hudson, Hosea. *Black Worker in the Deep South: A Personal Record*. New York: International Publishers, 1972.

Kautzer, Kathleen. "Moving against the Stream: An Organizational Study of the Older Women's League." Ph.D. thesis. Brandeis Univ., 1988.

Kelly, Rita Mae, and Mary Boutilier. *The Making of Political Women*. Chicago: Nelson-Hall, 1978.

Klehr, Harvey. *The Heyday of American Communism*. New York: Basic Books, 1984.

Koch, H. W. *The Hitler Youth*. London: Macdonald and Jane's, 1975.

Koedt, Anne, and Shulamuth Firestone, eds. *Notes from the Third Year*. New York: Notes from the Second Year, 1971.

Lessing, Doris. *Briefing for a Descent into Hell*. New York: Random House, 1981.

Lester, Julius. *Look Out Whitey! Black Power's Gon' Get Your Mama!* New York: Grove Press, 1968.

Lingeman, Richard R. *Don't You Know There's a War On? The American Home Front, 1941–45*. New York: G. P. Putnam's Sons, 1970.

MacLeish, Archibald. *Land of the Free*. New York: Da Capo, 1977.

Markowitz, Norman D. *The Rise and Fall of the People's Century: Henry A. Wallace and American Liberalism*. New York: Free Press, 1973.

Mazon, Mauricio. *The Zoot Suit Riots*. Austin: Univ. of Texas Press, 1984.

Meier, August, and Elliott Rudwick. *CORE: A Study in the Civil Rights Movement, 1942–1968*. New York: Oxford Univ. Press, 1973.

Miller, Jill. "Displaced Homemakers in the Employment and Training System." In *Job Training for Women*, ed. Sharon Horton and Ronnie J. Sternberg. Philadelphia: Temple Univ. Press, 1989.

Millett, Kate. *Sexual Politics*. Boston, MA: New England Free Press, 1968.

Mitford, Jessica. *A Fine Old Conflict*. New York: Alfred A. Knopf, 1977.

Moremen, Merrill Raymond. "The Independent Progressive Party in California." Master's thesis. Stanford Univ., 1950.

Nadeau, Remi A. *Los Angeles: From Mission to Modern City*. New York: Longmans, Green, 1960.

Nelson, Steve. *American Radical*. Pittsburgh: Univ. of Pittsburgh Press, 1981.

Painter, Nell. *The Narrative of Hosea Hudson*. Cambridge MA: Harvard Univ. Press, 1979.

Perrett, Geoffrey. *A Dream of Greatness: The American People, 1945–1963*. New York: Coward, McCann and Geoghegan, 1979.

Peterson, Deena. *A Practical Guide to the Women's Movement.* New York: Women's Action Alliance, 1975.

Plummer, Ken. *Documents of Life.* London: Allen and Unwin, 1983.

Politi, Leo. *Pedro, The Angel of Olvera Street.* New York: C. Scribner's Sons, 1946.

Rankers, Jess Elwood, Jr. "A Study of Juvenile Groups in the Hollenbeck Area of East Los Angeles." Master's thesis. Univ. of Southern California, 1957.

Rogin, Michael Paul, and John L. Shove. *Political Change in California.* Westport, CT.: Greenwood Publishing Corp., 1970.

Romo, Ricardo. *East Los Angeles: History of a Barrio.* Austin: Univ. of Texas Press, 1983.

Santiago, Danny. *Famous All Over Town.* New York: New American Library, 1983.

Scott, Robin Fitzgerald. "The Mexican-American in the Los Angeles Area, 1920–1950." Ph.D. thesis. Univ. of Southern California, 1971.

Seitz, William C. *Mark Tobey.* New York: Doubleday and Co, 1962.

Shannon, David A. *The Decline of American Communism: A History of the Communist Party of the United States since 1945.* New York: Harcourt, Brace and Co., 1959.

Shevky Eshref and Molly Levine. *Your Neighborhood: A Social Profile of Los Angeles.* Los Angeles: Haynes Foundation, 1949.

Shields, Laurie. *Displaced Homemakers: Organizing for a New Life.* New York: McGraw-Hill Book Co., 1981.

Sitkoff, Harvard. *The Struggle for Black Equality, 1954–1980.* New York: Hill and Wang, 1981.

Smith, Milo. "It's a Poor Hen That Can't Scratch." In *Out of the Frying Pan,* ed. Karol Hope and Nancy Young. New York: Anchor Books, 1979.

Snow, C. P. "J. D. Bernal, A Personal Portrait." In *Society and Science,* ed. Maurice Goldsmith and Allan Mackay. New York: Simon and Schuster, 1964.

Sommers, Joseph, and Tomas Ybarra-Frausto. *Modern Chicano Writers: A Collection of Critical Essays.* Englewood Cliffs, NJ: Prentice-Hall, 1979.

Sommers, Tish. *The Not-So-Helpless-Female.* New York: David O. McKay, 1973.

_____. "A Free Lance Agitator Confronts the Establishment." In *The New Old: Struggling for a Decent Aging,* ed. Ronald and Beatrice Gross and Sylvia Seidman. New York: Anchor Books, 1978.

_____. "Forward" and "Changing Society and Ourselves." In *Ourselves, Growing Older,* ed. Paula Brown Doress and Diana Laskin Siega. New York: Simon and Schuster, 1987.

Sommers, Tish, and Laurie Shields. *Women Take Care: The Consequences of Caregiving in Today's Society.* Gainesville, FL: Triad Publishing, 1987.

Sorenson, Roy. *Recreation for Everybody: A Community Plan for Recreation for Youth Services for Los Angeles.* Los Angeles: Welfare Council of Metropolitan Los Angeles, 1946.

Sorrell, Walter. *Hanya Holm: The Biography of an Artist.* Middletown, CT: Wesleyan Univ. Press, 1969.

————. *The Dancer's Image: Points and Counterpoints.* New York: Columbia Univ. Press, 1971.

————. *Dance in Its Time.* New York: Anchor Press/Doubleday, 1981.

Stanton, Elizabeth Cady. *Woman's Bible.* New York, 1895–98. Reprint. New York: Arno Press, 1974.

Starobin, Joseph. *American Communism in Crisis: 1943–1957.* Cambridge, MA: Harvard Univ. Press, 1972.

Stephenson, Jill. *The Nazi Organization of Women.* Totowa, NJ: Barnes and Noble, 1981.

Strachey, John (Evelyn John St. Loe). *The Coming Struggle for Power.* New York: H. Wolff, 1933.

Syfers, Judy. "Why I Want a Wife." In *Radical Feminism,* ed. Anne Koedt, Ellen Levine, and Anita Rapone. New York: Quadrangle/New York Times Book Co., 1976.

Troupe, Quincy, ed. *Watts Poets: A Book of New Poetry and Essays.* Los Angeles: House of Respect, 1968.

Ware, Cellestine. *Woman Power: The Movement for Women's Liberation.* New York: Tower Publications, 1970.

Warren, Larry. *Lester Horton, Modern Dance Pioneer.* New York: Dekker, 1977.

Watson, Lawrence C., and Maria-Barbara Watson-Frank. *Interpreting Life Histories: An Anthropological Inquiry.* New Brunswick, NJ: Rutgers Univ. Press, 1985.

Wigman, Mary. *The Language of Dance.* Middletown, CT: Wesleyan Univ. Press, 1966.

————. *The Mary Wigman Book: Her Writings Edited and Translated.* Edited by Walter Sorrell. Middletown, CT: Wesleyan Univ. Press, 1973.

Young, Michael. *The Elmhirsts of Dartington: The Creation of an Utopian Community.* London: Routledge and Kegan Paul, 1982.

Zaretsky, David. *President Johnson's War on Poverty.* Univ. of Alabama Press, 1986.

Periodicals, Reports, and Newspaper Articles

"A Feminist? Definition Varies with the Woman." *New York Times,* 8 Nov. 1975.

"Bachelor Joys Revive." *San Francisco Chronicle.* 23 Apr. 1926, 22.

Bales, Susan. "Spirit of the Place: A Tribute to 3800 Harrison Street." *OWL Observer,* Mar.–Apr. 1987, pp. 2–3.

Berkeley Tribe. 16 July 1971, TSC.

"Boy Drowns in Riptide." *San Francisco Chronicle.* 26 Sept. 1931, 1.

Burke, Sidney. "Labor Rally Goes Wild on His Arrival." *The People's World,* 17 May 1948, 1.

"Burned Bridge on Struck Railroad." *Life,* 9 May 1955, 34.

"Children's Fair for Refugee Youth." *California Arts and Architecture.* Apr. 1942, p. 12, TSC.

Cowl, Margaret. "Women's Struggle for Equality." *Political Affairs 53,* May 1974.

"Dancers Aid Democracy." *Dance Herald* 1, no. 6, Apr. 1938, Editorial, 2.

Dubin, Zan. "Horton Tribute: Credibility Out West." *Los Angeles Times,* 10 Nov. 1985, Calendar, 46.

Eisenberg, Emanuel. "Danse Macabre." *New Theatre,* 1936, pp. 22, 23, 27.

FBI files on Letitia Innes Burke Sommers. Nos. 100-23650, 100-345618, and 238,774. Copies in TSC.

Fisher, Lawrence. "Message From Older Women." *New York Times,* 29 Sept. 1986, 15.

Frankenstein, Alfred. "'Park' Ballet: The Emphasis Is on the Modern Side. *San Francisco Chronicle,* 25 Aug. 1941, 9.

Frontiers: A Journal of Women's Studies. Special Issue: Women's Oral History, 2, No. 2 (Summer 1977).

Frontiers: A Journal of Women's Studies. Special Issue: Women's Oral History Two, 7, No. 1 (1983).

Gardner, Marilyn. "Older Women—who cares about the care-givers?" *Christian Science Monitor,* 15 Apr. 1985, 29.

Gluck, Sherna. "What's So Special about Women? Women's Oral History." *Frontiers: A Journal of Women's Studies* 2 (1977): 3–14.

Gorney, Cynthia. "The Discarding of Ms. Hill." *Ladies Home Journal,* 21 Feb. 1976, 58+.

_____. Obituary, Tish Sommers. *The Washington Post.* 19 Oct. 1985, sec. G, 1.

Gore, W. and H. Costner. "Organizing the Poor: An Evaluation of a Strategy." *Social Science Quarterly,* Dec. 1969, pp. 643–56.

Hall, Sam. "South in Struggle." *The Daily Worker.* Harlem Edition. 13 Mar. 1949, 1.

Hamilton, Mildred. "The Resolve of Older Women." *San Francisco Chronicle,* 7 Oct. 1980, 16.

_____. "Older Women's League Gets First Black Chapter." *San Francisco Sunday Examiner* and *Chronicle,* 30 May 1982.

Hannula, Don. "Negro Leaders Hope People 'Get Message.'" *Seattle Times,* 1 Mar. 1968, 21.

"Hollywood Bowl Dancers Revolt, Demand Living Wage; Musicians and Famous Names Pledge Help." *The People's World,* 13 May 1938, 5.

"In California it's. . ." *The Californian,* 1, No. 6 (July 1945), 71, TSC.

Innes, Letitia, and Eleanor Brooks. "Dance Priorities." *Educational Dance,* 5 No. 2 (June–July 1942), TSC.

Kalman, Ted. "Accent on Youth." *The People's World,* 4 Jan. 1949, 8.

King, W. Ivan. "Maximizing Feasible Citizen Participation." Draft report (for consideration in analysis-recommendation section of OEO Social Change Evaluation Report), ca. 1968–69.

Klemesrud, Judy. "New Focus on Concerns of Older Women." *New York Times,* 13 Oct. 1980, 16.

————. "For Women 45 to 65, a Group to Promote Their Causes." *New York Times,* 24 Feb. 1981, 24.

————. "Conference on Aging Views Older Women." *New York Times.* 1 Dec. 1981.

————. "Older Women: No Longer 'Invisible.'" *New York Times.* 2 Dec. 1981.

————. "For Older Women, Parley Raises Hope." *New York Times,* 5 Dec. 1981, 22.

Koegler, Horst. "In the Shadow of the Swastika: Dance in Germany, 1927–1936." *Dance Perspectives,* Spring 1974, pp. 1, 48.

Krucoff, Carol. "Issues: The Older Woman." *The Washington Post,* 19 Apr. 1983.

Leonard, Fran. "Issues for Action: Older Women and Pensions—Catch 22." OWLEF *Gray Paper,* no. 4 (1980), TSC.

————, et al. "Issues for Action—The Disillusionment of Divorce for Older Women." OWLEF *Gray Paper,* no. 6 (n.d.), TSC.

Mann, Judy. "The Legacy of an Older Woman." *The Washington Post,* 23 Oct. 1985, sec. D, 3.

Miller, Alfred, "Camacho Holds Big 3-1 Lead." *The People's World,* 11 July 1940, 1.

Mills, Kay. "Aging Women Don't Agonize, Organize." *Los Angeles Times,* 21 Nov. 1982, sec. 4, 3.

Minnich, Elizabeth Karnarck. "Women: The Act of Feminist Biographies." *Feminist Studies* 2 (Summer 1985): 287–305.

Morse, Susan. "Final Requests—Preparing for Death." *The Washington Post,* 15 July 1985, sec. B, 5.

Nance, Merle. "Dancers Offer Program of Labor's Lost." *The People's World,* 22 Apr. 1938, 5.

National Organization for Women Task Force on Older Women. *Quarterly Newsletter*, 2, No. 2 (May 1975), TSC.

"1966 School for Community Action." *Northgate Journal*, 28 Sept. 1966, 7, TSC.

Obituary: Murray Innes. *San Diego Union*. 10 Aug. 1960, sec. B, 1.

Older Women's League. "Painless Alternatives to the Social Security Problem." Sept. 1981.

————. "Coming of Age." OWL Annual Report. Jan. 1984.

————. *Wingspan*. OWL Chapter Workbooks. 1984.

————. "The Second Wave: A Report of the Older Women's League." 1985.

————. "Taking Charge of the End of Your Life." 1985.

————. *Report on the Status of Midlife and Older Women in America*. 1986.

————. "Coming Into Our Own: A Report of the Older Women's League." 1987.

"One Thousand Join Women's Cavalcade for Peace." *The People's World*, 11 Aug. 1950, 1.

OWL Observer. Tish Sommers Memorial Edition. Vol. 4, no. 8 (Nov.–Dec. 1985).

OWL Observer. Memorial Issue for Laurie Shields, Mar.–Apr. 1989.

Pearldaughter, Andra, et al. "Issues for Action: Welfare—End of the Line for Women." OWLEF *Gray Paper*, no. 5 (n.d.), TSC.

"Peace, Unity Key Themes of His Talks." *The People's World*, 4 Oct. 1948, 1.

Pittman, John. "Dunham Dance Group Returns for Another San Francisco Triumph." *The People's World*, 2 Jan. 1942, 5.

"Plan for Nurseries Is Promoted in L.A." *The People's World*, 16 Mar. 1942, 5.

Porter, Sylvia. "New Older Women's League Helps That Invisible Group." *New York Times*, 13 Oct. 1980, 13.

Pratt, Edwin T. Excerpts from memorial pamphlet. Seattle Urban League, 1969, TSC.

Quinlan, Alice, OWL director of public policy. "Inequality of Sacrifice: The Impact of Reaganomics on Women." OWL reports, 1983–84.

"Return of Rosie the Riveter." *San Francisco Chronicle*, 23 Sept. 1974, 1.

Roderick, Kevin. "Case History of a 20-Year War on Poverty." *Los Angeles Times*, 31 July 1985, 8.

Rubin, Sylvia. "Fighting for the Rights of Older Women." *San Francisco Chronicle*, 22 Oct. 1980, 24.

Rupp, Leila J. "'Imagine My Surprise': Women's Relationships in Historical Perspective." *Frontiers: A Journal of Women's Studies*, 5, No. 3 (Fall 1980), 61–70.

Scheyer, Ernst. "The Shapes of Space: The Art of Mary Wigman and Oskar Schlemmer." *Dance Perspectives*, 1970, p. 57.

Schlafly, Phyllis. "The alternatives to women's lib." *Eagle Forum*. Aug. 1977.

Seattle–King County Economic Opportunity Board (SKCEOB). "Interim Report on the Central Area Motivation Program (CAMP)." 1966, TSC.

Seattle Urban League Annual Report, 1964. TSC.

"Senior Power." *Newsweek*, 16 Sept. 1974, 53–54.

Shaffer, Robert. "Women and the Communist Party, USA, 1930–40." *Socialist Review*, May–June 1979.

Silva, Nell. "Horton Dance Group Relates Life to Art." *The People's World*, 28 Apr. 1938, 5.

Silverman, Jan. "Two Oaklanders at the heart of the older-women's movement." *Oakland Tribune*, 6 Oct. 1980.

Smith, Lynn. "Older Women Who Quit Agonizing to Organize." *Los Angeles Times*. 26 Aug. 1984, sec. 4, 1.

––––––. "Older Women's Advocate Dies at 71." *Los Angeles Times*, 19 Oct. 1985, 7.

"Some 25,000 nonoperating L&N employees in 13 states went on strike 35 days ago." *Louisville Courier-Journal*, 17 Apr. 1955, 1.

"Sommers: Taking Charge of a Life." *COPE*. Aug. 86, p. 42.

Sommers, Tish. Report to the Los Angeles Youth Authority. 1947, TSC.

––––––. CAMP volunteer coordinator reports. 1965–69, TSC.

––––––. "Write On!" National Organization for Women pamphlet, ca. 1972.

––––––. "The Single Web of Human Rights: Women as Change Agents." Report to the International Assoc. of Official Human Rights Agencies, San Francisco. 12 July 1972, TSC.

––––––. "Fighting Back: A Call to Action by Older Women." *Prime Time*, 2, No. 1. (Jan. 1974), TSC.

––––––. "Sexism and Racism: Feminist Perspective." *Civil Rights Digest*, 6, No. 3, 1974, TSC.

––––––. "The Compounding Impact of Age and Sex," Draft submitted to *Civil Rights Digest*. Fall 1975, TSC.

––––––. "National Organization for Women Task Force on Older Women." *Quarterly Newsletter*, Vol. II, May 1975, TSC.

––––––. "On Growing Older Female: An Interview with Tish Sommers." *Aging* 253 (Nov. 1975): 111–12, TSC.

––––––. "Social Security: A Woman's Viewpoint." *Industrial Gerontology* 2 (Fall 1975): 266–80, TSC.

––––––. Testimony on Displaced Homemakers Act (SB 825) Health and Welfare Committee, California Senate, 14 May 1975, TSC.

––––––. "Here Comes the Older Woman." Statement by Sommers, Coordinator, NOW Task Force on Older Women, to U.S. Dept. of Health, Education and Welfare, Western Region. (21 Apr. 1975), TSC.

_____. "Differential Treatment by Sex," in *Social Security. How Social? How Secure?* Institute of Industrial Relations, UCLA., ca. 1975, TSC.

_____. "Moving From the Letter to the Spirit of Equality." Testimony about divorce and community property given to the Joint Committee on Legal Equality, State of California, ca.1975, TSC.

_____. "Do It NOW." Cover Picture of Tish at Alameda County Displaced Homemaker Center, 9, No. 11 (Dec. 1976), TSC.

_____. "Age Discrimination Within Reason." Testimony for the Age Discrimination Study of the U.S. Commission on Civil Rights. (1977), TSC.

_____. "Employment Problems of Older Women." Testimony before the U.S. House of Representatives Select Committee on Aging (1977), TSC.

_____. "Look Out Job Market!" *Generations*, Western Gerontological Society, (Winter 1978), TSC.

_____. "Death—A Feminist Perspective." *Quest,* a feminist quarterly. (Summer 1978), TSC.

_____. "To Our Good Health." Cover letter. *OWLEF* (Oct. 1979), TSC.

_____. "Older Women and Public Policy," OWLEF *Gray Paper*, no. 1 (1979).

_____. *How to Tame the CETA Beast: An Advocacy Manual for Older Women.* Developed collectively with Andra Pearldaughter, Laurie Shields, Donna Ambrogi, Gail Antler, Martha Gresham, Margaret Malberti, with suggestions from others and cartoons by bülbul (Genny Guracar). Older Women's League Education Fund (OWLEF), 1979, TSC.

_____. "The Best Things in Life Are . . . Costing More." Cover letter. *OWLEF,* (May 1980), TSC.

_____. "Growing Numbers, Growing Force." Report from White House Mini-Conference on Older Women. OWLEF and Western Gerontological Society, 1981, TSC.

_____. "Caregiving: A Woman's Issue." *Generations,* Fall 1985, pp. 99–113, TSC.

_____. "Long-Term Care: Biggest Dilemma, Toughest Problem, Greatest Challenge." *Perspective on Aging,* 9, No. 4 (July–Aug. 1985), TSC.

Sommers, Tish, and Kerstin Joslyn. "Volunteer Beware!" National Organization for Women pamphlet, ca. 1971, TSC.

Sommers, Tish, and Laurie Shields. "Displaced Homemakers: 'Forced Retirement' Leaves Many Penniless." *Civil Rights Digest*, U.S. Commission on Civil Rights. (Winter 1978).

_____. "ERA and Older Woman." *Perspective on Aging,* 1978, TSC.

_____. "Issues for Action: Social Security—Adequacy and Equity for Older Women." OWLEF *Gray Paper,* no. 2 (1979), TSC.

_____. "We're Stronger Than We Think" Cover letter. *OWLEF*, Apr. 1979, TSC.

_____. "What to Do With a 'Very Austere' Budget." Cover letter. *OWLEF*, July 1979, TSC.

_____. "An OWL's Eye View of the 80's." Cover letter. *OWLEF*, Jan. 1980, TSC.

_____. "When Will They Listen." Cover letter. *OWLEF*, May 1981, TSC.

Sommers, Tish, et al. "Issues for Action: Older Women and Health Care— Strategy for Survival." OWLEF *Gray Paper*, no. 3 (1980).

Stephen, Beverly. "Older Women: Reversing an Image." *Los Angeles Times*, 27 Feb. 1983, 7.

Storm, Walter. "The World Youth Festival in Prague." *The People's World*, 13 Sept. 1947, 5.

"Story in News about Red Puts Fireman on Spot." *Birmingham News*, 12 Aug. 1957, local news page.

Strickland, Edwin. "Pinks Worked under Noses of Union, City." *Birmingham News*, 11 Aug. 1957, 1.

Sweet, Ellen. "Tish Sommers: Organize—Don't Agonize!" *Ms.* 10 (Jan. 1982): 60–61.

U.S. Public Law No. 95-524. Comprehensive Employment and Training Act. 27 Oct. 1978.

U.S. Senate Committee on Labor and Human Resources. Tish Sommers and Laurie Shields Displaced Homemakers Training and Economic Self-Sufficiency Assistance Act of 1989. Hearing S1107. 1 June 1989.

"We Should Live So Long: A Program on Women and Aging." Script for KQED-TV public service program, 1974. Members of We Should Live So Long collective: Milo Smith, Lucile Dunham, Ruth Sheer, Tish Sommers, Jean Weinberg, Kay Nollenberger, Isabel Van Frank, Ethel Mengel, Pat O'Brian.

Weaver, Peter. "Health Insurance for Older Women." *Los Angeles Times*, 6 May 1984, sec. 4, 14.

"While Wallace Was in L.A." *The People's World*, 4 Oct. 1948, 3.

"Whirlwind Tour Slated for Wallace." *The People's Choice*, 15 May 1948, 1.

Letters

Kate Innes to Murray Innes. 10 Apr. 1929.

Kate Innes to Murray Innes. Jan. 1932.

Murray Innes, Sr., to J. J. Lerman, Attorney. 6 June 1933.

Tish Sommers. Letters to Kate Innes. 1933–35.

Mary Wigman to Kate Innes. 6 June 1934.

Murray Innes, Sr., to son Bill Innes. 19 Dec. 1939.

Mrs. Sigmund Stern to Letitia Innes. May 1941.

Aliso Village Victory Council to Los Angeles War Chest. 6 Aug. 1945.

Elsie D. Newton to Mrs. Edith Terry Bremer, American Federation of International Institutes. 21 Nov. 1945.

Tish Sommers to Alita Letwin. ca. 1965.

Tish Sommers. Letters to author. July and Aug. 1970.

Tish Sommers to Ruth McElhinney. 15 Oct. 1972.

Tish Sommers to Cine Manifest, Connie Field, and Susan Lyne. 22 Nov. 1974.

Tish Sommers to NOW board members. 4 Dec. 1977.

Tish Sommers to Arlie Scott. 1 May 1978.

Annette K. Smail to Tish Sommers. 1 Nov. 1980.

Tish Sommers response to Annette K. Smail. 11 Nov. 1980.

Laurie Shields to Virginia Matthews. 28 Feb. 1982.

Tish Sommers to K. M. 2 Mar. 1985.

Tish Sommers to Carroll Estes. 24 May 1985.

Laurie Shields to Ann Zimmerman. 7 July 1985.

Doris Notestein to author. 1986.

Dorothy Pitts to author. 1988.

Jeanne Saletan to author. 27 July 1988.

Index

Tish Sommers, Activist was designed by Dariel Mayer and composed at the University of Tennessee Press on the Apple Macintosh IIcx with Aldus *PageMaker*. Linotronic camera pages were generated by AMPM, Inc. The book is set in Garamond No. 3, with ITC Garamond used for display, and printed on 60-lb Glatfelter Natural, B-16. Manufactured in the United States of America by Cushing/Malloy, Inc.